Talbot~

THE TALE OF
ONE BAD RAT

for Mary

Published by Jonathan Cape 2008

2 4 6 8 10 9 7 5 3 1

Copyright © Bryan Talbot, 1995, 2008

Bryan Talbot has asserted his right under the Copyright, Designs
and Patents Act 1988 to be identified as the author of this work

Lettered by Ellie DeVille

This book collects issues one through four of the Dark Horse comic-book series
The Tale of One Bad Rat

First published in the USA in 1995 by Dark Horse Comics, Inc.

First published in Great Britain in 2008 by
Jonathan Cape
Random House, 20 Vauxhall Bridge Road,
London SW1V 2SA

www.rbooks.co.uk

www. bryan-talbot.com

Addresses for companies within The Random House Group Limited can be
found at: www.randomhouse.co.uk/offices.htm

The Random House Group Limited Reg. No. 954009

A CIP catalogue record for this book is available from the British Library

ISBN 9780224084703

The Random House Group Limited supports The Forest Stewardship
Council (FSC), the leading international forest certification organisation.
All our titles that are printed on Greenpeace approved FSC certified paper
carry the FSC logo. Our paper procurement policy can be found at
www.rbooks.co.uk/environment

Printed and bound in China by C&C Offset Printing Co., Ltd

THE TALE OF
ONE BAD RAT

by

BRYAN TALBOT

JONATHAN CAPE
LONDON

THE RAT'S WHISKERS

THERE have been rats in Bryan Talbot's kitchen for longer than I care to remember. I don't mean the kind that scratch around under the floorboards, dodging traps and ignoring poison and finally being dispatched by a couple of council workers with a quick eye and a cricket bat; Bryan's rats have been bright-eyed little charmers with their own immaculate quarters and a taste for boiled rice and chapati.

Their owner has become well acquainted with their ways, too. Very few visitors can have left the house without concluding that, over the years, rats have had a pretty one-sided press. Vermin, plague-bearers, traditional objects of terror; rats, like wolves, have been forced to carry a certain burden of the human imagination. When a rat dives across the path of someone out walking and surprises them, it's never a rat of normal size. In the retelling, it's always at least the size of a cat. A squirrel on the lawn is something to smile at. But stick it on all fours and shave its tail, and there's an instant pucker-factor.

Ever since we lived in caves, we've had to demonise *something* out there; and after a while, it's as if the demons are the only truth we can know. We're born into a world that's full of such received ideas, automatic ways of seeing things, and they surround us as we grow. They're hard-to question; the world tends to resist having its assumptions challenged, and its non-conformist thinkers have been given a hard time throughout history. It's much easier to accept the general line. Do otherwise, and you're a rebel, you're weird . . . and the weird and rebellious are always suspect.

So how do you handle it, then, if you happen to be brought up in an atmosphere of certainty that the demon is *you*?

That's how it can be when you're a child if the adults in your life can't be relied upon, and they seem to get some consolation out of projecting their inadequacies onto you. I don't know why it's such a human trait, to react to feeling badly by looking for someone weaker, that you can make feel worse, but there it is. In every generation, there's this urge among a number to damage the next. Sometimes because it makes them feelbetter. Sometimes just because they can.

And children, of course, believe what they're told. They're credulous in the most open way because they simply haven't the data to know otherwise. Make them think that they're guilty, and they'll wonder what it was they did. Let them think they're worthless, and they'll assume it must be a true valuation.

Bad rats, all.

When a soul's been starved in this way and kept in darkness, its only hope lies in making its own journey out of there. And when the darkness is your entire world, even starting such a journey requires a faith in yourself that can be very hard to muster.

What you are about to read is the tale of such a journey. Picked from among countless numbers, this is *The Tale of One Bad Rat*.

Watching this book as it has moved toward its final form has been rather like seeing the offspring of a close friend growing up and heading out into the world. You feel as if you can share a little bit of the glow of satisfaction while knowing full well that you didn't do a single stroke of all the hard work that was required. I was, Bryan reckons, about the third person ever to hear him recount the story that was to become the graphic novel you now hold. We were driving back from a joint signing somewhere at the other end of the country, and he wanted to tell it as a way of getting it clear in his own mind.

Since then, I've witnessed the long process of development, the phenomenal concentration, the research, the dedication, and the genuine sacrifice that were to go into the creation of the work you're about to enter. More than one of those small house guests came and went during the process; life is short, but even a good rat's life is shorter than most.

You, of course, will see none of this. You'll see only the *Tale*.

Which is exactly the way it should be.

STEPHEN GALLAGHER
author of *Red, Red Robin*
and *Nightmare, With Angel & co.*.

TOWN

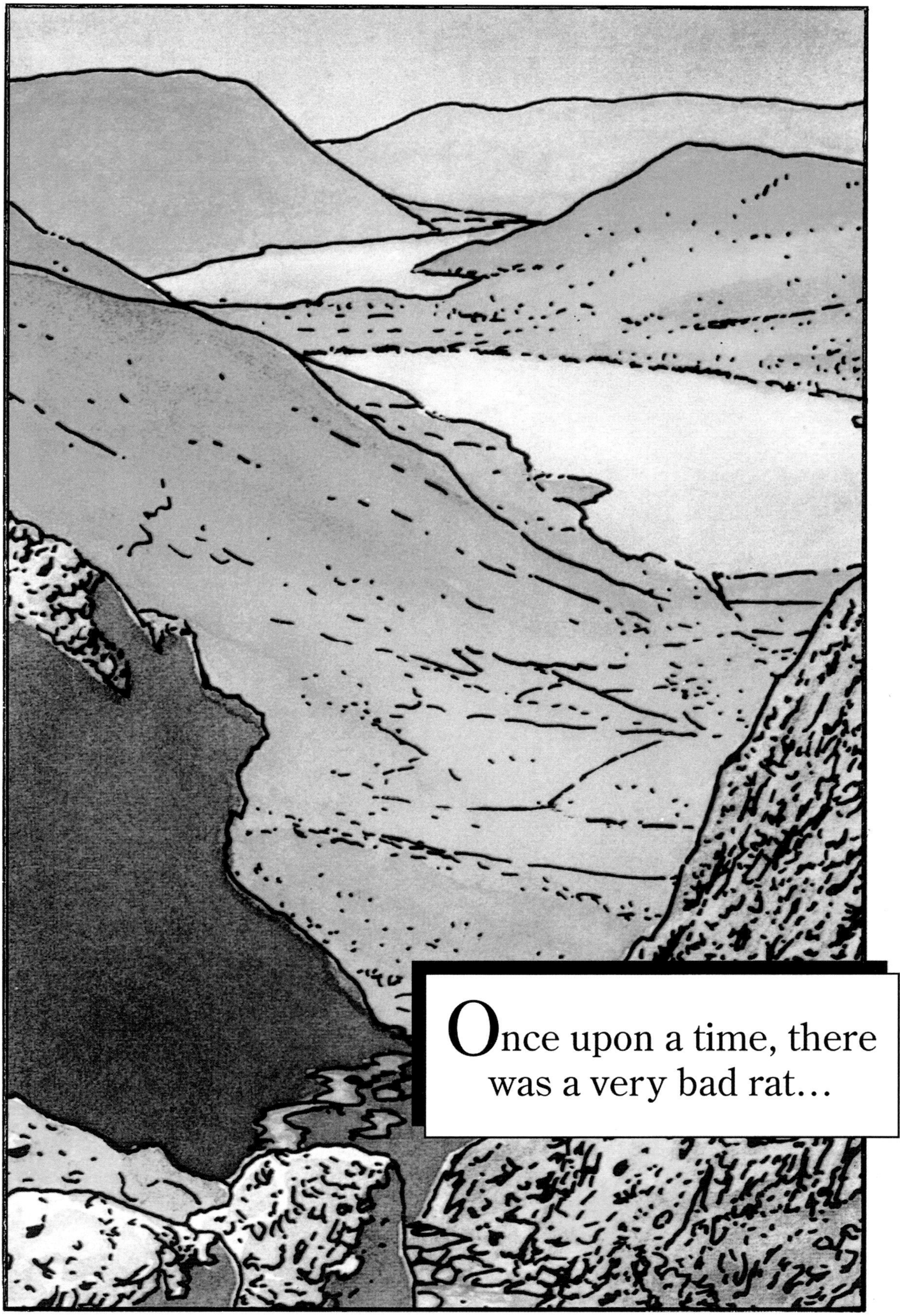
Once upon a time, there was a very bad rat…

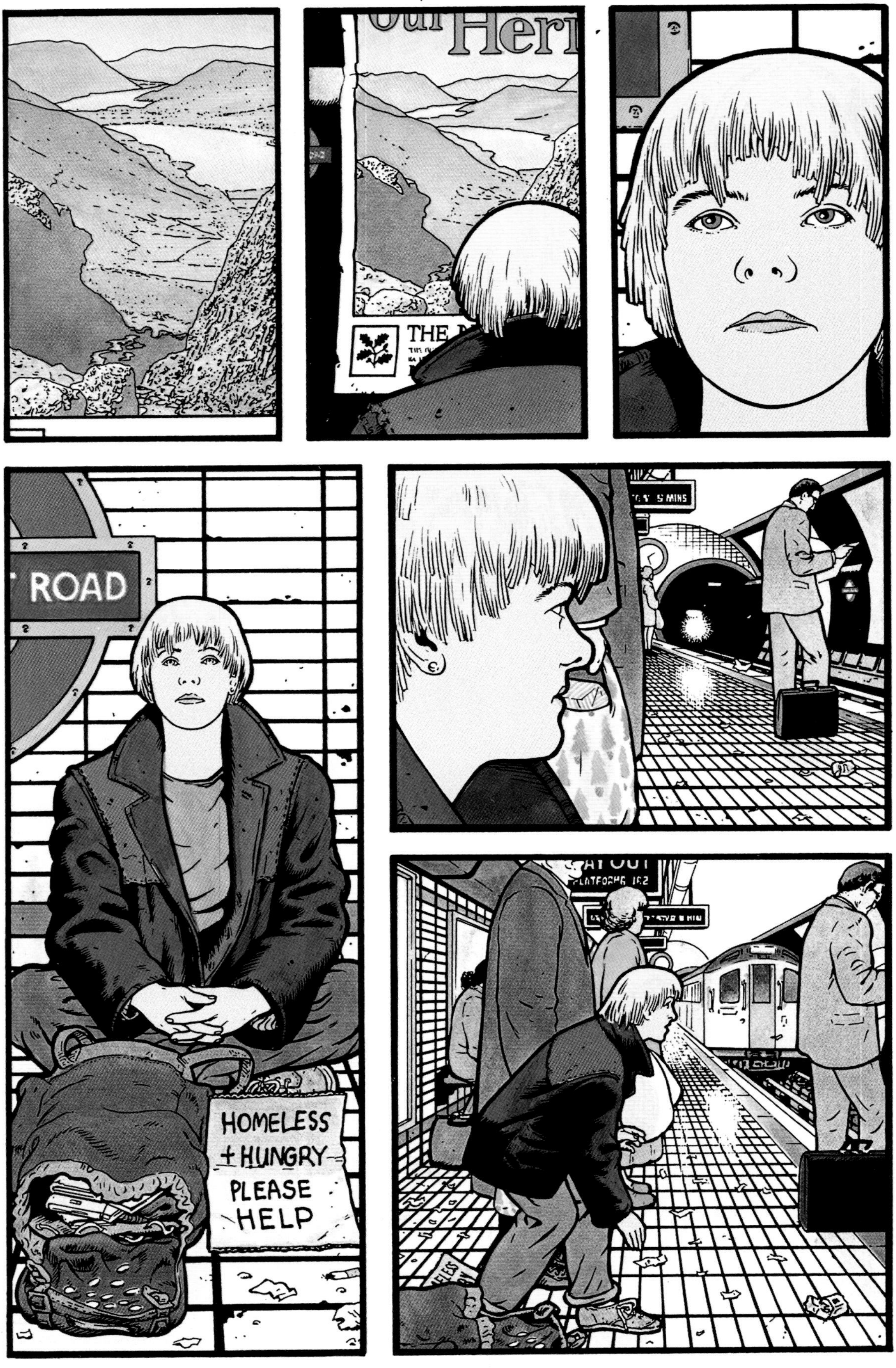
Our
THE
ROAD
HOMELESS
+ HUNGRY
PLEASE
HELP

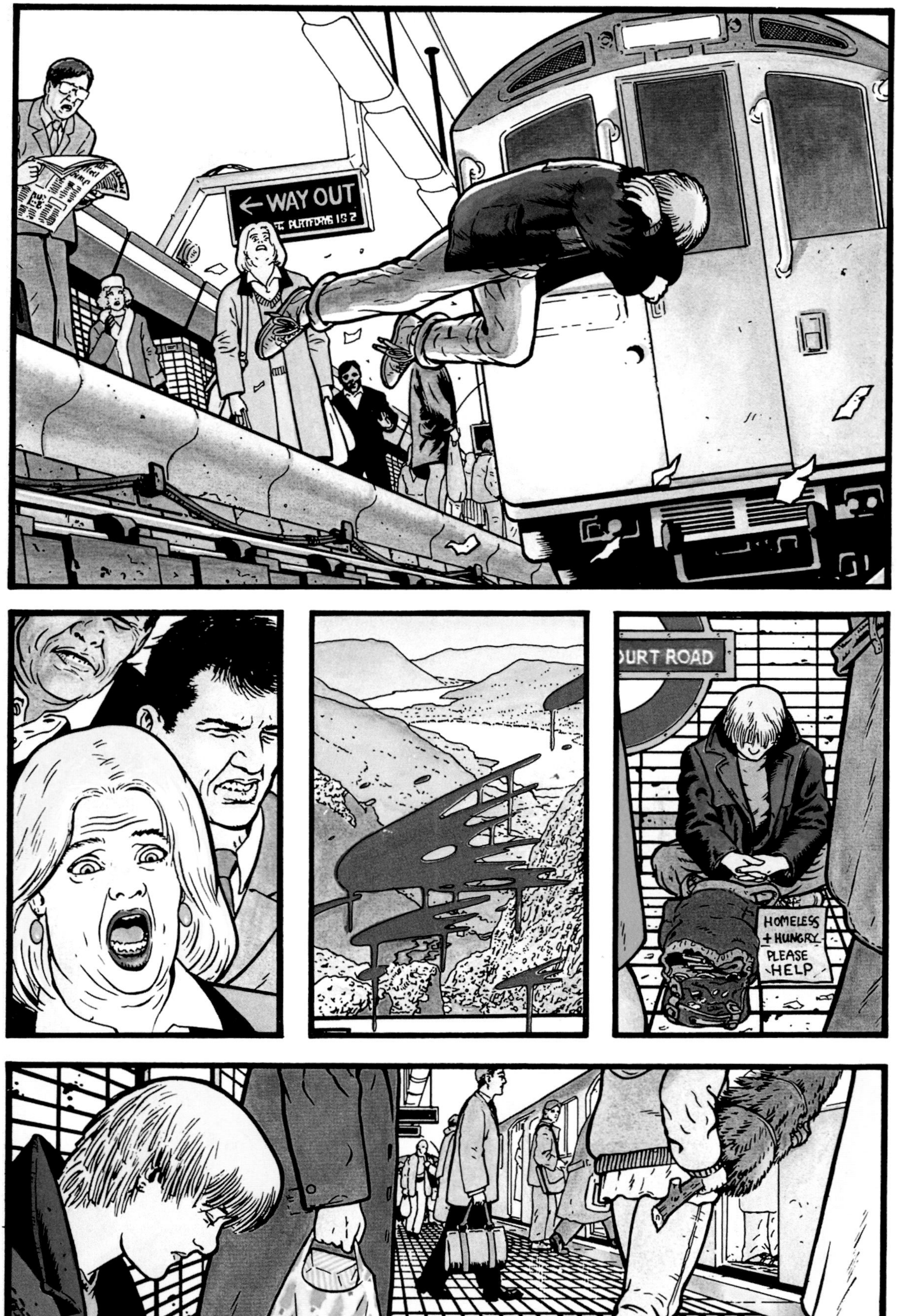
← WAY OUT
OURT ROAD
HOMELESS
+ HUNGRY
PLEASE
HELP

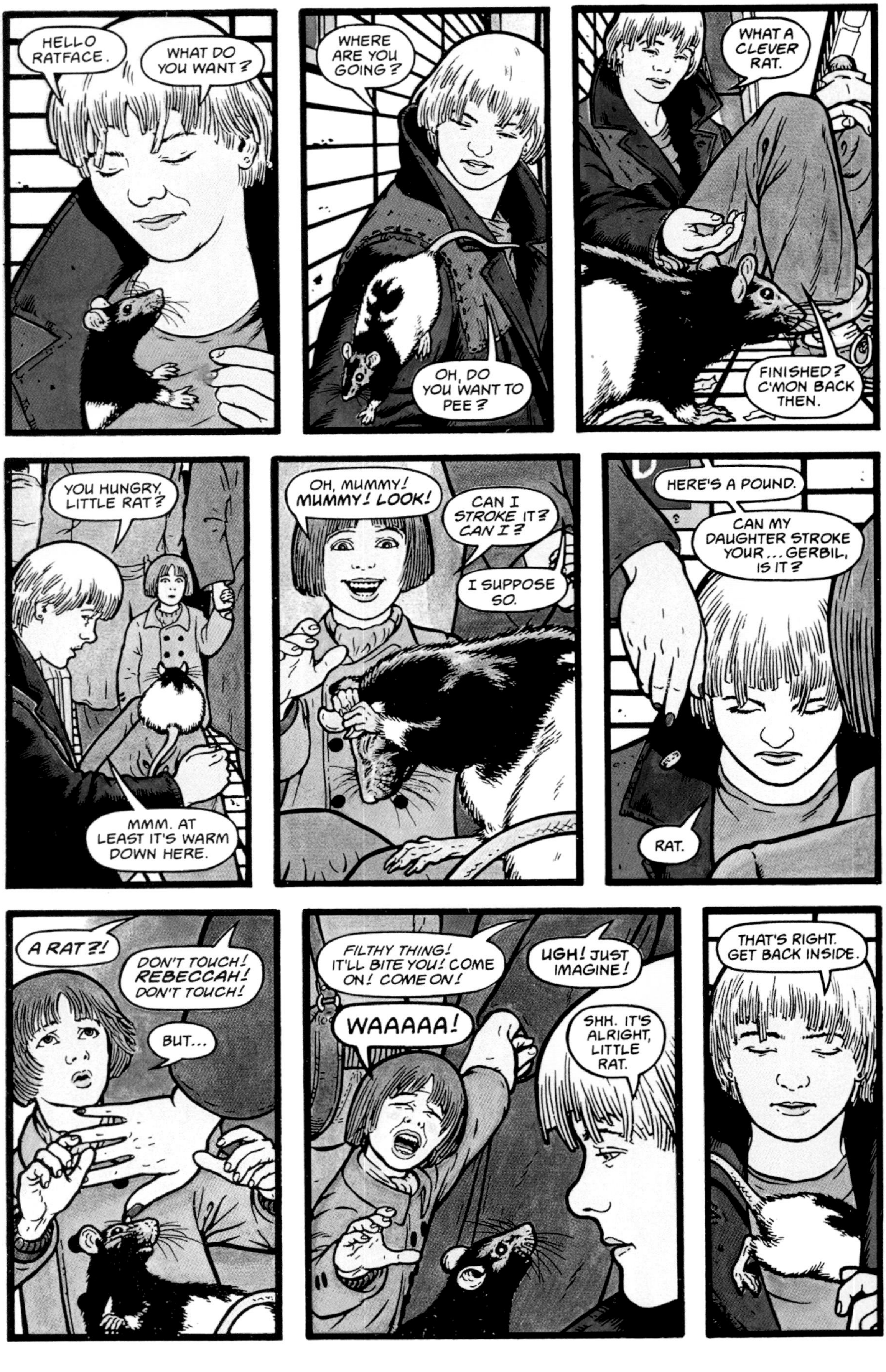
HELLO RATFACE.
WHAT DO YOU WANT?
WHERE ARE YOU GOING?
OH, DO YOU WANT TO PEE?
WHAT A CLEVER RAT.
FINISHED? C'MON BACK THEN.
YOU HUNGRY, LITTLE RAT?
MMM. AT LEAST IT'S WARM DOWN HERE.
OH, MUMMY! MUMMY! LOOK!
CAN I STROKE IT? CAN I?
I SUPPOSE SO.
HERE'S A POUND.
CAN MY DAUGHTER STROKE YOUR... GERBIL, IS IT?
RAT.
A RAT?!
DON'T TOUCH! REBECCAH! DON'T TOUCH!
BUT...
FILTHY THING! IT'LL BITE YOU! COME ON! COME ON!
UGH! JUST IMAGINE!
WAAAAA!
SHH. IT'S ALRIGHT, LITTLE RAT.
THAT'S RIGHT. GET BACK INSIDE.

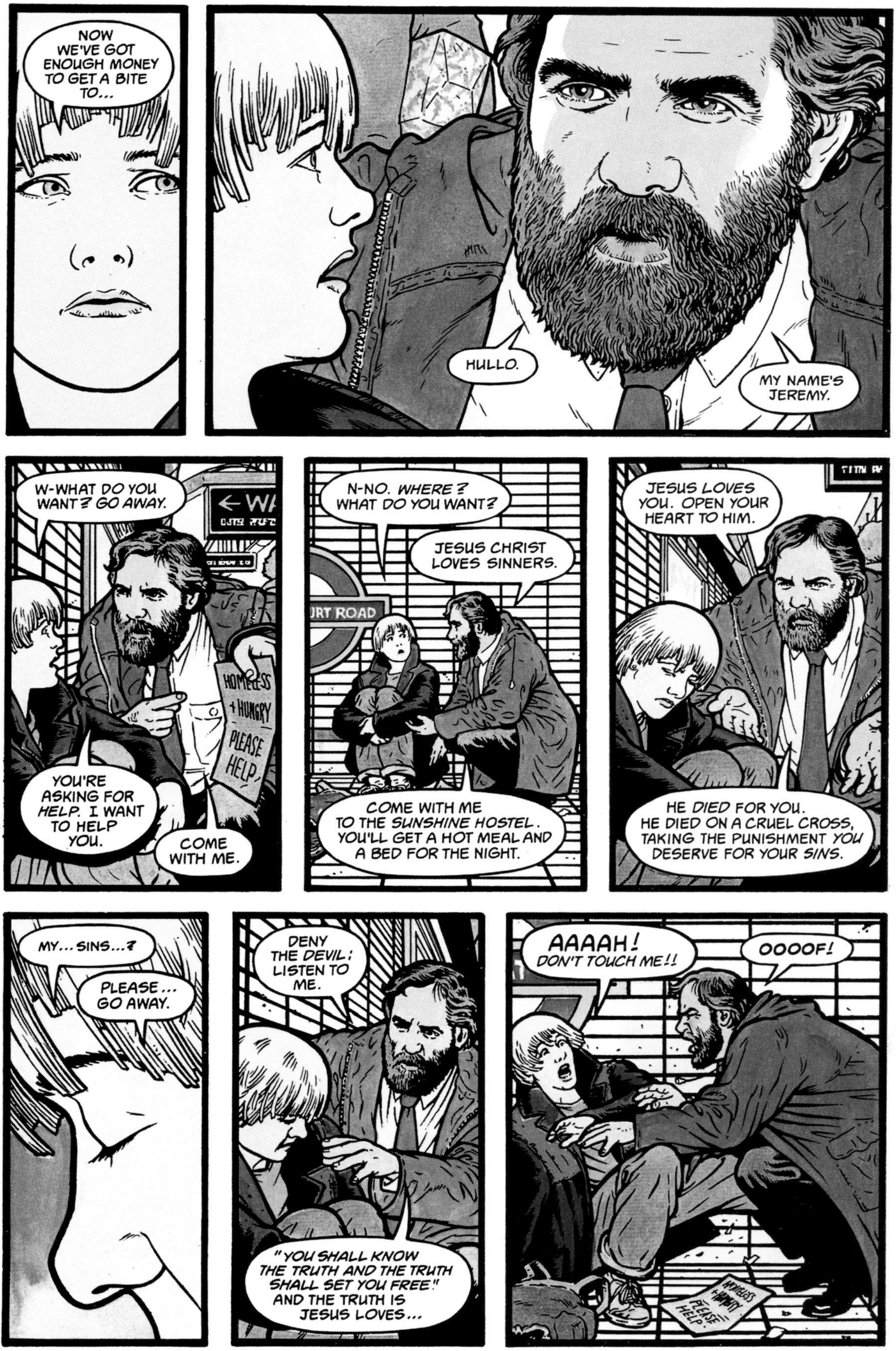
NOW WE'VE GOT ENOUGH MONEY TO GET A BITE TO...
HULLO.
MY NAME'S JEREMY.
W-WHAT DO YOU WANT? GO AWAY.
HOMELESS + HUNGRY PLEASE HELP.
YOU'RE ASKING FOR *HELP*. I WANT TO HELP YOU.
COME WITH ME.
N-NO. *WHERE?* WHAT DO YOU WANT?
JESUS CHRIST LOVES SINNERS.
URT ROAD
COME WITH ME TO THE *SUNSHINE HOSTEL*. YOU'LL GET A HOT MEAL AND A BED FOR THE NIGHT.
JESUS *LOVES* YOU. OPEN YOUR HEART TO HIM.
HE *DIED* FOR YOU. HE DIED ON A CRUEL CROSS, TAKING THE PUNISHMENT *YOU* DESERVE FOR YOUR *SINS*.
MY... SINS...?
PLEASE... GO AWAY.
DENY THE *DEVIL*; LISTEN TO ME.
"YOU SHALL KNOW THE TRUTH AND THE TRUTH SHALL SET YOU FREE" AND THE TRUTH IS JESUS LOVES...
AAAAH! *DON'T TOUCH ME!!*
OOOOF!

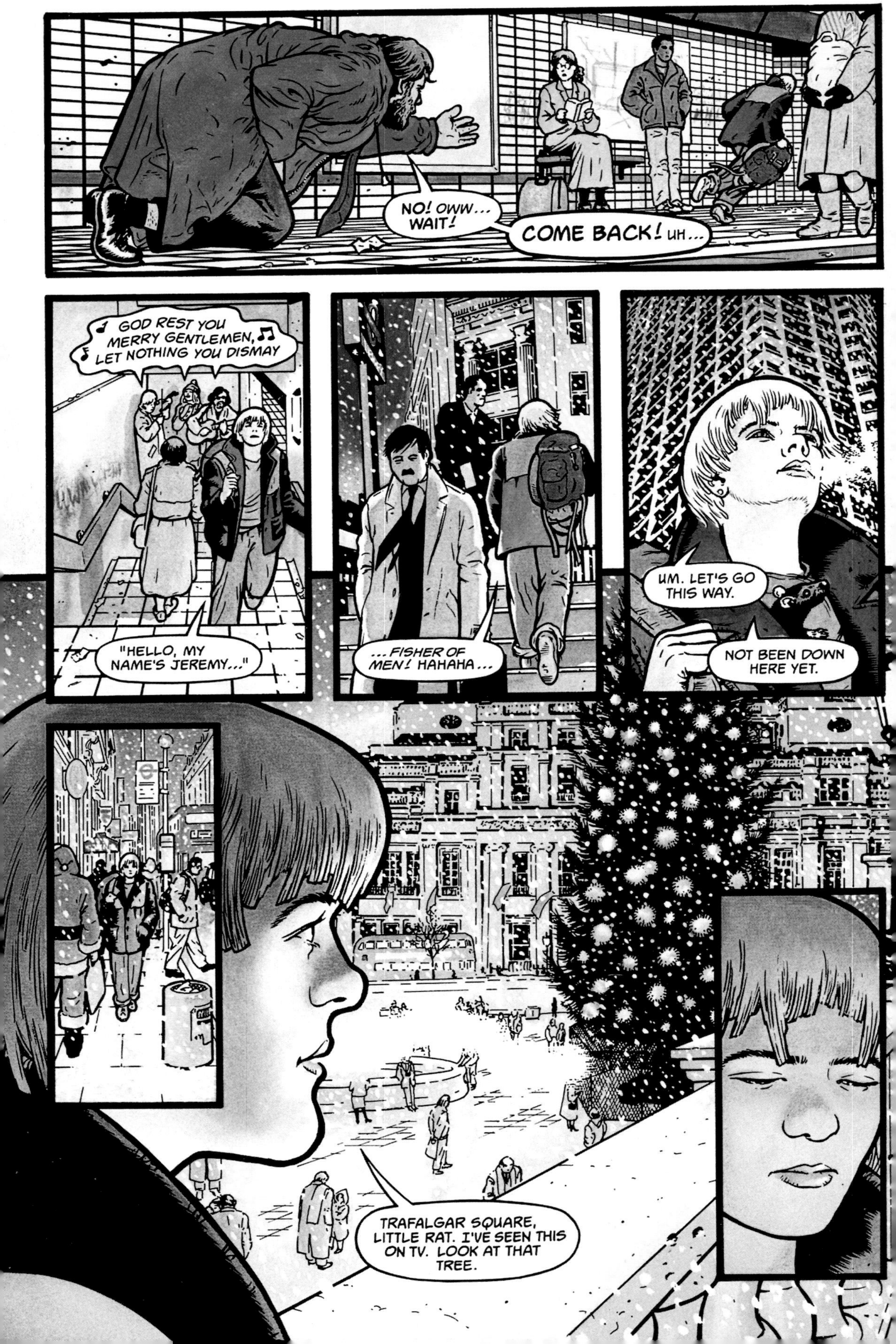

NO! OWW... WAIT!
COME BACK! UH...
GOD REST YOU MERRY GENTLEMEN, LET NOTHING YOU DISMAY
"HELLO, MY NAME'S JEREMY..."
...FISHER OF MEN! HAHAHA...
UM. LET'S GO THIS WAY.
NOT BEEN DOWN HERE YET.
TRAFALGAR SQUARE, LITTLE RAT. I'VE SEEN THIS ON TV. LOOK AT THAT TREE.

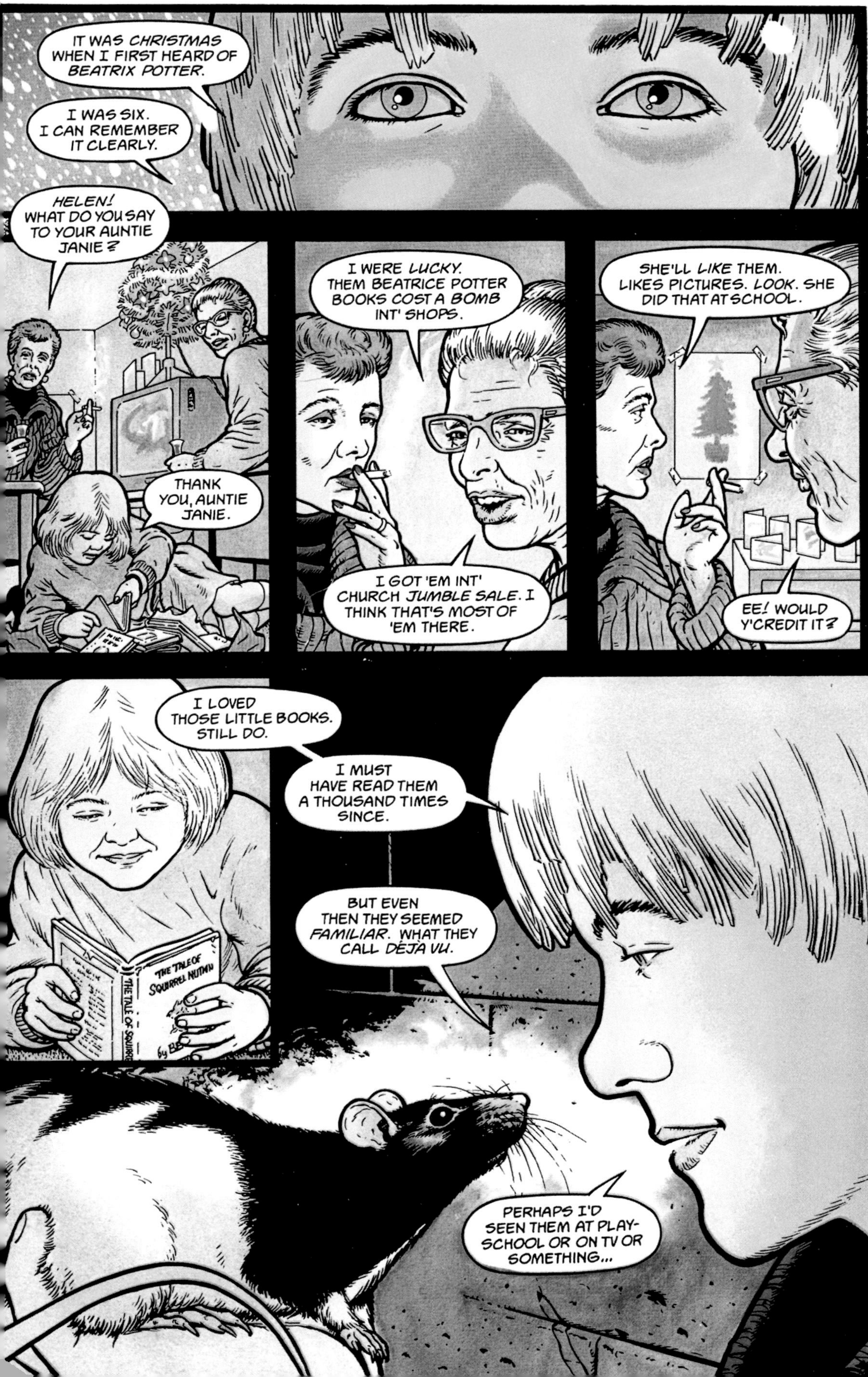
IT WAS CHRISTMAS WHEN I FIRST HEARD OF BEATRIX POTTER.
I WAS SIX. I CAN REMEMBER IT CLEARLY.
HELEN! WHAT DO YOU SAY TO YOUR AUNTIE JANIE?
THANK YOU, AUNTIE JANIE.
I WERE LUCKY. THEM BEATRICE POTTER BOOKS COST A BOMB INT' SHOPS.
I GOT 'EM INT' CHURCH JUMBLE SALE. I THINK THAT'S MOST OF 'EM THERE.
SHE'LL LIKE THEM. LIKES PICTURES. LOOK. SHE DID THAT AT SCHOOL.
EE! WOULD Y'CREDIT IT?
I LOVED THOSE LITTLE BOOKS. STILL DO.
I MUST HAVE READ THEM A THOUSAND TIMES SINCE.
THE TALE OF SQUIRREL NUTKIN
BUT EVEN THEN THEY SEEMED FAMILIAR. WHAT THEY CALL DÉJÀ VU.
PERHAPS I'D SEEN THEM AT PLAY-SCHOOL OR ON TV OR SOMETHING...

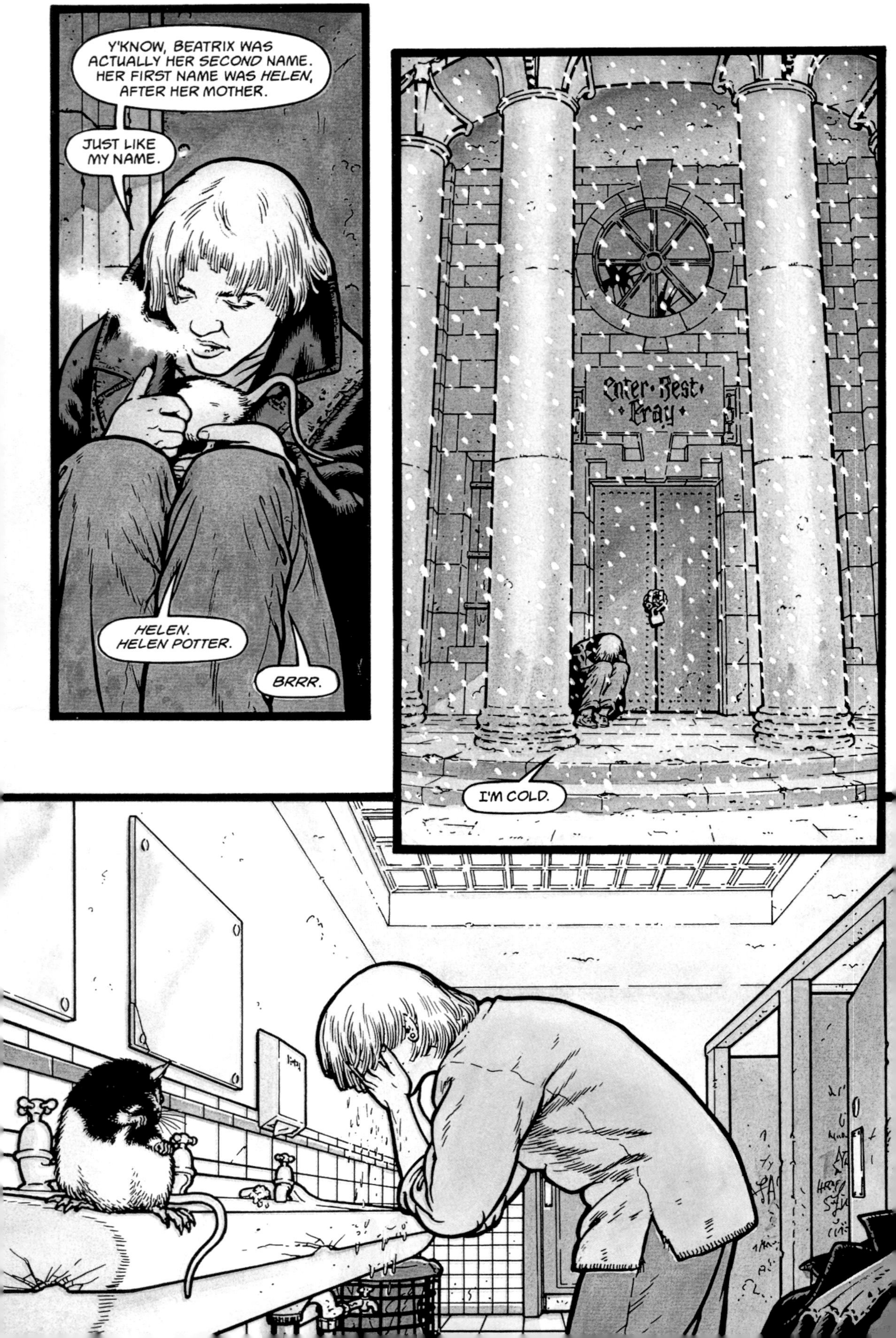
Y'KNOW, BEATRIX WAS ACTUALLY HER SECOND NAME. HER FIRST NAME WAS HELEN, AFTER HER MOTHER.
JUST LIKE MY NAME.
HELEN. HELEN POTTER.
BRRR.
Enter·Rest·Pray
I'M COLD.

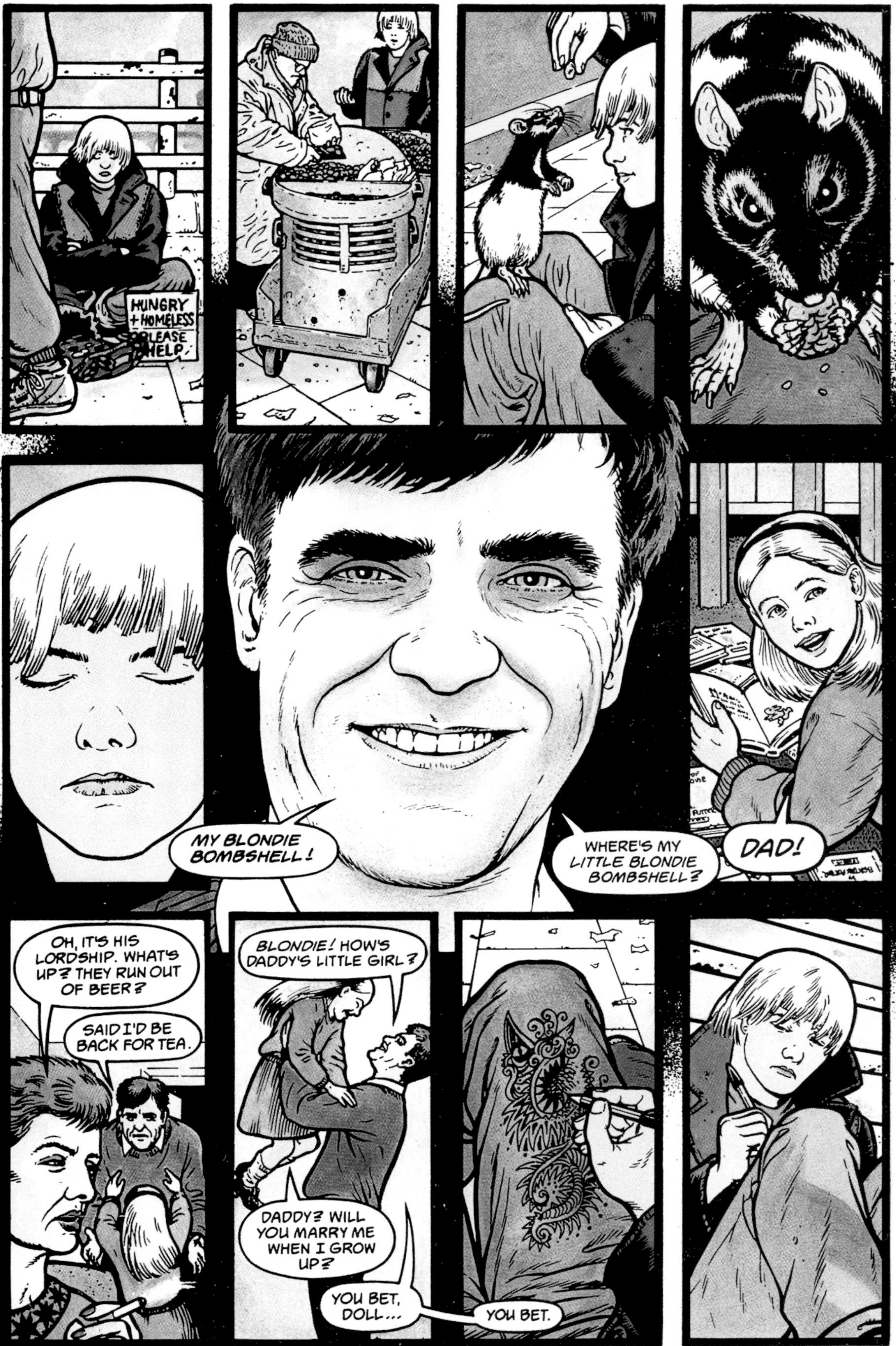

HUNGRY + HOMELESS PLEASE HELP
MY BLONDIE BOMBSHELL!
WHERE'S MY LITTLE BLONDIE BOMBSHELL?
DAD!
OH, IT'S HIS LORDSHIP. WHAT'S UP? THEY RUN OUT OF BEER?
SAID I'D BE BACK FOR TEA.
BLONDIE! HOW'S DADDY'S LITTLE GIRL?
DADDY? WILL YOU MARRY ME WHEN I GROW UP?
YOU BET, DOLL...
YOU BET.

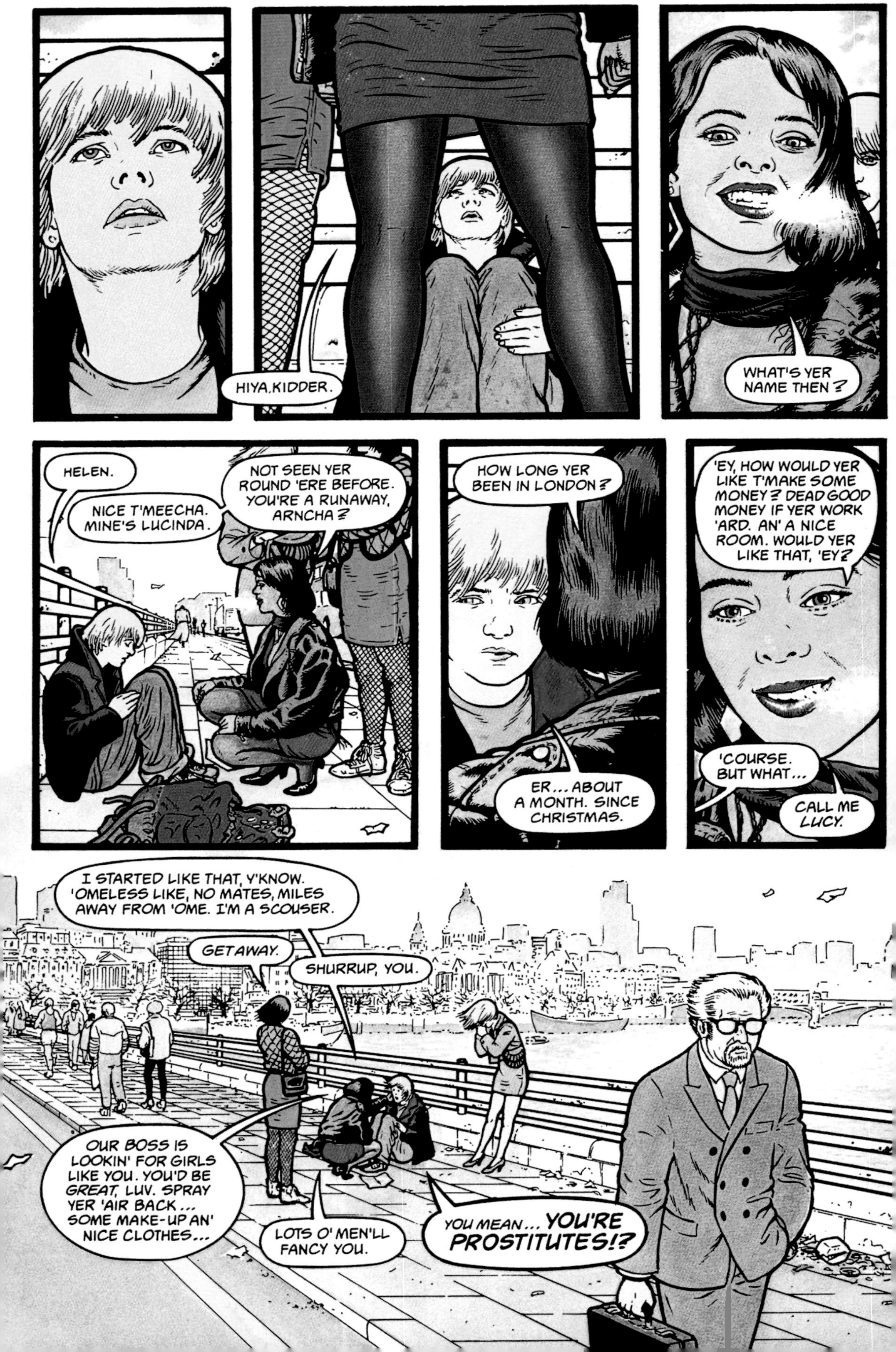
HIYA, KIDDER.
WHAT'S YER NAME THEN?
HELEN.
NICE T'MEECHA. MINE'S LUCINDA.
NOT SEEN YER ROUND 'ERE BEFORE. YOU'RE A RUNAWAY, ARNCHA?
HOW LONG YER BEEN IN LONDON?
ER... ABOUT A MONTH. SINCE CHRISTMAS.
'EY, HOW WOULD YER LIKE T'MAKE SOME MONEY? DEAD GOOD MONEY IF YER WORK 'ARD. AN' A NICE ROOM. WOULD YER LIKE THAT, 'EY?
'COURSE. BUT WHAT...
CALL ME *LUCY.*
I STARTED LIKE THAT, Y'KNOW. 'OMELESS LIKE, NO MATES, MILES AWAY FROM 'OME. I'M A SCOUSER.
GETAWAY.
SHURRUP, YOU.
OUR BOSS IS LOOKIN' FOR GIRLS LIKE YOU. YOU'D BE GREAT, LUV. SPRAY YER 'AIR BACK... SOME MAKE-UP AN' NICE CLOTHES...
LOTS O' MEN'LL FANCY YOU.
YOU MEAN... **YOU'RE PROSTITUTES!?**

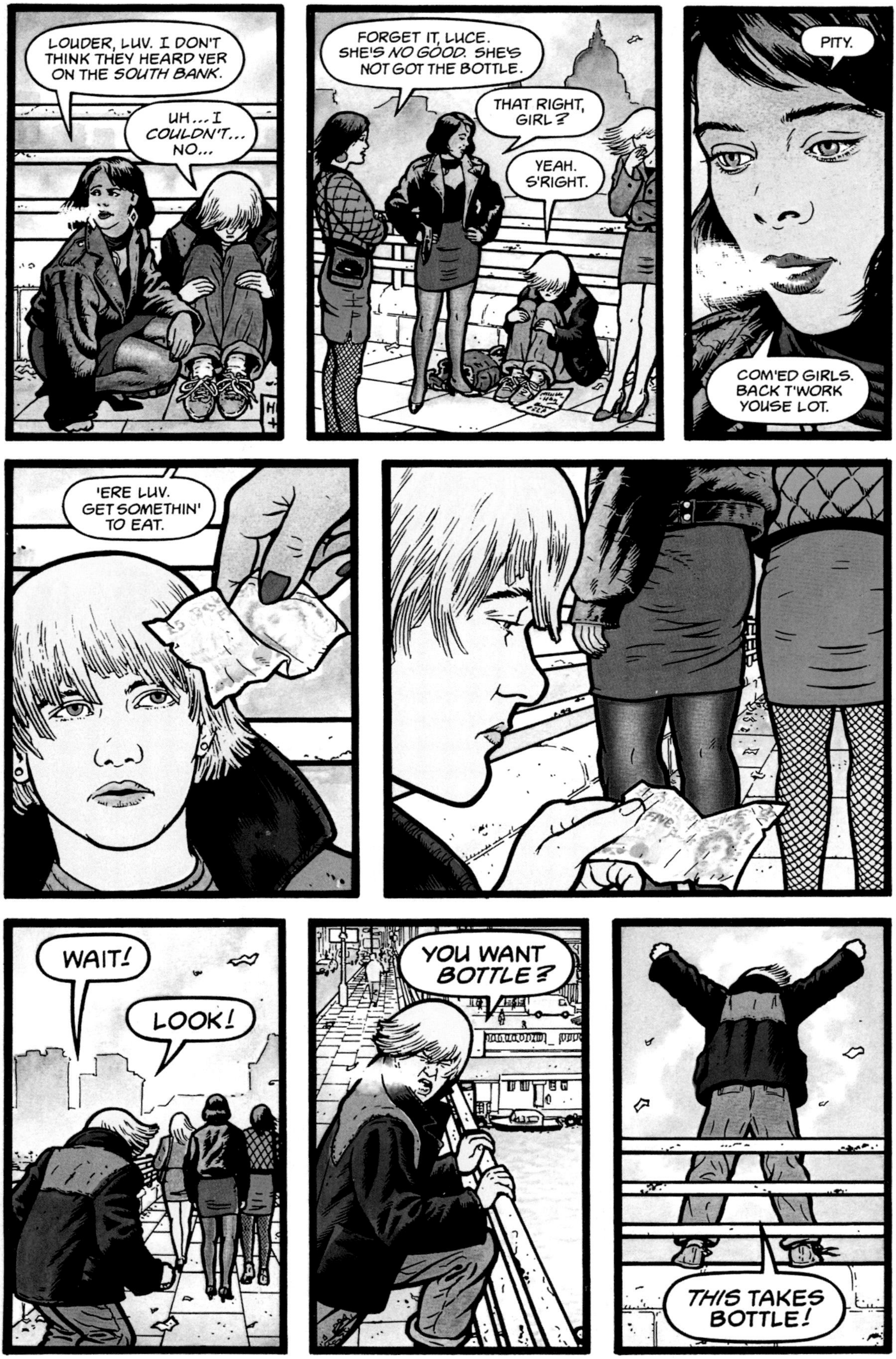
LOUDER, LUV. I DON'T THINK THEY HEARD YER ON THE SOUTH BANK.
UH... I COULDN'T... NO...
FORGET IT, LUCE. SHE'S NO GOOD. SHE'S NOT GOT THE BOTTLE.
THAT RIGHT, GIRL?
YEAH. S'RIGHT.
PITY.
COM'ED GIRLS. BACK T'WORK YOUSE LOT.
'ERE LUV. GET SOMETHIN' TO EAT.
WAIT!
LOOK!
YOU WANT BOTTLE?
THIS TAKES BOTTLE!

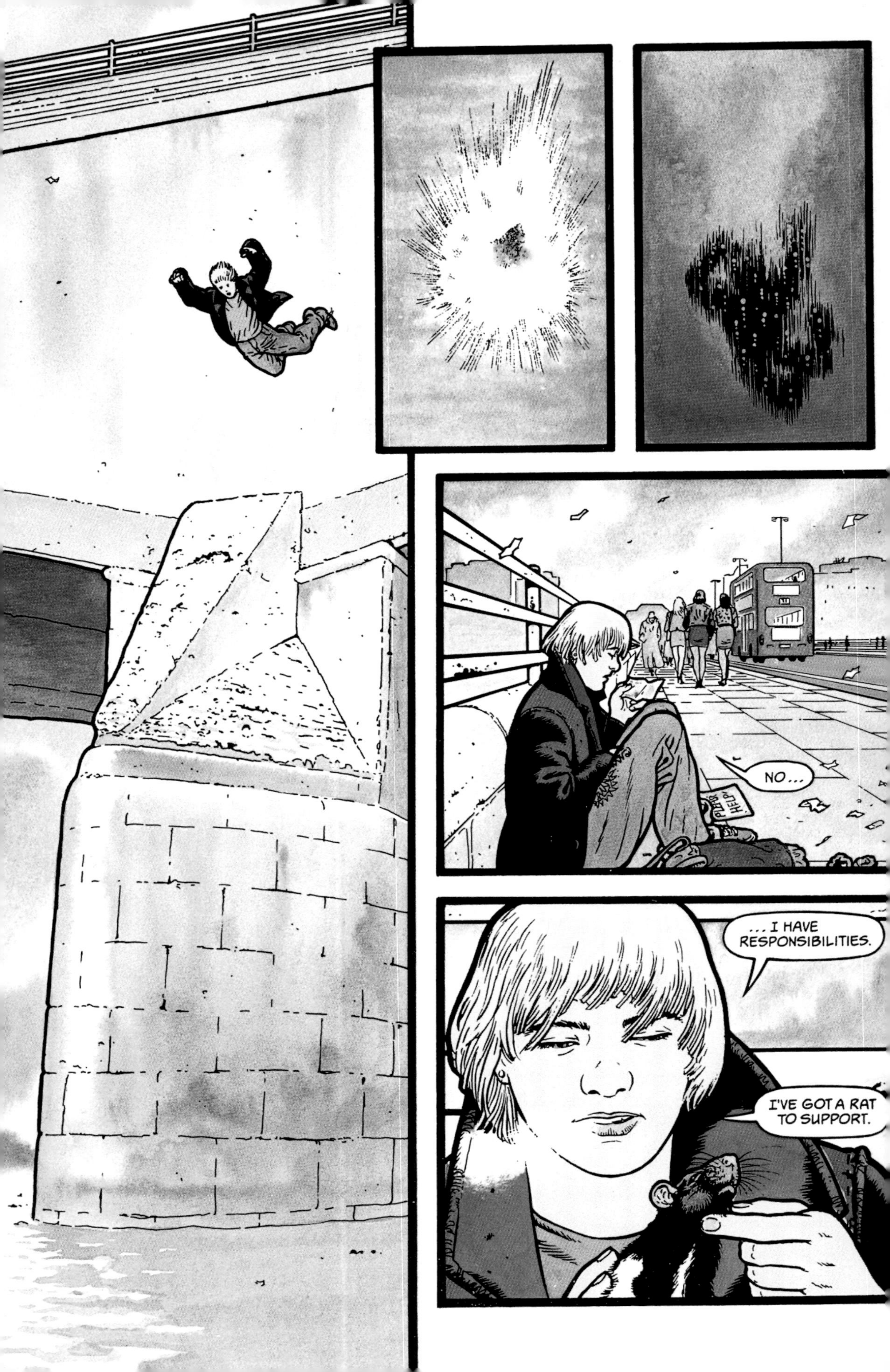

PLEASE HELP
NO...
...I HAVE RESPONSIBILITIES.
I'VE GOT A RAT TO SUPPORT.

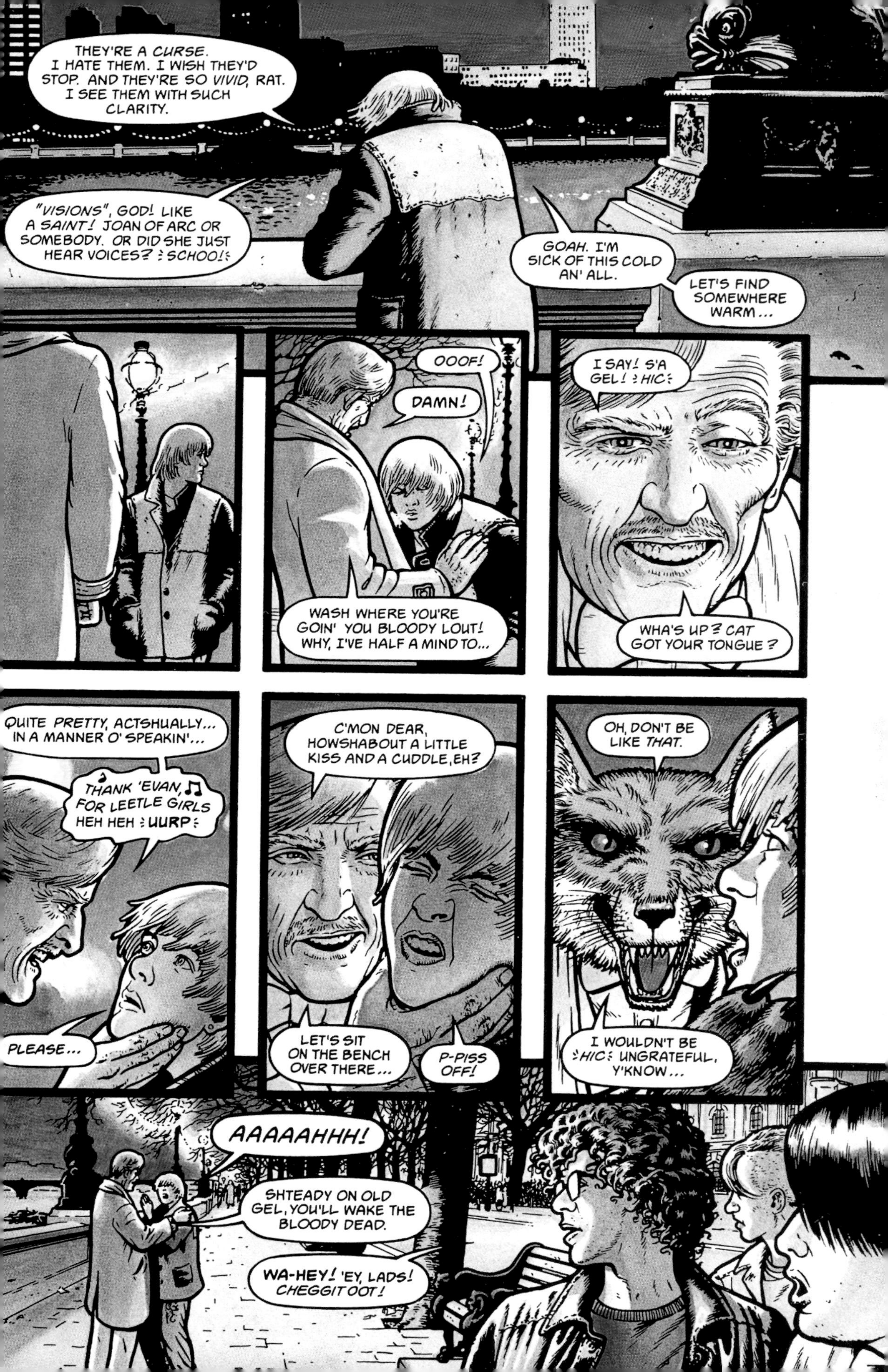
THEY'RE A CURSE. I HATE THEM. I WISH THEY'D STOP. AND THEY'RE SO VIVID, RAT. I SEE THEM WITH SUCH CLARITY.
"VISIONS", GOD! LIKE A SAINT! JOAN OF ARC OR SOMEBODY. OR DID SHE JUST HEAR VOICES? SCHOO!
GOAH. I'M SICK OF THIS COLD AN' ALL.
LET'S FIND SOMEWHERE WARM...
OOOF!
DAMN!
WASH WHERE YOU'RE GOIN' YOU BLOODY LOUT! WHY, I'VE HALF A MIND TO...
I SAY! S'A GEL! HIC
WHA'S UP? CAT GOT YOUR TONGUE?
QUITE PRETTY, ACTSHUALLY... IN A MANNER O' SPEAKIN'...
THANK 'EVAN, FOR LEETLE GIRLS HEH HEH UURP
PLEASE...
C'MON DEAR, HOWSHABOUT A LITTLE KISS AND A CUDDLE, EH?
LET'S SIT ON THE BENCH OVER THERE...
P-PISS OFF!
OH, DON'T BE LIKE THAT.
I WOULDN'T BE HIC UNGRATEFUL, Y'KNOW...
AAAAAHHH!
SHTEADY ON OLD GEL, YOU'LL WAKE THE BLOODY DEAD.
WA-HEY! 'EY, LADS! CHEGGIT OOT!

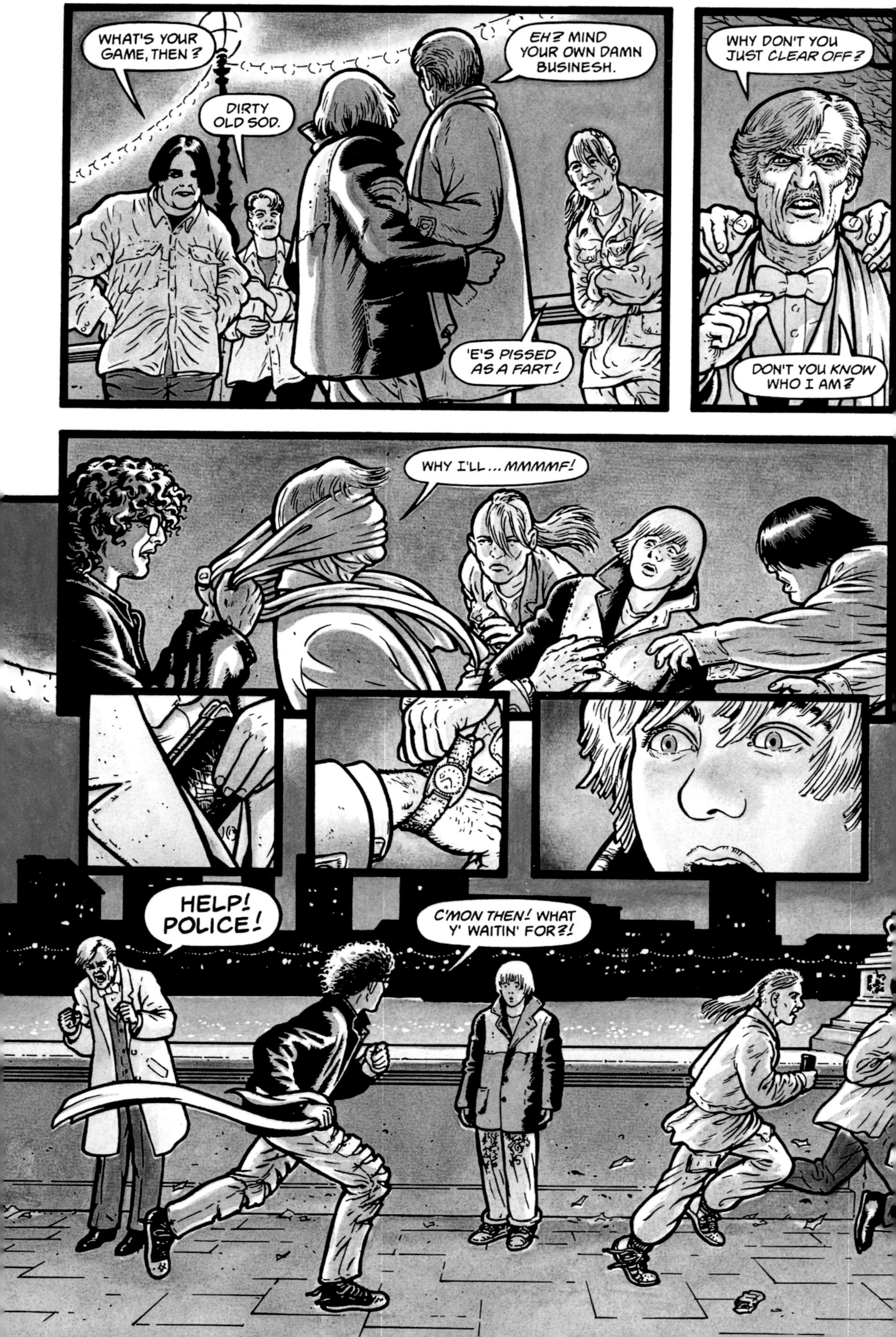
WHAT'S YOUR GAME, THEN?
DIRTY OLD SOD.
EH? MIND YOUR OWN DAMN BUSINESH.
'E'S PISSED AS A FART!
WHY DON'T YOU JUST CLEAR OFF?
DON'T YOU KNOW WHO I AM?
WHY I'LL ... MMMMF!
HELP! POLICE!
C'MON THEN! WHAT Y' WAITIN' FOR?!

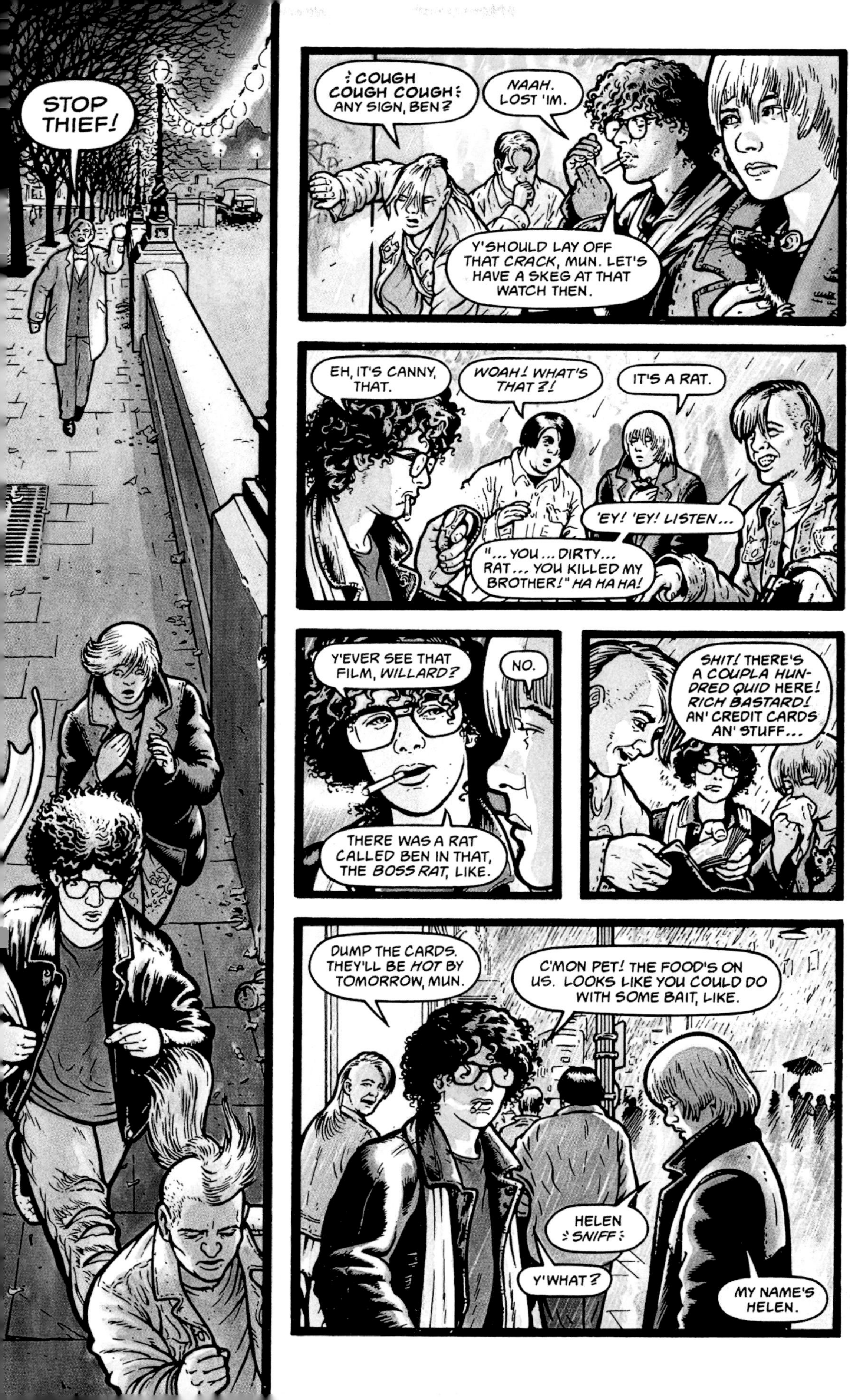
STOP THIEF!
⁝COUGH COUGH COUGH⁝ ANY SIGN, BEN?
NAAH. LOST 'IM.
Y'SHOULD LAY OFF THAT CRACK, MUN. LET'S HAVE A SKEG AT THAT WATCH THEN.
EH, IT'S CANNY, THAT.
WOAH! WHAT'S THAT?!
IT'S A RAT.
'EY! 'EY! LISTEN...
"...YOU...DIRTY... RAT... YOU KILLED MY BROTHER!" HA HA HA!
Y'EVER SEE THAT FILM, WILLARD?
NO.
THERE WAS A RAT CALLED BEN IN THAT, THE BOSS RAT, LIKE.
SHIT! THERE'S A COUPLA HUNDRED QUID HERE! RICH BASTARD! AN' CREDIT CARDS AN' STUFF...
DUMP THE CARDS. THEY'LL BE HOT BY TOMORROW, MUN.
C'MON PET! THE FOOD'S ON US. LOOKS LIKE YOU COULD DO WITH SOME BAIT, LIKE.
HELEN ⁝SNIFF⁝
Y'WHAT?
MY NAME'S HELEN.

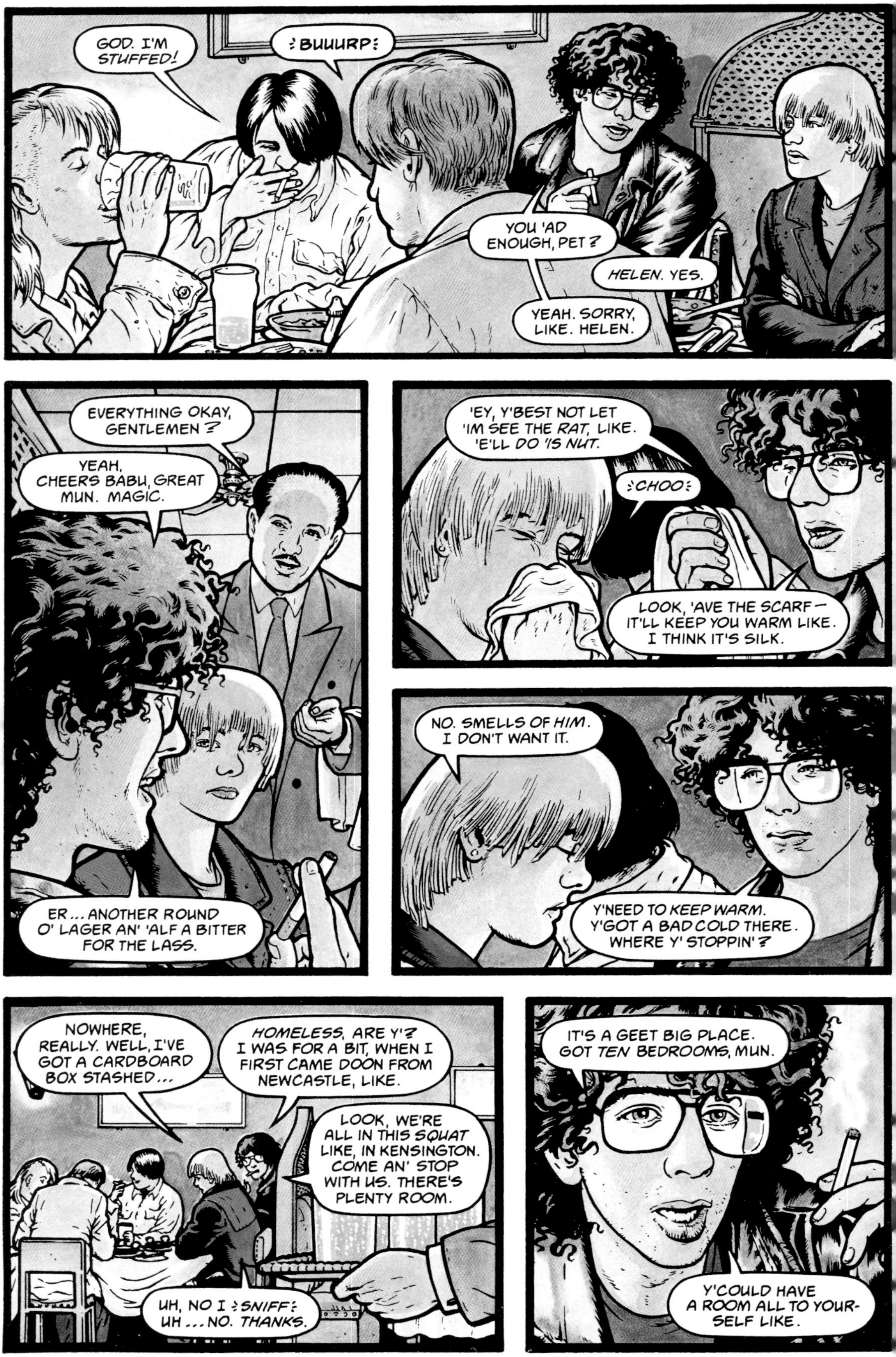
GOD. I'M STUFFED!
BUUURP
YOU 'AD ENOUGH, PET?
HELEN. YES.
YEAH. SORRY, LIKE. HELEN.
EVERYTHING OKAY, GENTLEMEN?
YEAH, CHEERS BABU, GREAT MUN. MAGIC.
ER... ANOTHER ROUND O' LAGER AN' 'ALF A BITTER FOR THE LASS.
'EY, Y'BEST NOT LET 'IM SEE THE RAT, LIKE. 'E'LL DO 'IS NUT.
CHOO
LOOK, 'AVE THE SCARF — IT'LL KEEP YOU WARM LIKE. I THINK IT'S SILK.
NO. SMELLS OF HIM. I DON'T WANT IT.
Y'NEED TO KEEP WARM. Y'GOT A BAD COLD THERE. WHERE Y' STOPPIN'?
NOWHERE, REALLY. WELL, I'VE GOT A CARDBOARD BOX STASHED...
HOMELESS, ARE Y'? I WAS FOR A BIT, WHEN I FIRST CAME DOON FROM NEWCASTLE, LIKE.
LOOK, WE'RE ALL IN THIS SQUAT LIKE, IN KENSINGTON. COME AN' STOP WITH US. THERE'S PLENTY ROOM.
UH, NO I SNIFF UH ... NO. THANKS.
IT'S A GEET BIG PLACE. GOT TEN BEDROOMS, MUN.
Y'COULD HAVE A ROOM ALL TO YOURSELF LIKE.

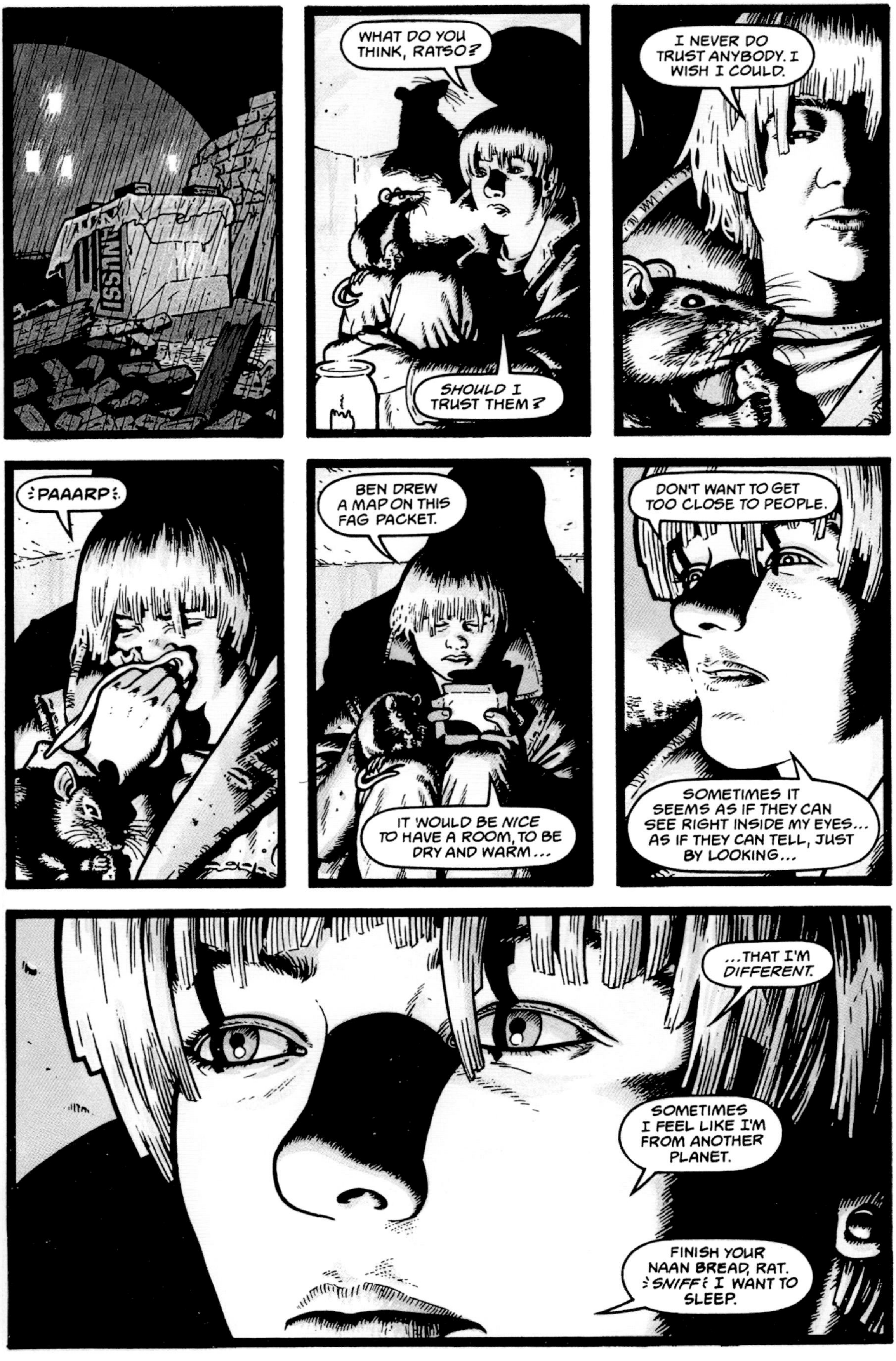
WHAT DO YOU THINK, RATSO?
SHOULD I TRUST THEM?
I NEVER DO TRUST ANYBODY. I WISH I COULD.
PAAARP
BEN DREW A MAP ON THIS FAG PACKET.
IT WOULD BE *NICE* TO HAVE A ROOM, TO BE DRY AND WARM...
DON'T WANT TO GET TOO CLOSE TO PEOPLE.
SOMETIMES IT SEEMS AS IF THEY CAN SEE RIGHT INSIDE MY EYES... AS IF THEY CAN TELL, JUST BY LOOKING...
...THAT I'M *DIFFERENT.*
SOMETIMES I FEEL LIKE I'M FROM ANOTHER PLANET.
FINISH YOUR NAAN BREAD, RAT. *SNIFF* I WANT TO SLEEP.

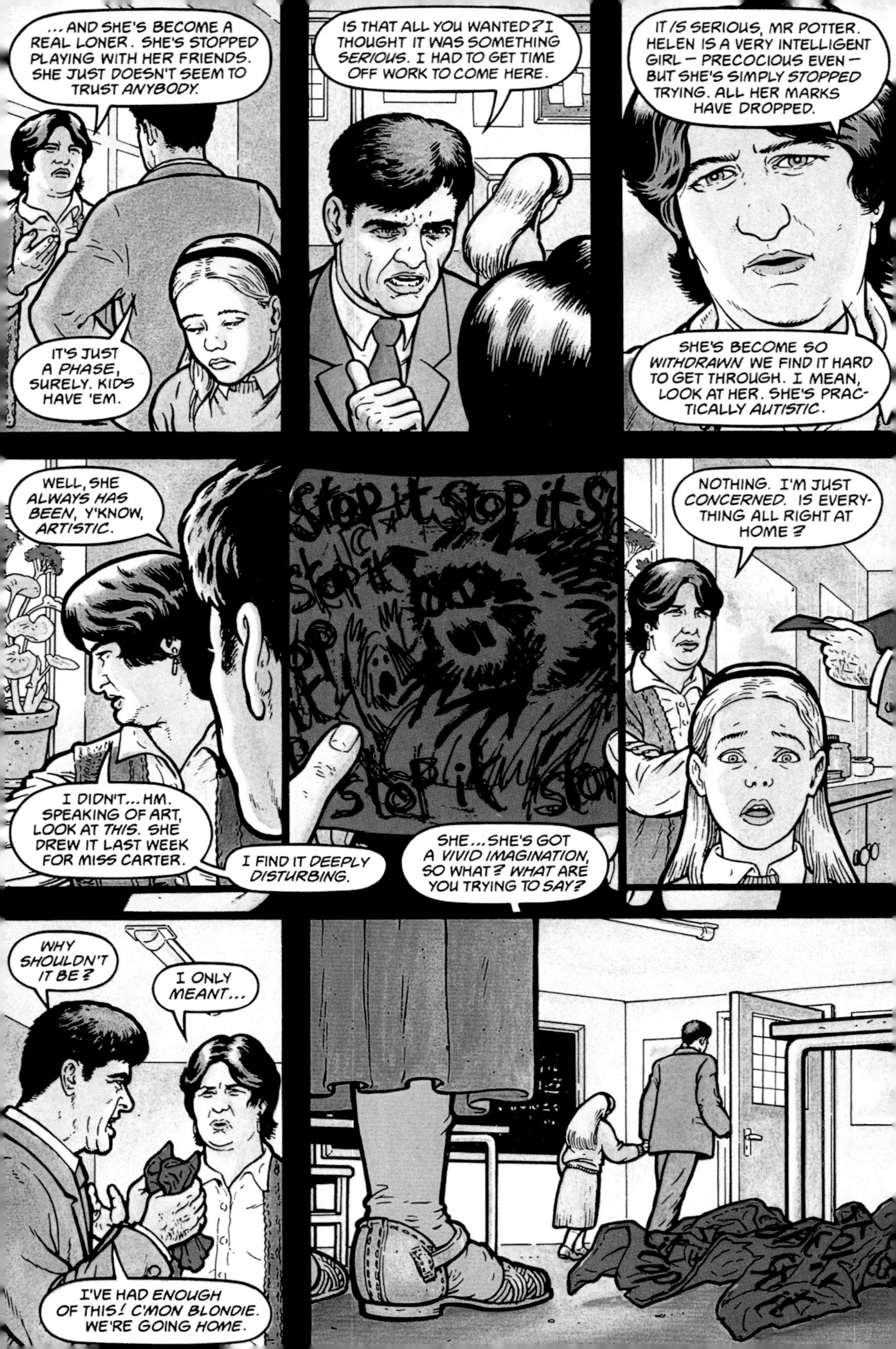
...AND SHE'S BECOME A REAL LONER. SHE'S STOPPED PLAYING WITH HER FRIENDS. SHE JUST DOESN'T SEEM TO TRUST ANYBODY.
IT'S JUST A PHASE, SURELY. KIDS HAVE 'EM.
IS THAT ALL YOU WANTED? I THOUGHT IT WAS SOMETHING SERIOUS. I HAD TO GET TIME OFF WORK TO COME HERE.
IT IS SERIOUS, MR POTTER. HELEN IS A VERY INTELLIGENT GIRL — PRECOCIOUS EVEN — BUT SHE'S SIMPLY STOPPED TRYING. ALL HER MARKS HAVE DROPPED.
SHE'S BECOME SO WITHDRAWN WE FIND IT HARD TO GET THROUGH. I MEAN, LOOK AT HER. SHE'S PRACTICALLY AUTISTIC.
WELL, SHE ALWAYS HAS BEEN, Y'KNOW, ARTISTIC.
I DIDN'T... HM. SPEAKING OF ART, LOOK AT THIS. SHE DREW IT LAST WEEK FOR MISS CARTER.
I FIND IT DEEPLY DISTURBING.
STOP IT STOP IT
SHE... SHE'S GOT A VIVID IMAGINATION, SO WHAT? WHAT ARE YOU TRYING TO SAY?
NOTHING. I'M JUST CONCERNED. IS EVERYTHING ALL RIGHT AT HOME?
WHY SHOULDN'T IT BE?
I ONLY MEANT...
I'VE HAD ENOUGH OF THIS! C'MON BLONDIE. WE'RE GOING HOME.

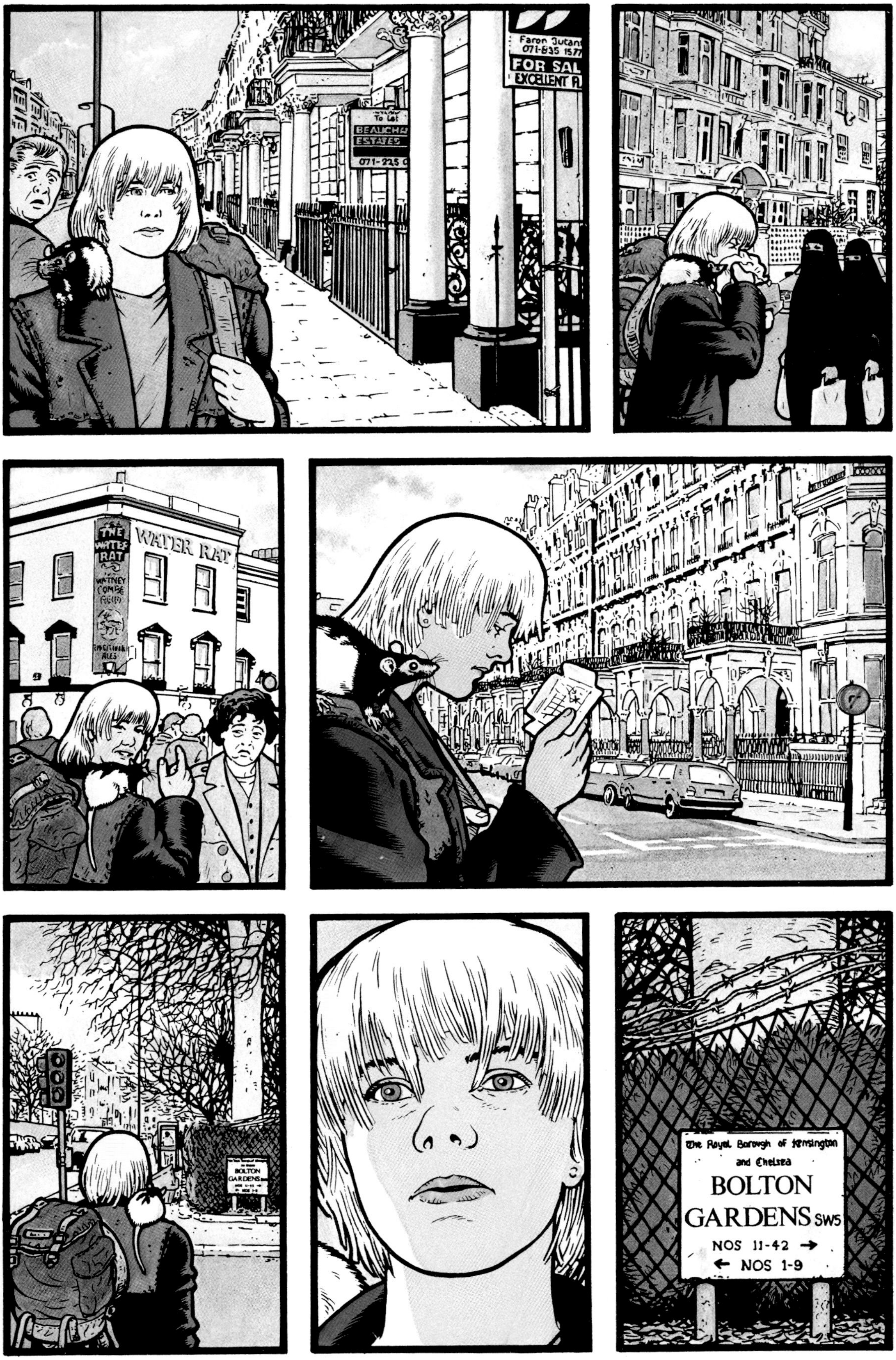
071-835 1577
FOR SAL
EXCELLENT F
To Let
BEAUCHA
ESTATES
071-225 C
THE WATER RAT
WATER RAT
TRADITIONAL ALES
BOLTON
GARDENS
The Royal Borough of Kensington
and Chelsea
BOLTON
GARDENS SW5
NOS 11-42 →
← NOS 1-9

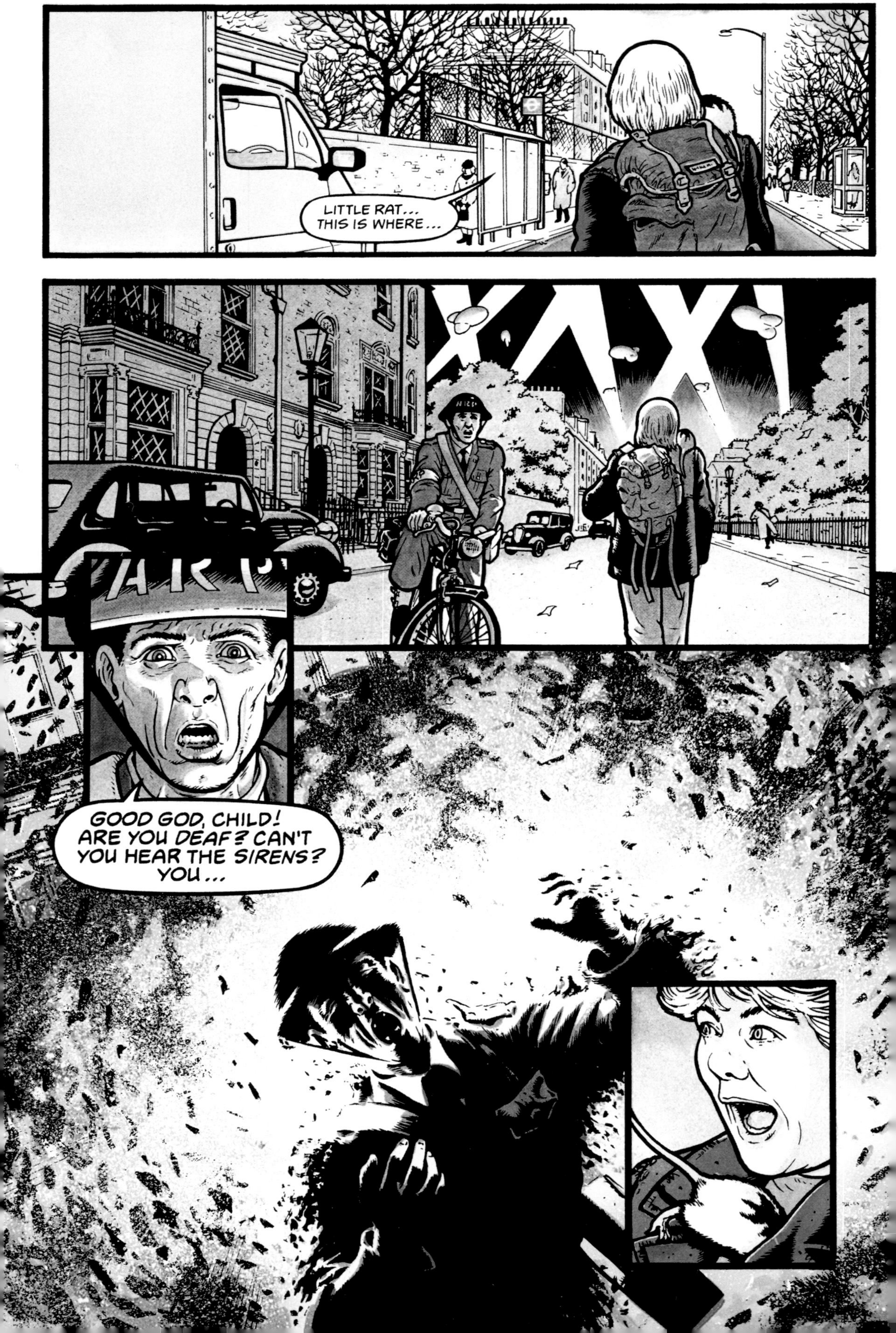

LITTLE RAT... THIS IS WHERE...
ARP
GOOD GOD, CHILD! ARE YOU DEAF? CAN'T YOU HEAR THE SIRENS? YOU...

BEATRIX POTTER
Writer and Artist
1866 to 1943
Lived in a house on this site from 1866 w...
... THE BOLTONS ASSOCIATION, THE BEATRIX POTTER SOCIETY AND FREDERICK WARNE &...

"MY UNLOVED BIRTHPLACE".

AND, JUST ACROSS THE ROAD...

THAT'S THE ONE, RAT. MIDDLE ONE OF THE THREE FOR SALE. WE'VE GOT TO SNEAK ROUND THE BACK.

...TEN...ELEVEN... TWELVE. THIS IS IT. THERE'S SUPPOSED TO BE A LOOSE BOARD...

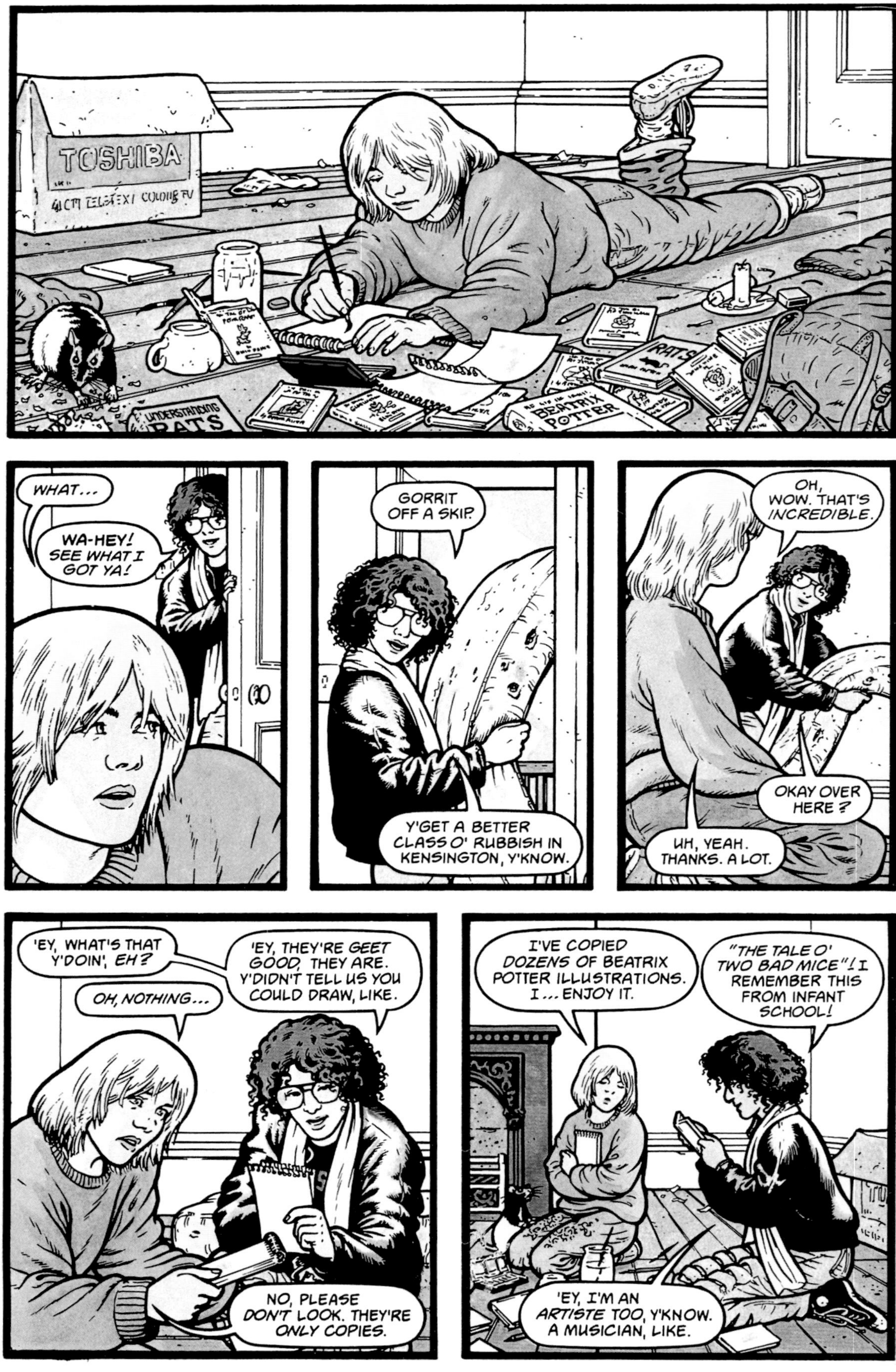

TOSHIBA
BEATRIX POTTER
RATS
UNDERSTANDING RATS
WHAT...
WA-HEY! SEE WHAT I GOT YA!
GORRIT OFF A SKIP.
Y'GET A BETTER CLASS O' RUBBISH IN KENSINGTON, Y'KNOW.
OH, WOW. THAT'S *INCREDIBLE*.
OKAY OVER HERE?
UH, YEAH. THANKS. A LOT.
'EY, WHAT'S THAT Y'DOIN', *EH?*
OH, NOTHING...
'EY, THEY'RE *GEET GOOD*, THEY ARE. Y'DIDN'T TELL US YOU COULD DRAW, LIKE.
NO, PLEASE *DON'T* LOOK. THEY'RE *ONLY* COPIES.
I'VE COPIED *DOZENS* OF BEATRIX POTTER ILLUSTRATIONS. I... ENJOY IT.
"THE TALE O' TWO BAD MICE"! I REMEMBER THIS FROM INFANT SCHOOL!
'EY, I'M AN *ARTISTE* TOO, Y'KNOW. A MUSICIAN, LIKE.

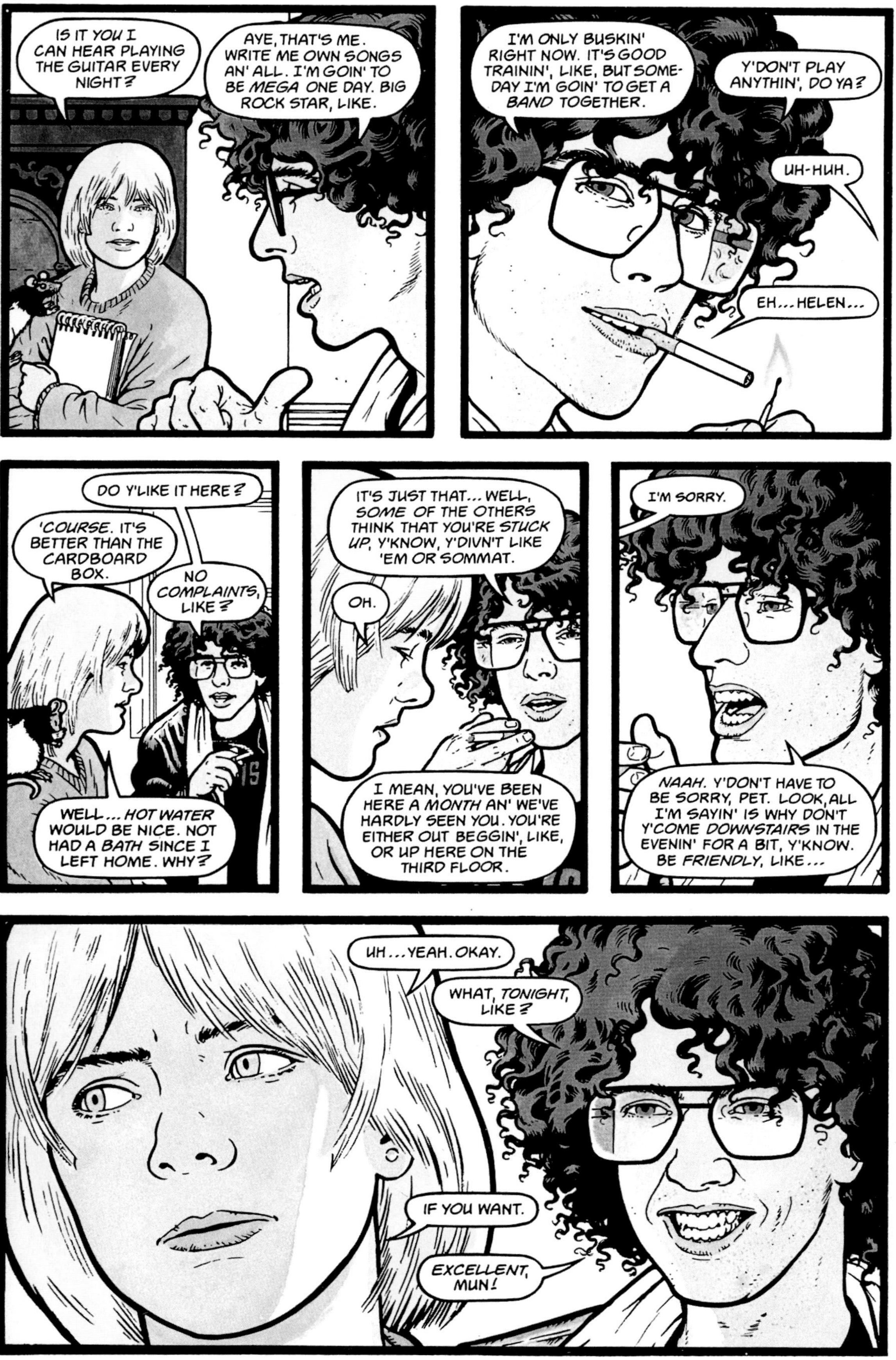
IS IT YOU I CAN HEAR PLAYING THE GUITAR EVERY NIGHT?
AYE, THAT'S ME. WRITE ME OWN SONGS AN' ALL. I'M GOIN' TO BE MEGA ONE DAY. BIG ROCK STAR, LIKE.
I'M ONLY BUSKIN' RIGHT NOW. IT'S GOOD TRAININ', LIKE, BUT SOMEDAY I'M GOIN' TO GET A BAND TOGETHER.
Y'DON'T PLAY ANYTHIN', DO YA?
UH-HUH.
EH... HELEN...
DO Y'LIKE IT HERE?
'COURSE. IT'S BETTER THAN THE CARDBOARD BOX.
NO COMPLAINTS, LIKE?
WELL... HOT WATER WOULD BE NICE. NOT HAD A BATH SINCE I LEFT HOME. WHY?
IT'S JUST THAT... WELL, SOME OF THE OTHERS THINK THAT YOU'RE STUCK UP, Y'KNOW, Y'DIVN'T LIKE 'EM OR SOMMAT.
OH.
I MEAN, YOU'VE BEEN HERE A MONTH AN' WE'VE HARDLY SEEN YOU. YOU'RE EITHER OUT BEGGIN', LIKE, OR UP HERE ON THE THIRD FLOOR.
I'M SORRY.
NAAH. Y'DON'T HAVE TO BE SORRY, PET. LOOK, ALL I'M SAYIN' IS WHY DON'T Y'COME DOWNSTAIRS IN THE EVENIN' FOR A BIT, Y'KNOW. BE FRIENDLY, LIKE...
UH... YEAH. OKAY.
WHAT, TONIGHT, LIKE?
IF YOU WANT.
EXCELLENT, MUN!

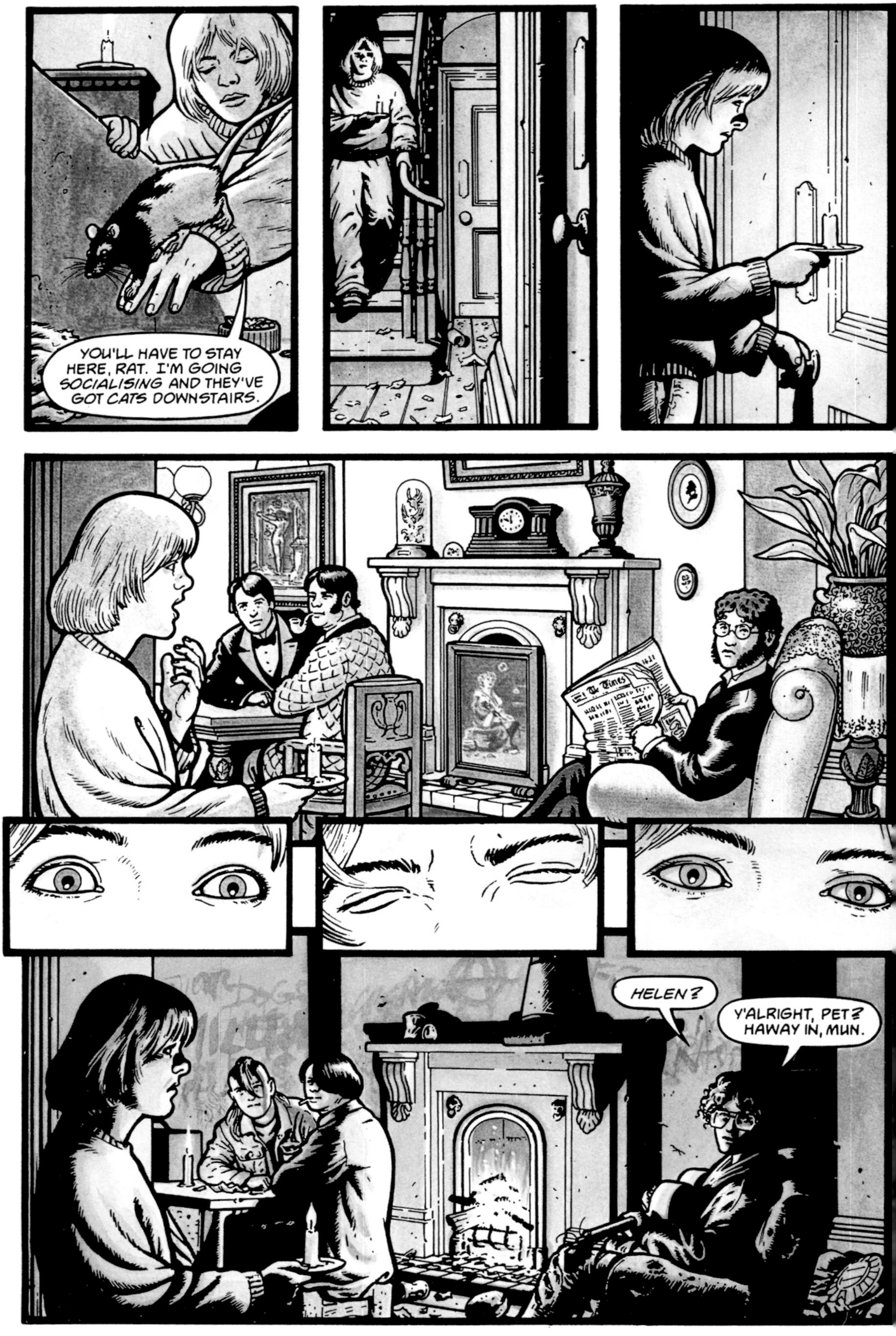
YOU'LL HAVE TO STAY HERE, RAT. I'M GOING SOCIALISING AND THEY'VE GOT CATS DOWNSTAIRS.
HELEN?
Y'ALRIGHT, PET? HAWAY IN, MUN.

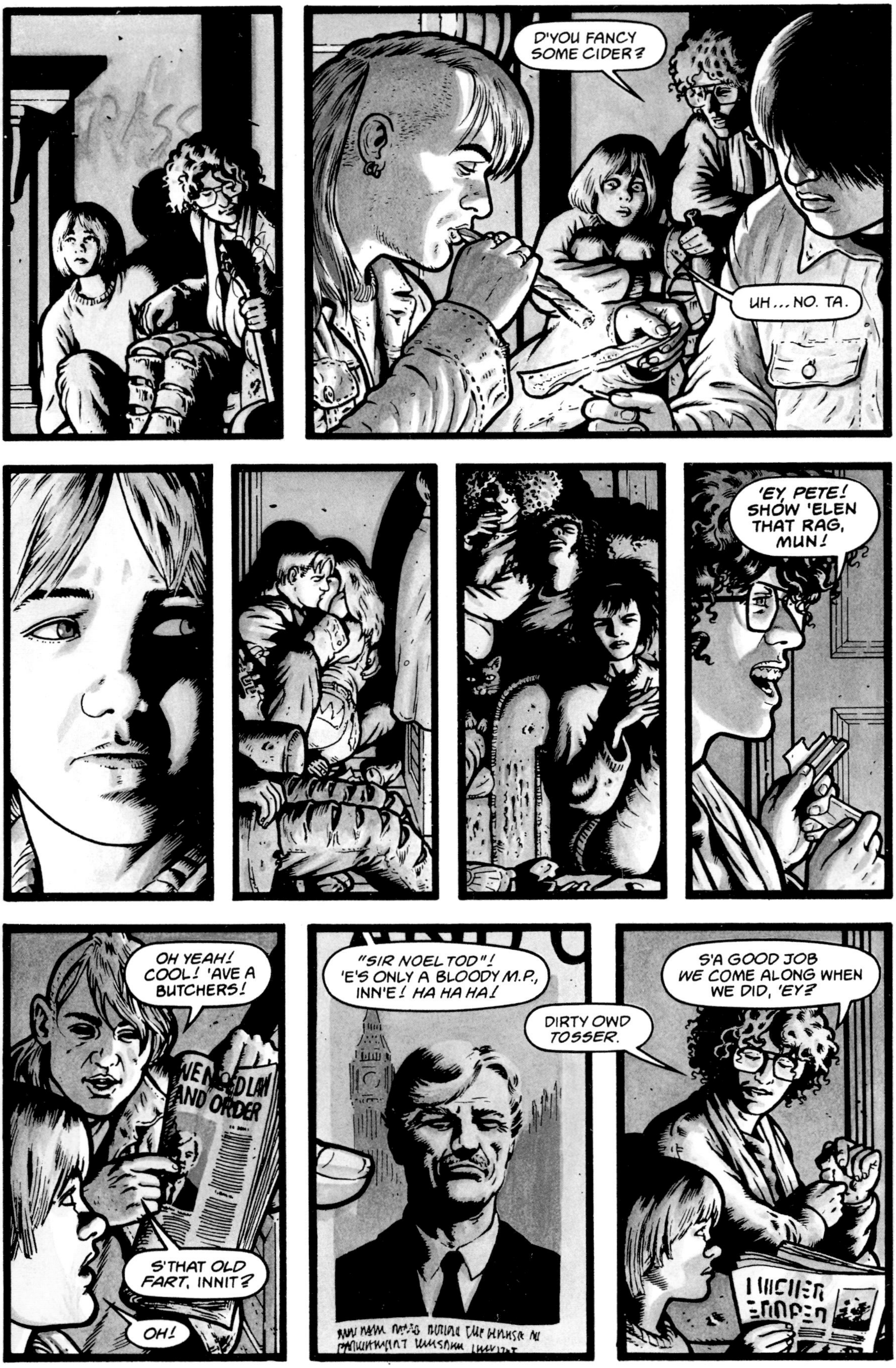
D'YOU FANCY SOME CIDER?
UH... NO. TA.
'EY, PETE! SHOW 'ELEN THAT RAG, MUN!
OH YEAH! COOL! 'AVE A BUTCHERS!
WE NEED LAW AND ORDER
S'THAT OLD FART, INNIT?
OH!
"SIR NOEL TOD"! 'E'S ONLY A BLOODY M.P., INN'E! HA HA HA!
DIRTY OWD TOSSER.
S'A GOOD JOB WE COME ALONG WHEN WE DID, 'EY?

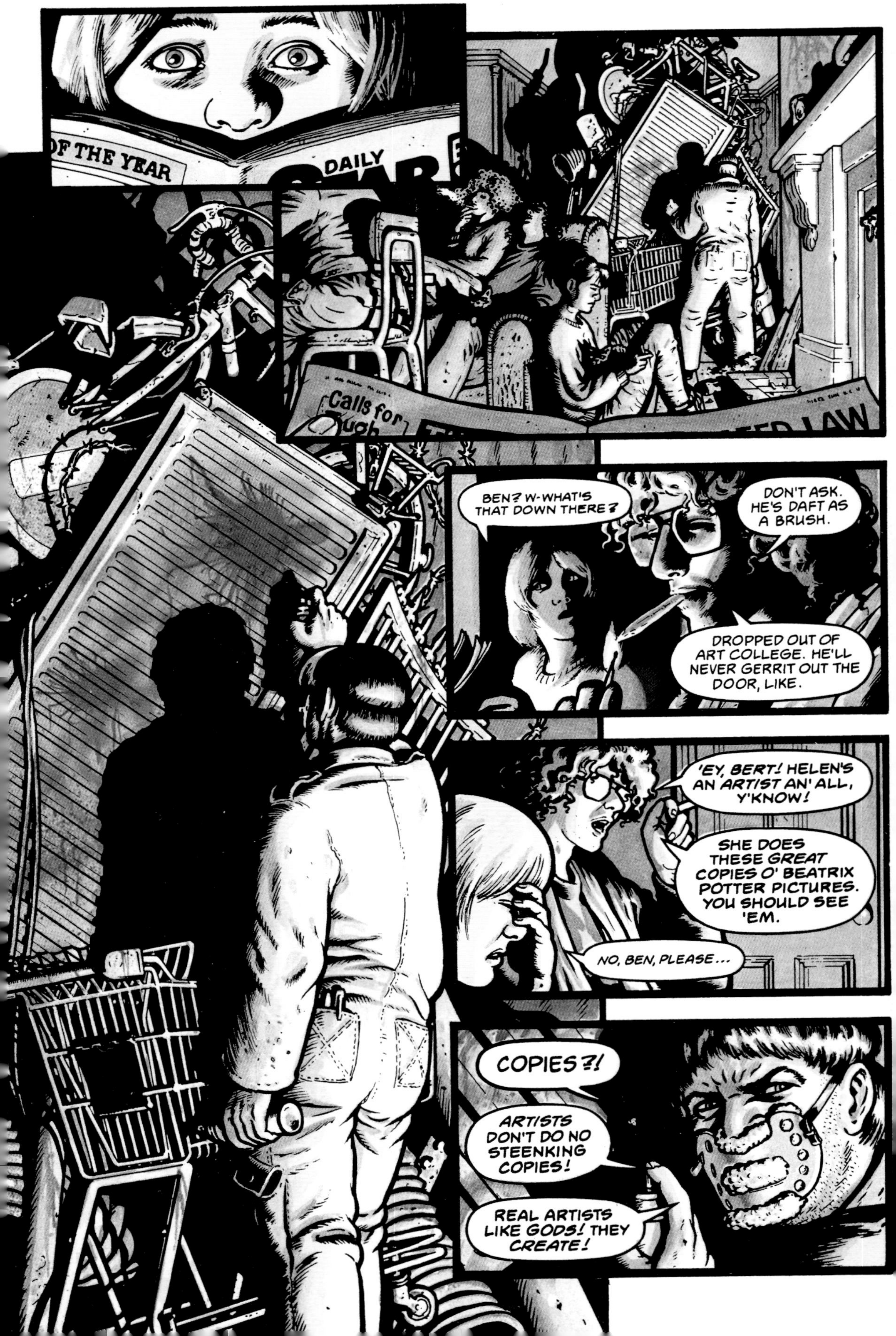
OF THE YEAR
DAILY
Calls for
BEN? W-WHAT'S THAT DOWN THERE?
DON'T ASK. HE'S DAFT AS A BRUSH.
DROPPED OUT OF ART COLLEGE. HE'LL NEVER GERRIT OUT THE DOOR, LIKE.
'EY, BERT! HELEN'S AN ARTIST AN' ALL, Y'KNOW!
SHE DOES THESE GREAT COPIES O' BEATRIX POTTER PICTURES. YOU SHOULD SEE 'EM.
NO, BEN, PLEASE...
COPIES?!
ARTISTS DON'T DO NO STEENKING COPIES!
REAL ARTISTS LIKE GODS! THEY CREATE!

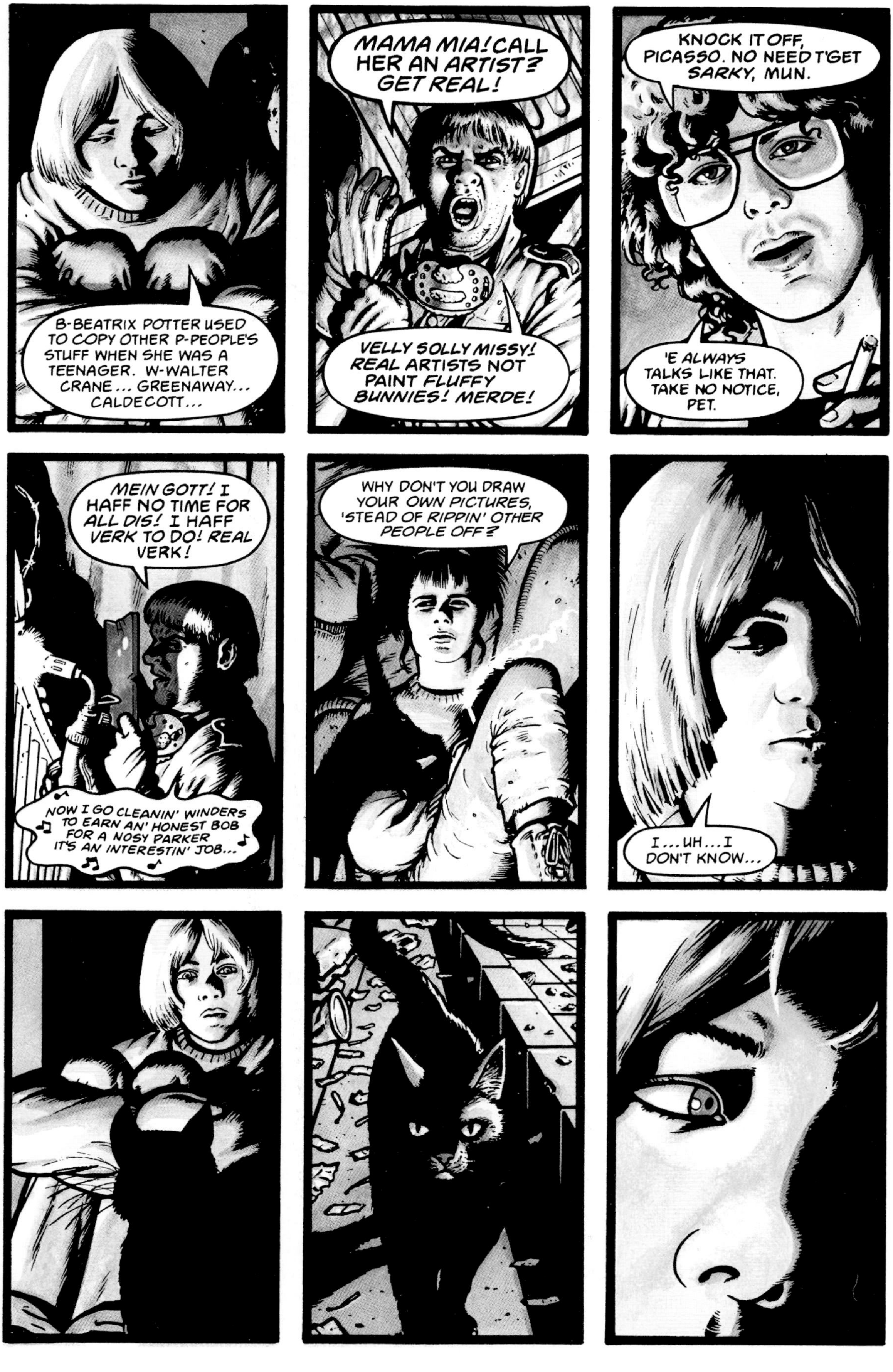
B-BEATRIX POTTER USED TO COPY OTHER P-PEOPLE'S STUFF WHEN SHE WAS A TEENAGER. W-WALTER CRANE... GREENAWAY... CALDECOTT...
MAMA MIA! CALL HER AN ARTIST? GET REAL!
VELLY SOLLY MISSY! REAL ARTISTS NOT PAINT FLUFFY BUNNIES! MERDE!
KNOCK IT OFF, PICASSO. NO NEED T'GET SARKY, MUN.
'E ALWAYS TALKS LIKE THAT. TAKE NO NOTICE, PET.
MEIN GOTT! I HAFF NO TIME FOR ALL DIS! I HAFF VERK TO DO! REAL VERK!
NOW I GO CLEANIN' WINDERS TO EARN AN' HONEST BOB FOR A NOSY PARKER IT'S AN INTERESTIN' JOB...
WHY DON'T YOU DRAW YOUR OWN PICTURES, 'STEAD OF RIPPIN' OTHER PEOPLE OFF?
I... UH... I DON'T KNOW...

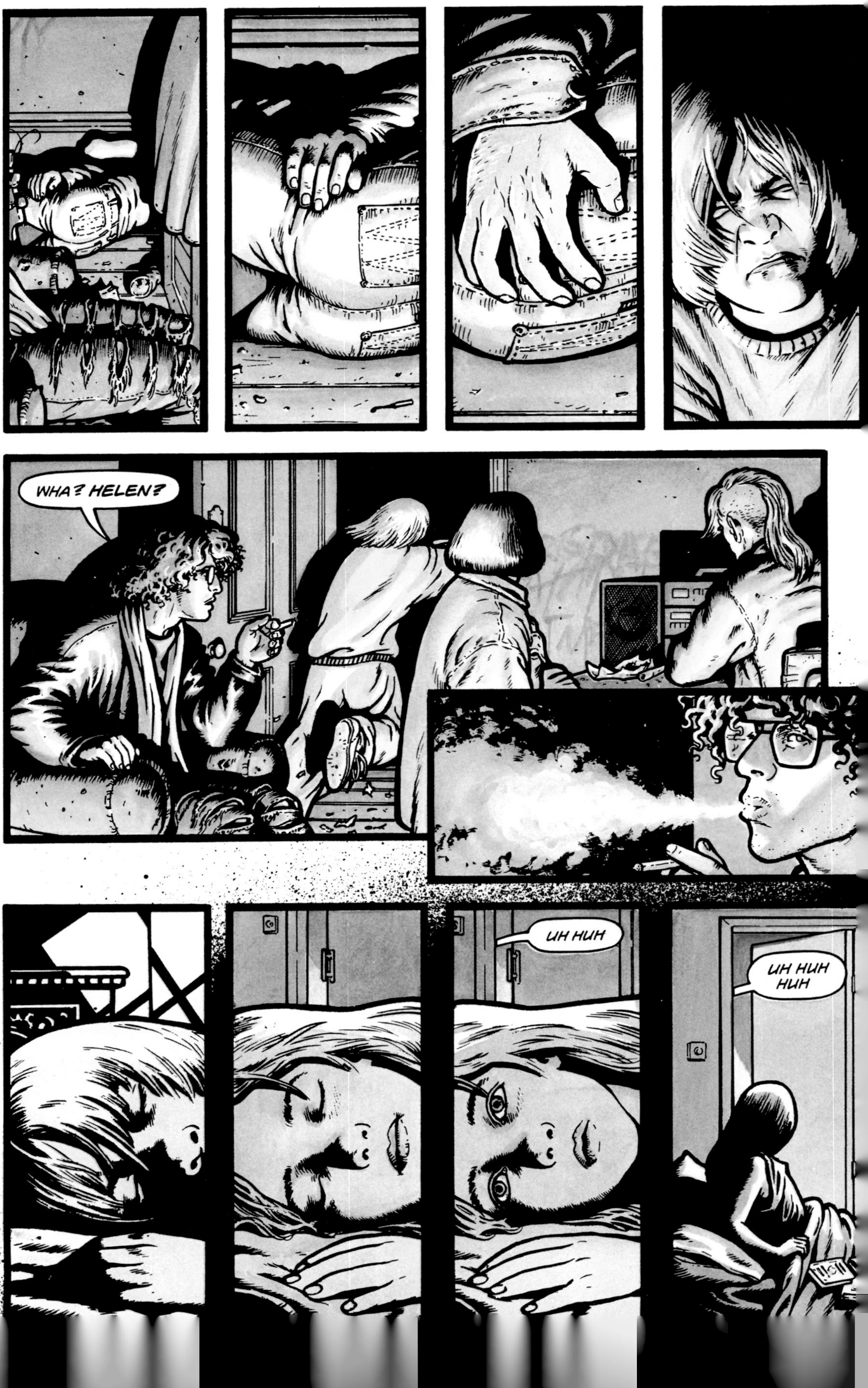
WHA? HELEN?
UH HUH
UH HUH
HUH

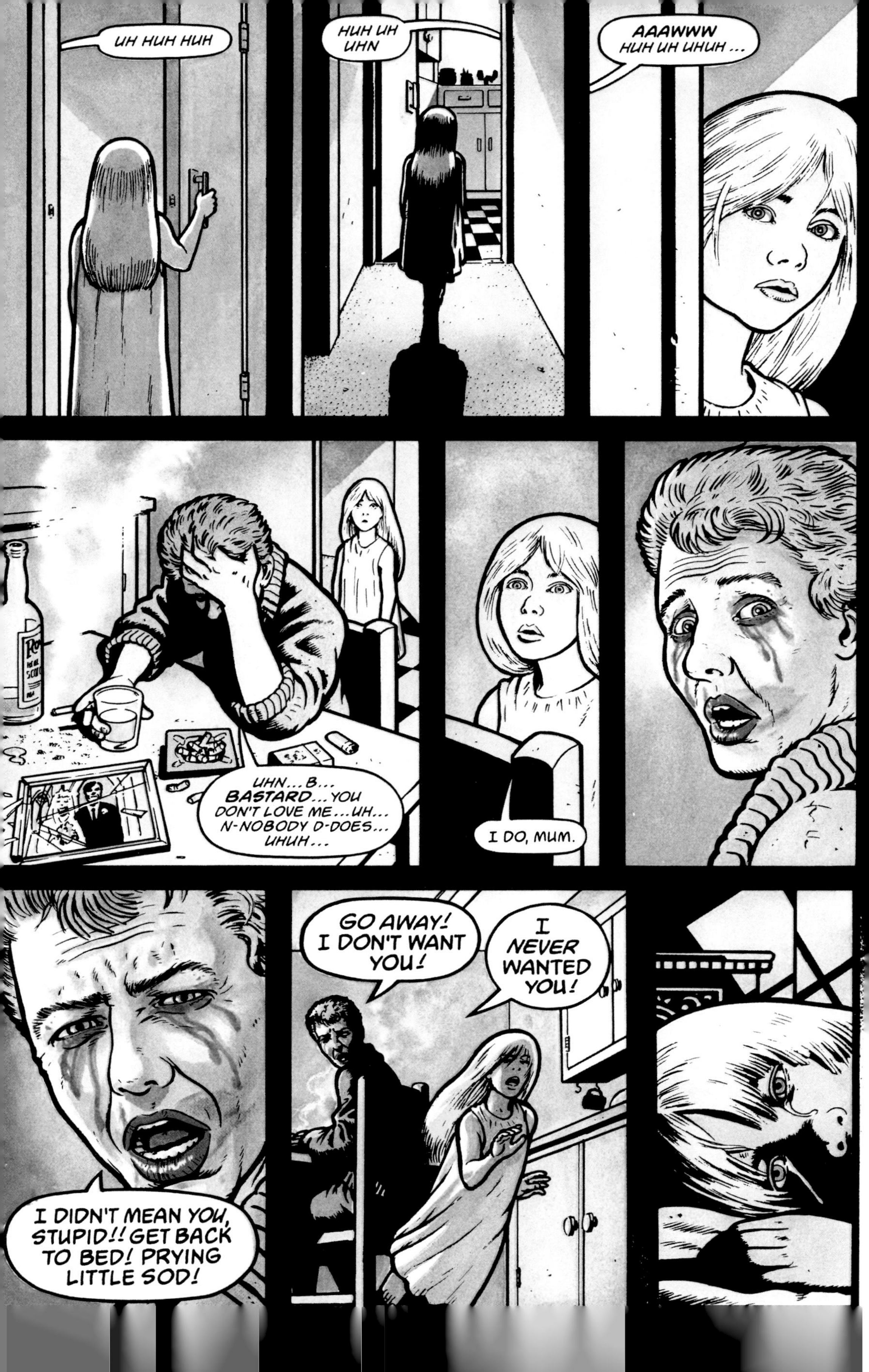
UH HUH HUH
HUH UH UHN
AAAWWW HUH UH UHUH ...
UHN... B... BASTARD... YOU DON'T LOVE ME... UH... N-NOBODY D-DOES... UHUH...
I DO, MUM.
I DIDN'T MEAN YOU, STUPID!! GET BACK TO BED! PRYING LITTLE SOD!
GO AWAY! I DON'T WANT YOU!
I NEVER WANTED YOU!

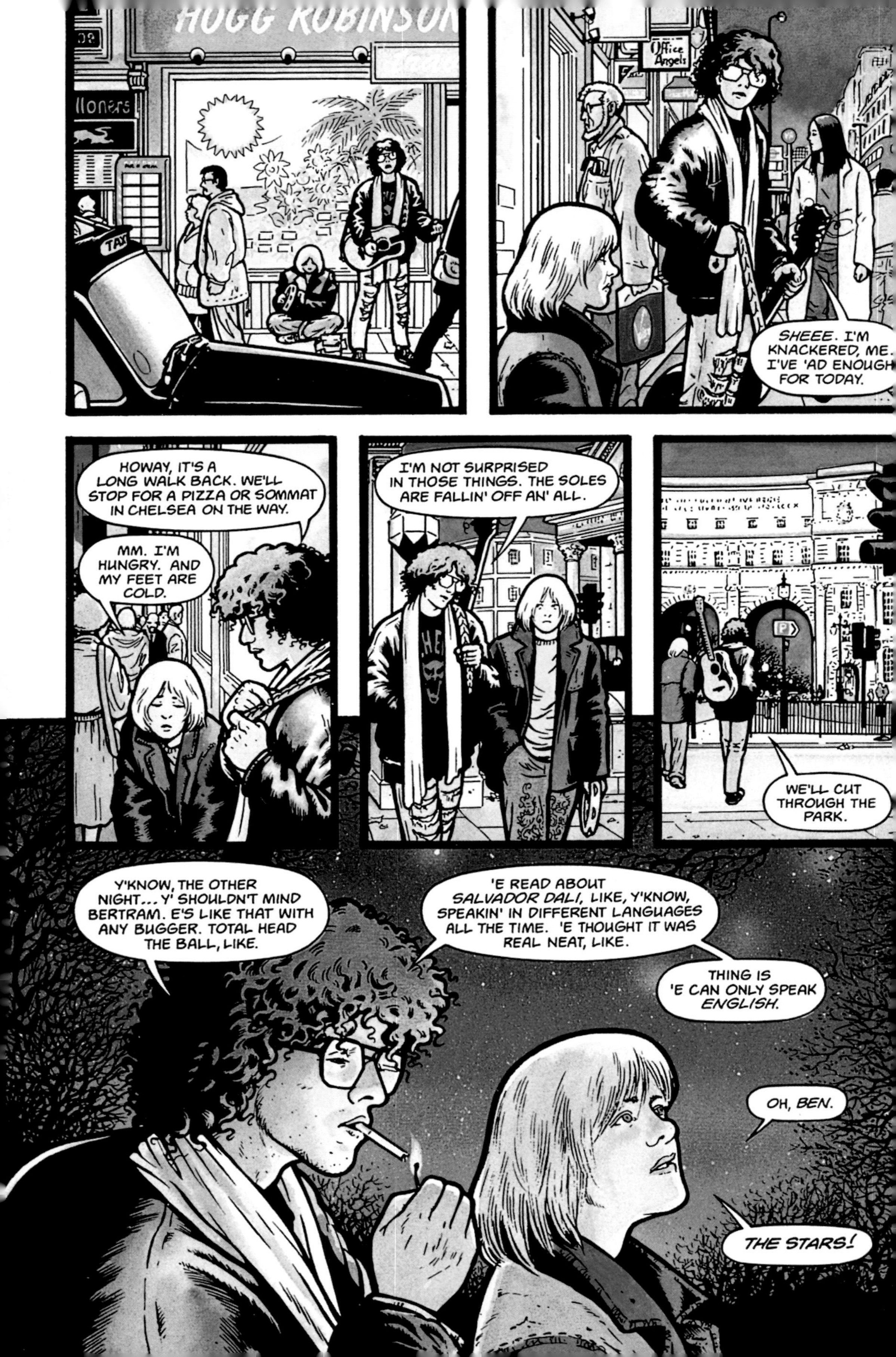
HOGG ROBINSON
Office Angels
SHEEE. I'M KNACKERED, ME. I'VE 'AD ENOUGH FOR TODAY.
HOWAY, IT'S A LONG WALK BACK. WE'LL STOP FOR A PIZZA OR SOMMAT IN CHELSEA ON THE WAY.
MM. I'M HUNGRY. AND MY FEET ARE COLD.
I'M NOT SURPRISED IN THOSE THINGS. THE SOLES ARE FALLIN' OFF AN' ALL.
WE'LL CUT THROUGH THE PARK.
Y'KNOW, THE OTHER NIGHT... Y' SHOULDN'T MIND BERTRAM. E'S LIKE THAT WITH ANY BUGGER. TOTAL HEAD THE BALL, LIKE.
'E READ ABOUT *SALVADOR DALI*, LIKE, Y'KNOW, SPEAKIN' IN DIFFERENT LANGUAGES ALL THE TIME. 'E THOUGHT IT WAS REAL NEAT, LIKE.
THING IS 'E CAN ONLY SPEAK *ENGLISH*.
OH, *BEN*.
THE STARS!

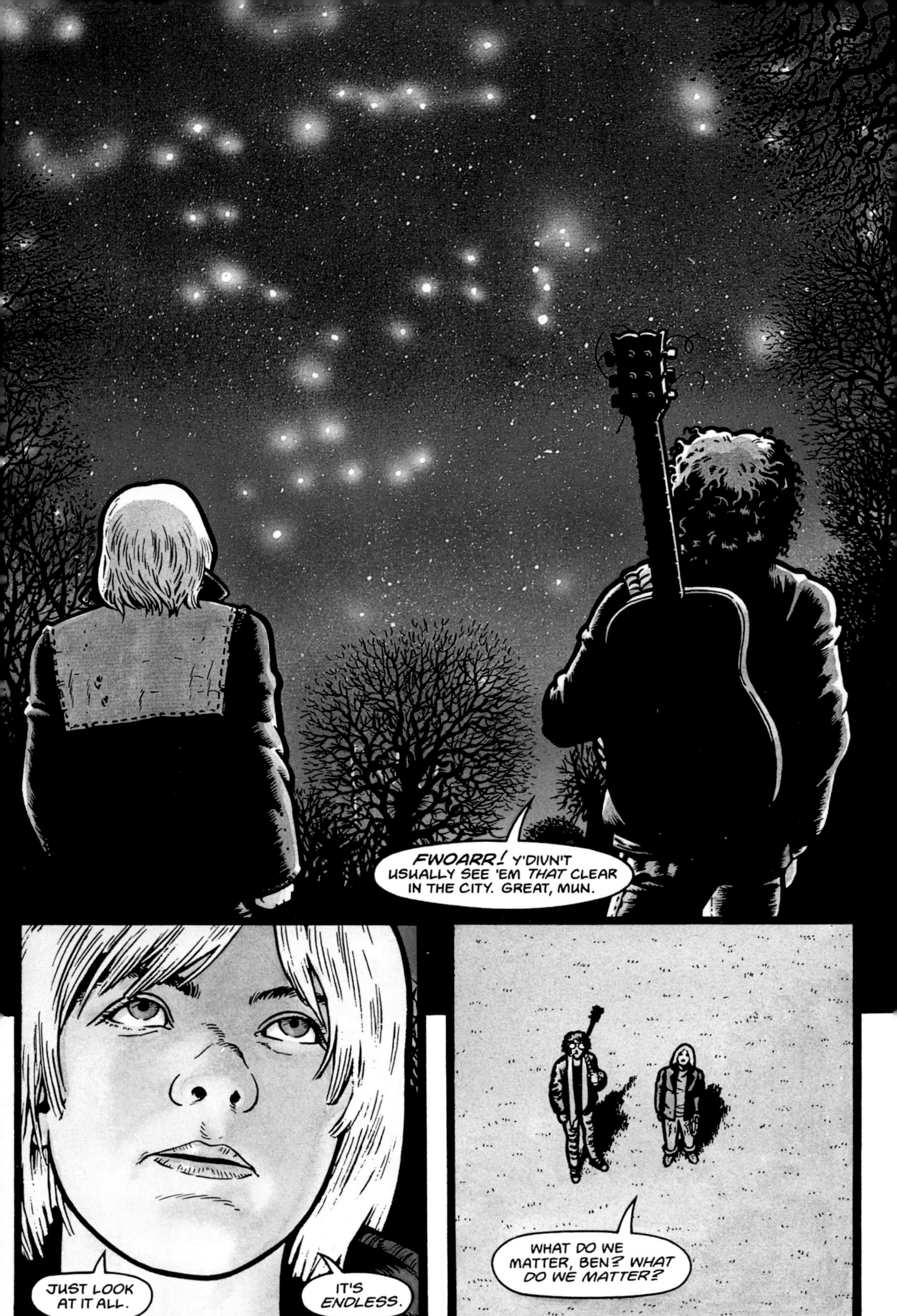
FWOARR! Y'DIVN'T USUALLY SEE 'EM THAT CLEAR IN THE CITY. GREAT, MUN.
JUST LOOK AT IT ALL.
IT'S ENDLESS.
WHAT DO WE MATTER, BEN? WHAT DO WE MATTER?

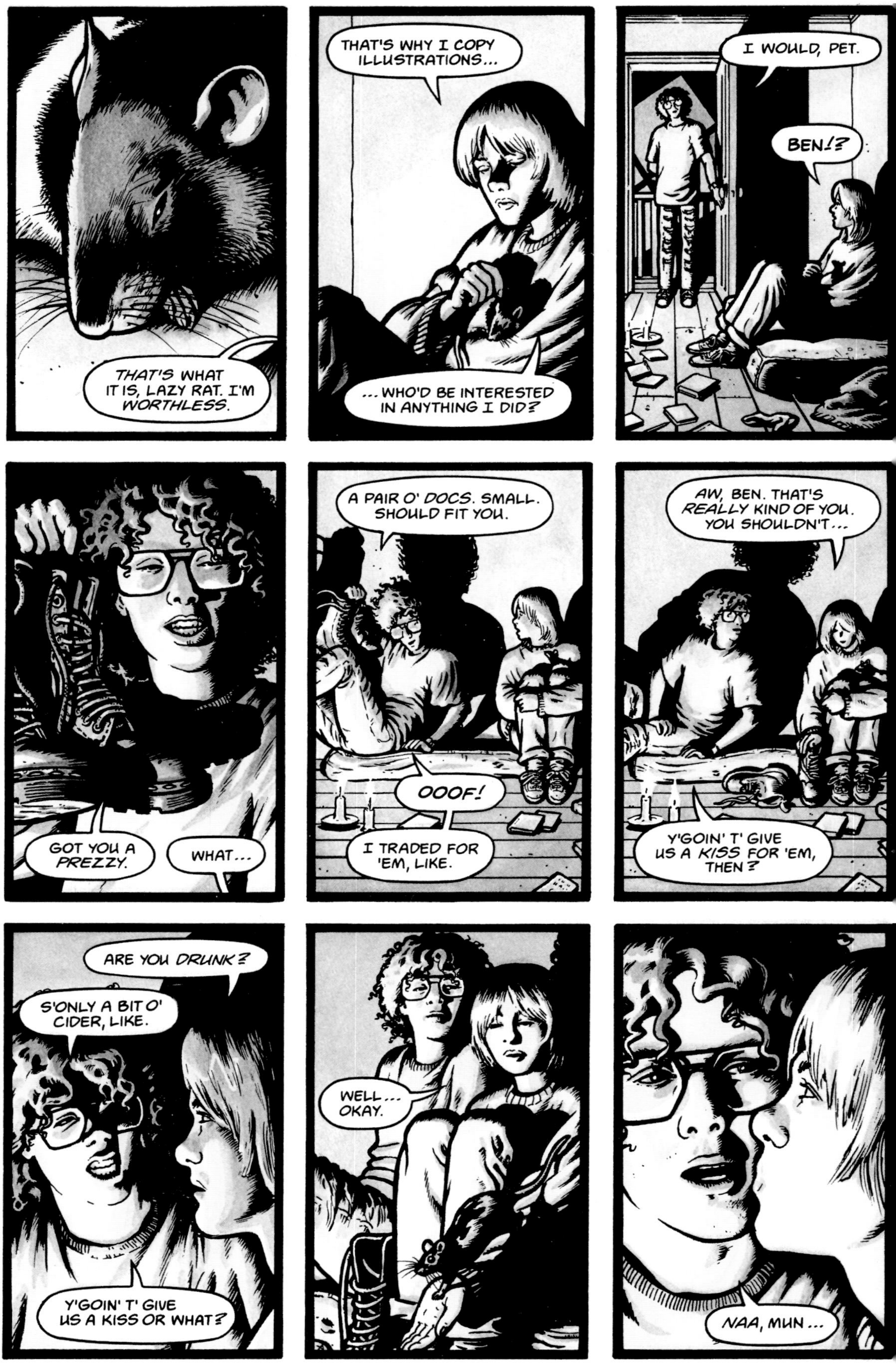
THAT'S WHAT IT IS, LAZY RAT. I'M WORTHLESS.
THAT'S WHY I COPY ILLUSTRATIONS...
...WHO'D BE INTERESTED IN ANYTHING I DID?
I WOULD, PET.
BEN!?
GOT YOU A PREZZY.
WHAT...
A PAIR O' DOCS. SMALL. SHOULD FIT YOU.
OOOF!
I TRADED FOR 'EM, LIKE.
AW, BEN. THAT'S REALLY KIND OF YOU. YOU SHOULDN'T...
Y'GOIN' T' GIVE US A KISS FOR 'EM, THEN?
ARE YOU DRUNK?
S'ONLY A BIT O' CIDER, LIKE.
Y'GOIN' T' GIVE US A KISS OR WHAT?
WELL... OKAY.
NAA, MUN...

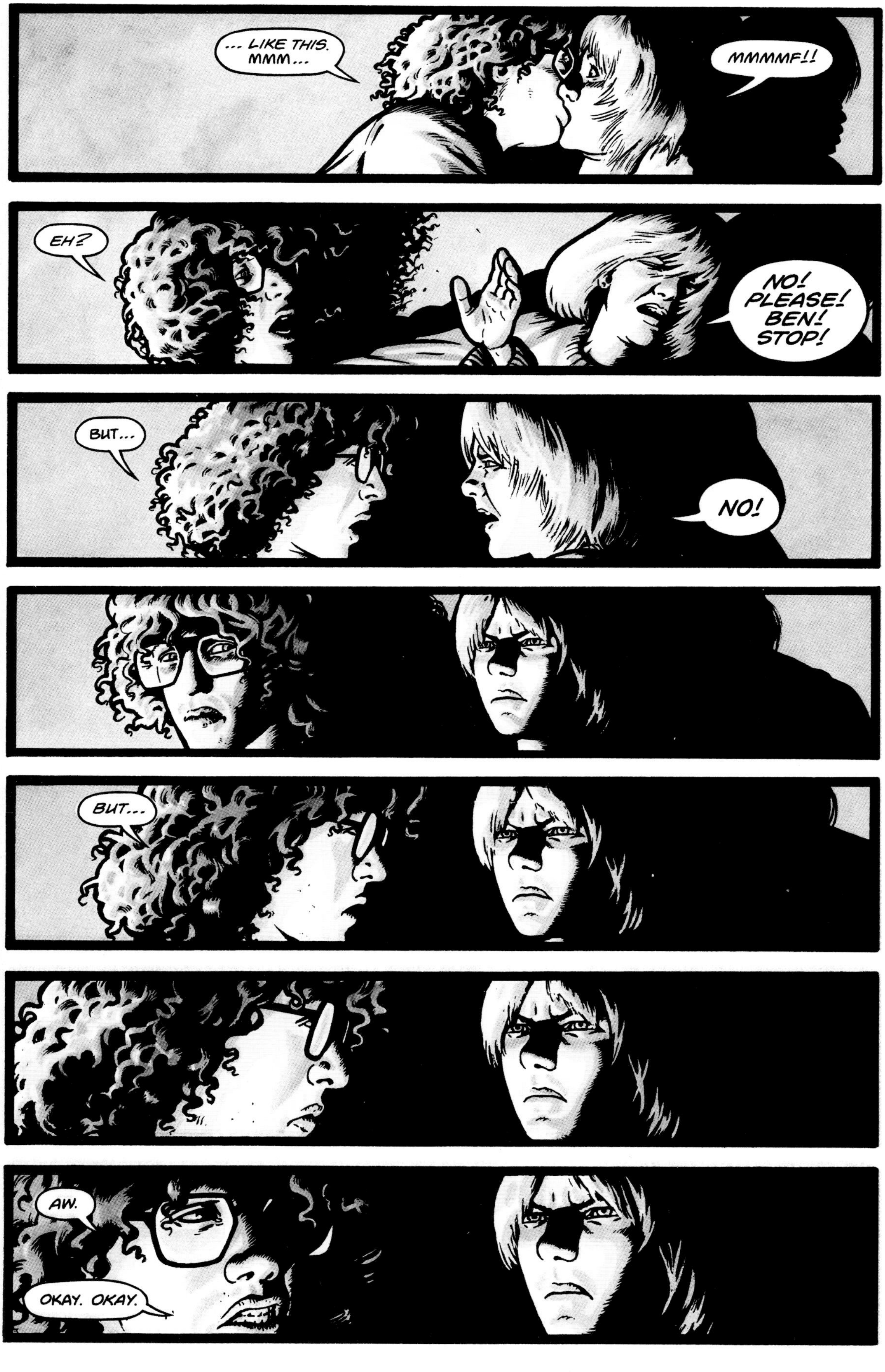
... LIKE THIS. MMM...
MMMMF!!
EH?
NO! PLEASE! BEN! STOP!
BUT...
NO!
BUT...
AW.
OKAY. OKAY.

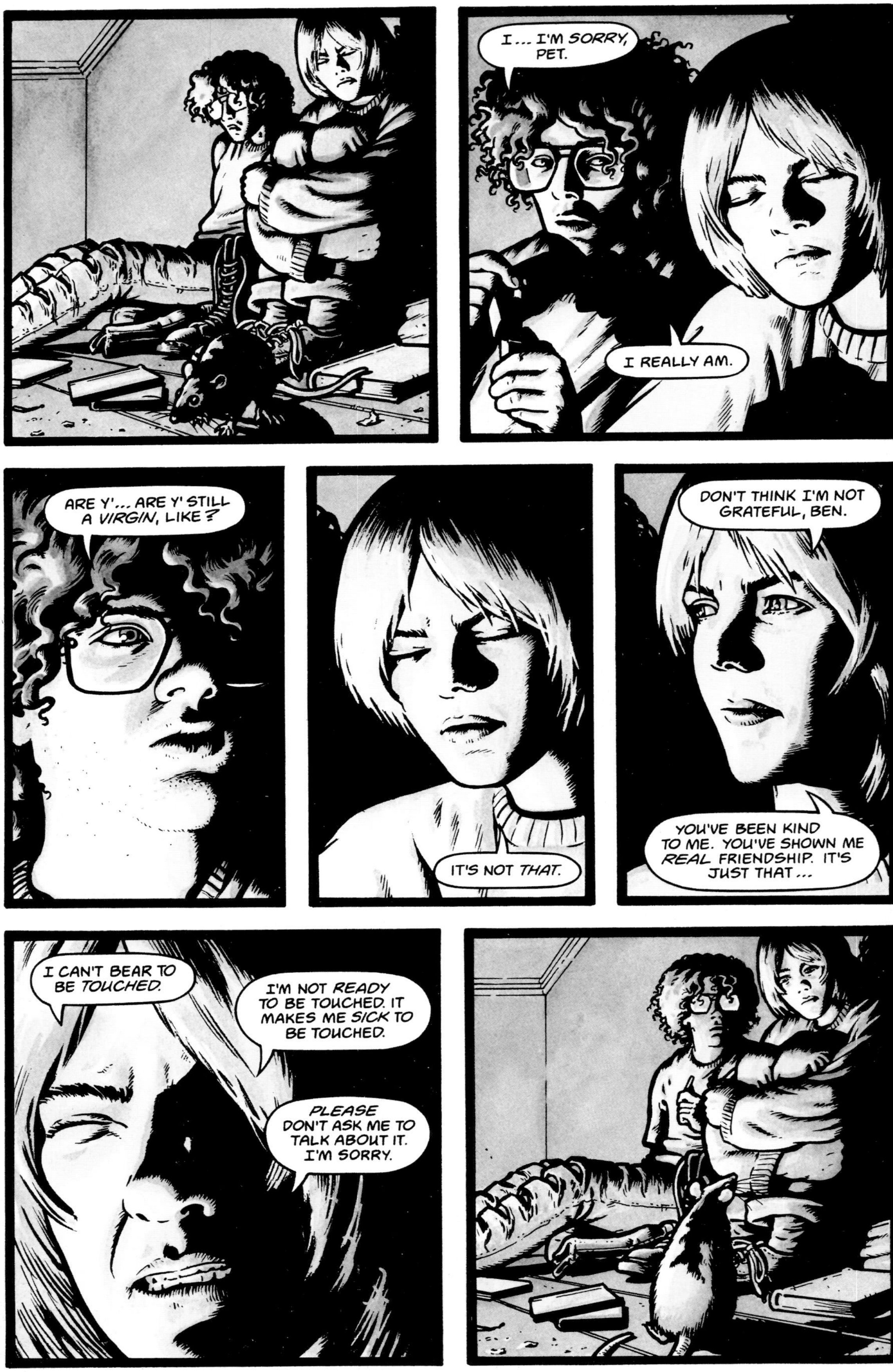

I... I'M SORRY, PET.
I REALLY AM.
ARE Y'... ARE Y' STILL A VIRGIN, LIKE?
IT'S NOT THAT.
DON'T THINK I'M NOT GRATEFUL, BEN.
YOU'VE BEEN KIND TO ME. YOU'VE SHOWN ME REAL FRIENDSHIP. IT'S JUST THAT...
I CAN'T BEAR TO BE TOUCHED.
I'M NOT READY TO BE TOUCHED. IT MAKES ME SICK TO BE TOUCHED.
PLEASE DON'T ASK ME TO TALK ABOUT IT. I'M SORRY.

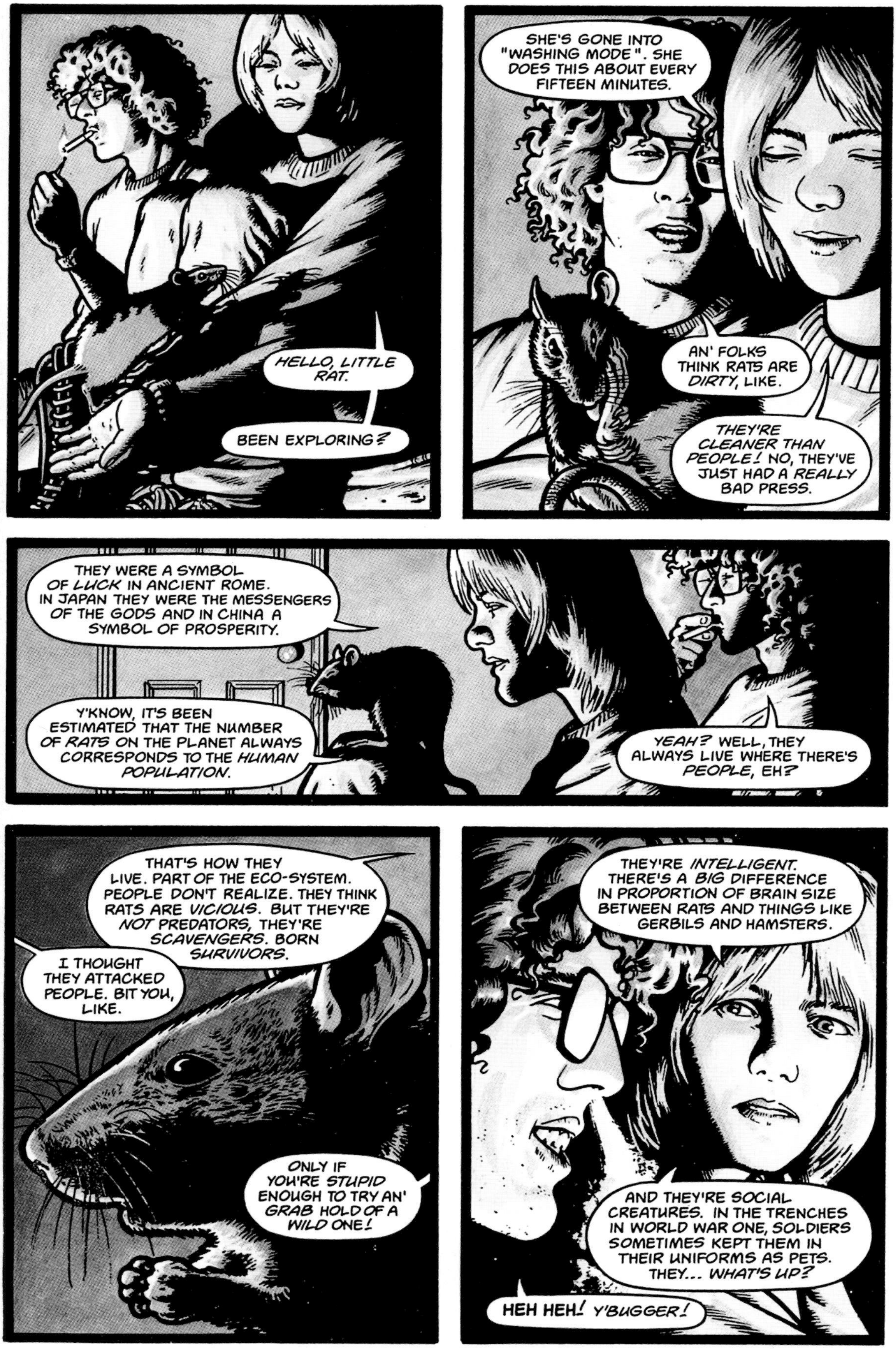
HELLO, LITTLE RAT.
BEEN EXPLORING?
SHE'S GONE INTO "WASHING MODE". SHE DOES THIS ABOUT EVERY FIFTEEN MINUTES.
AN' FOLKS THINK RATS ARE DIRTY, LIKE.
THEY'RE CLEANER THAN PEOPLE! NO, THEY'VE JUST HAD A REALLY BAD PRESS.
THEY WERE A SYMBOL OF LUCK IN ANCIENT ROME. IN JAPAN THEY WERE THE MESSENGERS OF THE GODS AND IN CHINA A SYMBOL OF PROSPERITY.
Y'KNOW, IT'S BEEN ESTIMATED THAT THE NUMBER OF RATS ON THE PLANET ALWAYS CORRESPONDS TO THE HUMAN POPULATION.
YEAH? WELL, THEY ALWAYS LIVE WHERE THERE'S PEOPLE, EH?
THAT'S HOW THEY LIVE. PART OF THE ECO-SYSTEM. PEOPLE DON'T REALIZE. THEY THINK RATS ARE VICIOUS. BUT THEY'RE NOT PREDATORS, THEY'RE SCAVENGERS. BORN SURVIVORS.
I THOUGHT THEY ATTACKED PEOPLE. BIT YOU, LIKE.
ONLY IF YOU'RE STUPID ENOUGH TO TRY AN' GRAB HOLD OF A WILD ONE!
THEY'RE INTELLIGENT. THERE'S A BIG DIFFERENCE IN PROPORTION OF BRAIN SIZE BETWEEN RATS AND THINGS LIKE GERBILS AND HAMSTERS.
AND THEY'RE SOCIAL CREATURES. IN THE TRENCHES IN WORLD WAR ONE, SOLDIERS SOMETIMES KEPT THEM IN THEIR UNIFORMS AS PETS. THEY... WHAT'S UP?
HEH HEH! Y'BUGGER!

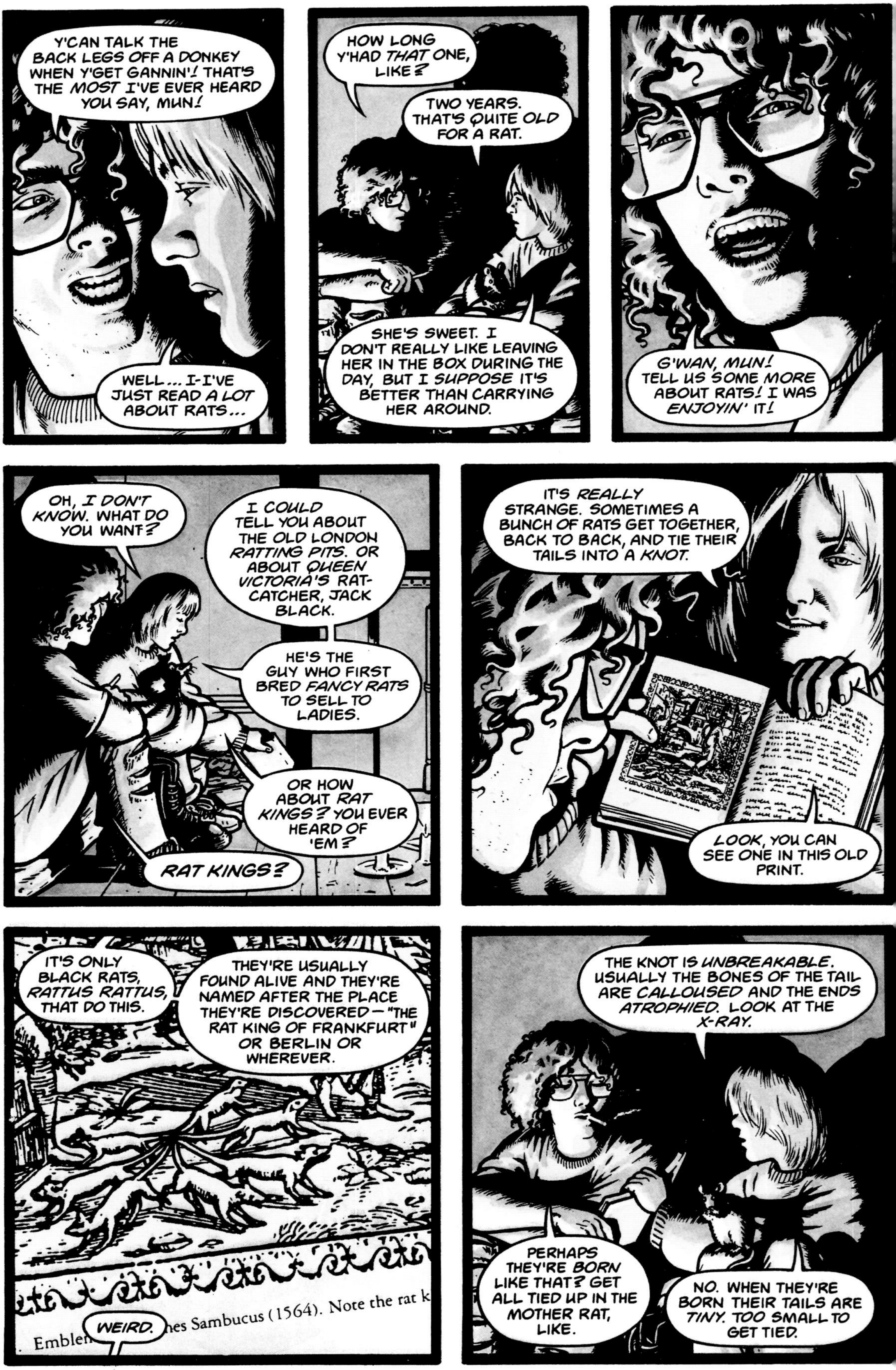

Y'CAN TALK THE BACK LEGS OFF A DONKEY WHEN Y'GET GANNIN'! THAT'S THE *MOST* I'VE EVER HEARD YOU SAY, MUN!
WELL... I-I'VE JUST READ A *LOT* ABOUT RATS...
HOW LONG Y'HAD *THAT* ONE, LIKE?
TWO YEARS. THAT'S QUITE *OLD* FOR A RAT.
SHE'S SWEET. I DON'T REALLY LIKE LEAVING HER IN THE BOX DURING THE DAY, BUT I *SUPPOSE* IT'S BETTER THAN CARRYING HER AROUND.
G'WAN, MUN! TELL US SOME MORE ABOUT RATS! I WAS *ENJOYIN'* IT!
OH, *I DON'T KNOW.* WHAT DO YOU WANT?
I COULD TELL YOU ABOUT THE OLD LONDON *RATTING PITS.* OR ABOUT *QUEEN VICTORIA'S* RAT-CATCHER, JACK BLACK.
HE'S THE GUY WHO FIRST BRED *FANCY RATS* TO SELL TO LADIES.
OR HOW ABOUT *RAT KINGS?* YOU EVER HEARD OF 'EM?
RAT KINGS?
IT'S *REALLY* STRANGE. SOMETIMES A BUNCH OF RATS GET TOGETHER, BACK TO BACK, AND TIE THEIR TAILS INTO A *KNOT.*
LOOK, YOU CAN SEE ONE IN THIS OLD PRINT.
IT'S ONLY BLACK RATS, *RATTUS RATTUS,* THAT DO THIS.
THEY'RE USUALLY FOUND ALIVE AND THEY'RE NAMED AFTER THE PLACE THEY'RE *DISCOVERED* — "THE RAT KING OF FRANKFURT" OR BERLIN OR WHEREVER.
Emblen hes Sambucus (1564). Note the rat k
WEIRD.
THE KNOT IS *UNBREAKABLE.* USUALLY THE BONES OF THE TAIL ARE *CALLOUSED* AND THE ENDS *ATROPHIED.* LOOK AT THE *X-RAY.*
PERHAPS THEY'RE *BORN* LIKE THAT? GET ALL TIED UP IN THE MOTHER RAT, LIKE.
NO. WHEN THEY'RE BORN THEIR TAILS ARE *TINY.* TOO SMALL TO GET TIED.

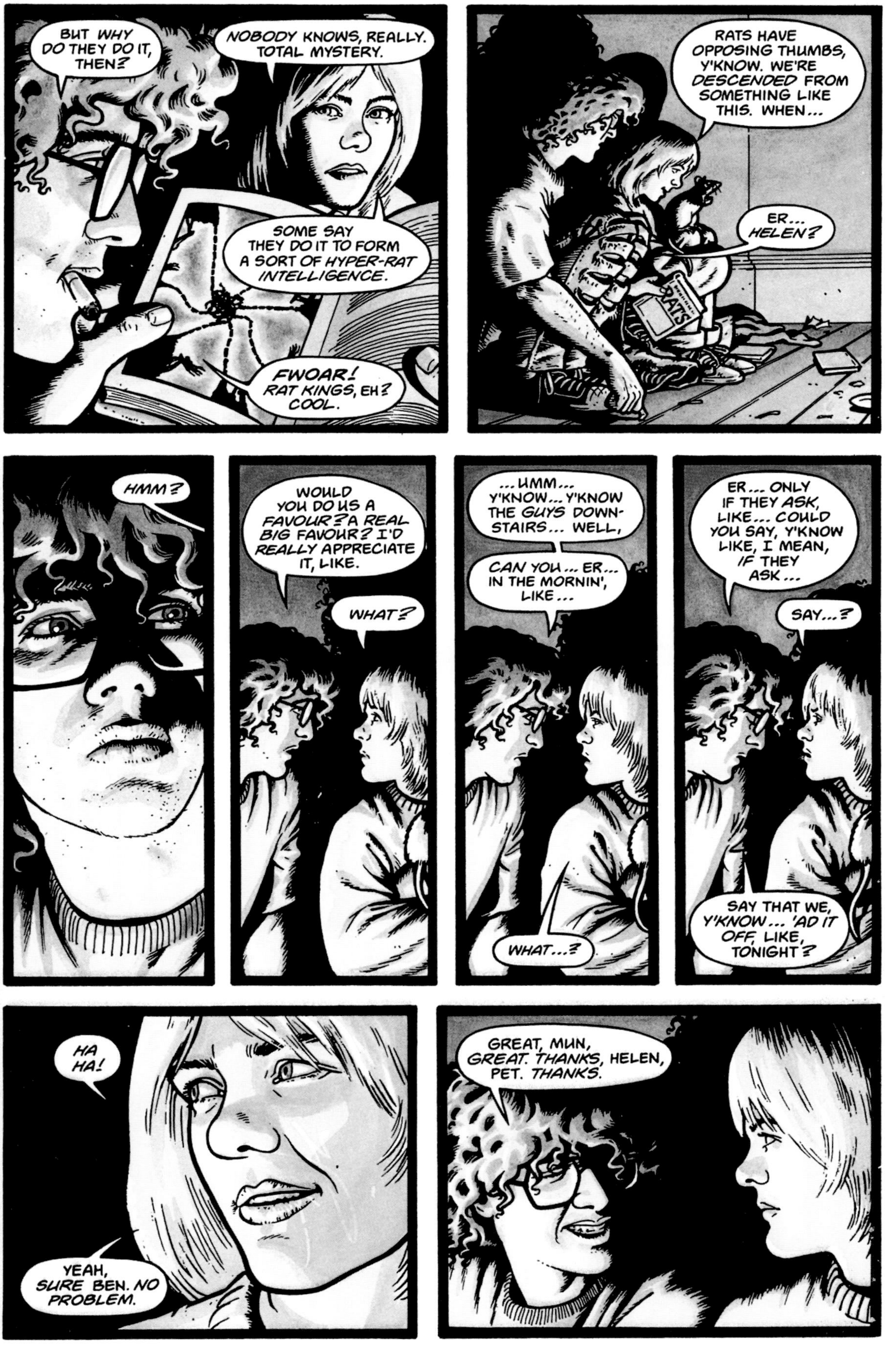
BUT WHY DO THEY DO IT, THEN?
NOBODY KNOWS, REALLY. TOTAL MYSTERY.
SOME SAY THEY DO IT TO FORM A SORT OF HYPER-RAT INTELLIGENCE.
FWOAR! RAT KINGS, EH? COOL.
RATS HAVE OPPOSING THUMBS, Y'KNOW. WE'RE DESCENDED FROM SOMETHING LIKE THIS. WHEN...
ER... HELEN?
RATS
HMM?
WOULD YOU DO US A FAVOUR? A REAL BIG FAVOUR? I'D REALLY APPRECIATE IT, LIKE.
WHAT?
...UMM... Y'KNOW... Y'KNOW THE GUYS DOWN-STAIRS... WELL,
CAN YOU... ER... IN THE MORNIN', LIKE...
WHAT...?
ER... ONLY IF THEY ASK, LIKE... COULD YOU SAY, Y'KNOW LIKE, I MEAN, IF THEY ASK...
SAY...?
SAY THAT WE, Y'KNOW... 'AD IT OFF, LIKE, TONIGHT?
HA HA!
YEAH, SURE BEN. NO PROBLEM.
GREAT, MUN, GREAT. THANKS, HELEN, PET. THANKS.

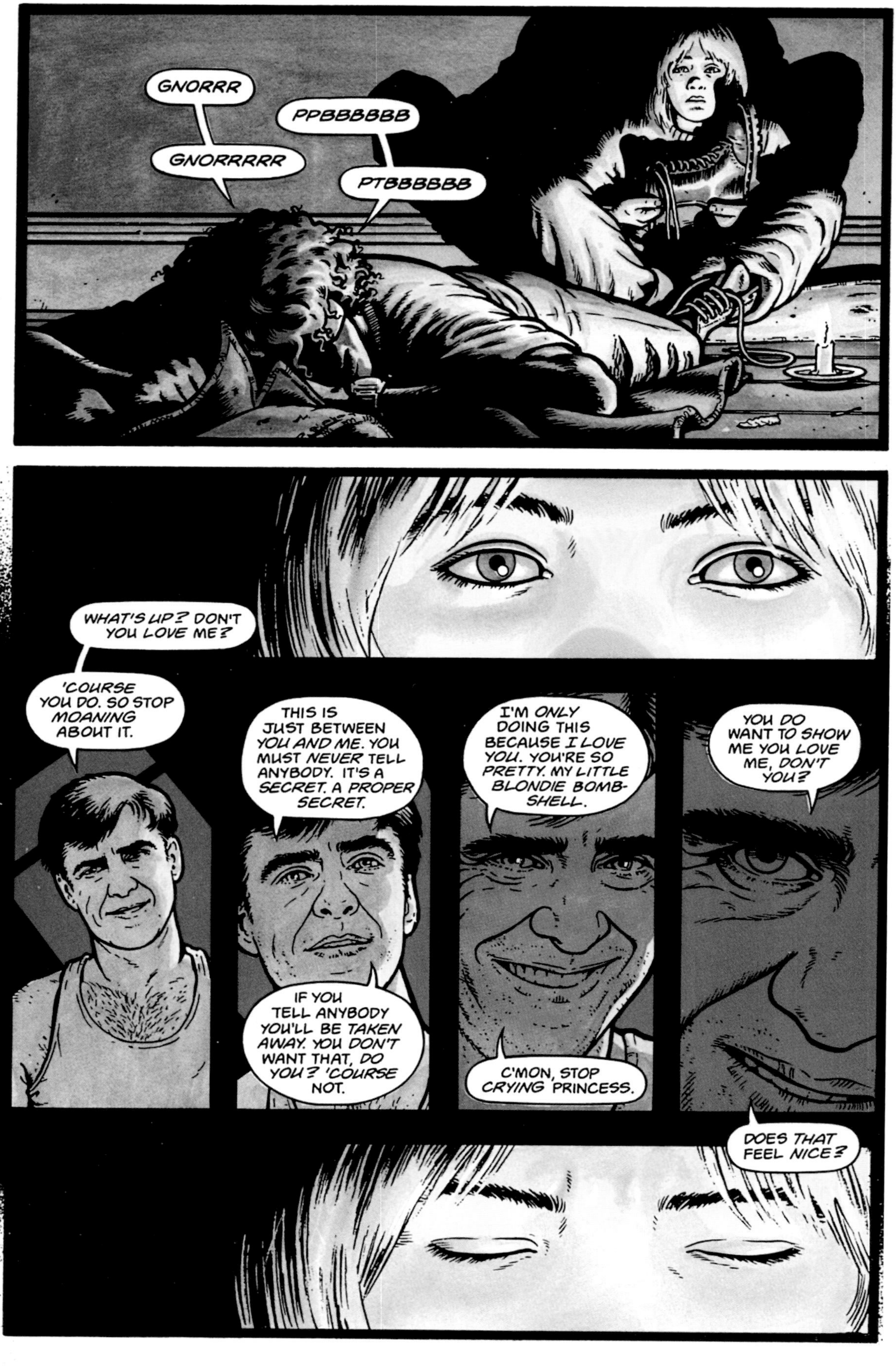
GNORRR
GNORRRRR
PPBBBBBB
PTBBBBBB
WHAT'S UP? DON'T YOU LOVE ME?
'COURSE YOU DO. SO STOP MOANING ABOUT IT.
THIS IS JUST BETWEEN YOU AND ME. YOU MUST NEVER TELL ANYBODY. IT'S A SECRET. A PROPER SECRET.
IF YOU TELL ANYBODY YOU'LL BE TAKEN AWAY. YOU DON'T WANT THAT, DO YOU? 'COURSE NOT.
I'M ONLY DOING THIS BECAUSE I LOVE YOU. YOU'RE SO PRETTY. MY LITTLE BLONDIE BOMB-SHELL.
C'MON, STOP CRYING PRINCESS.
YOU DO WANT TO SHOW ME YOU LOVE ME, DON'T YOU?
DOES THAT FEEL NICE?

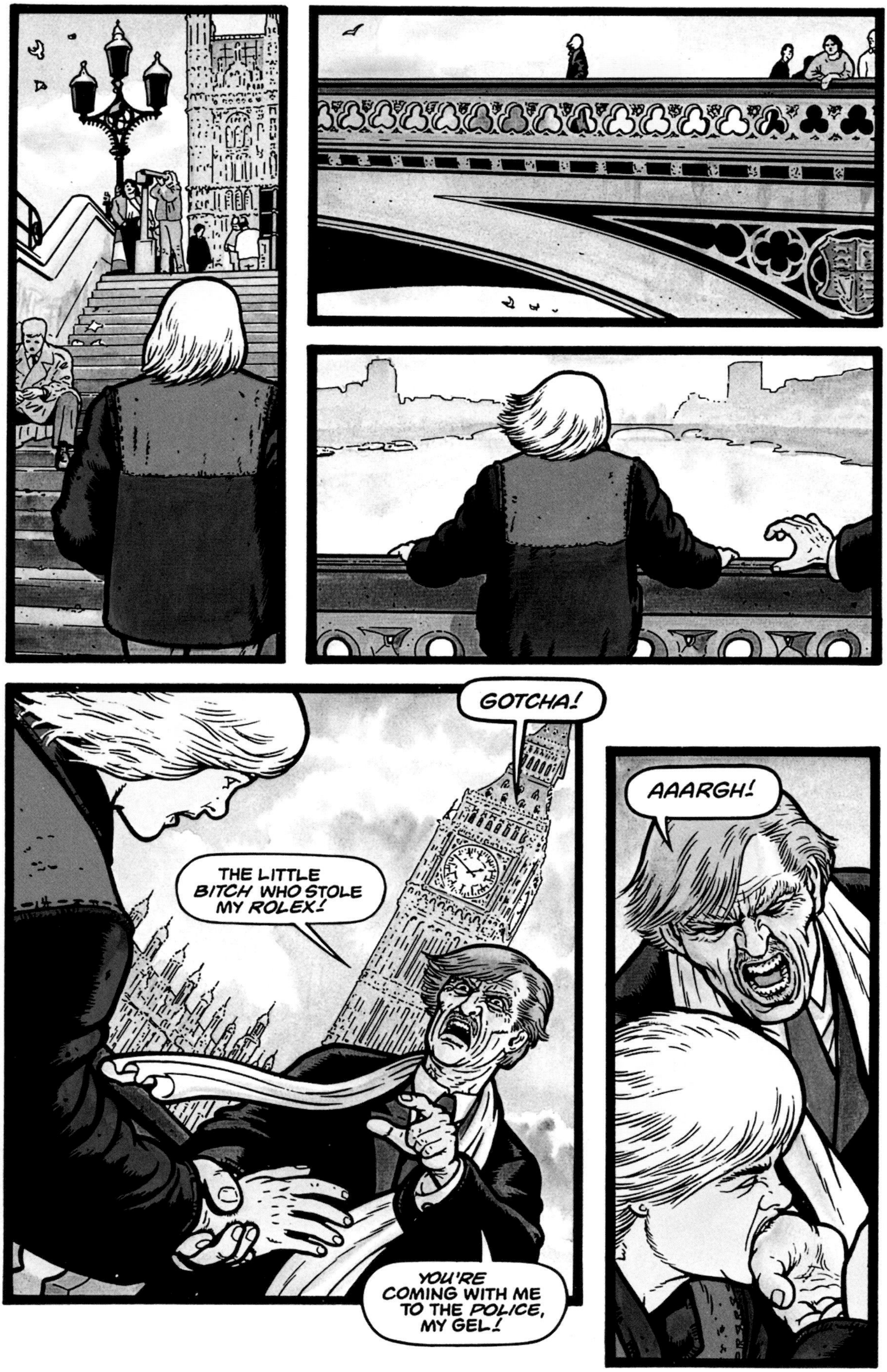
GOTCHA!
THE LITTLE BITCH WHO STOLE MY ROLEX!
YOU'RE COMING WITH ME TO THE POLICE, MY GEL!
AAARGH!

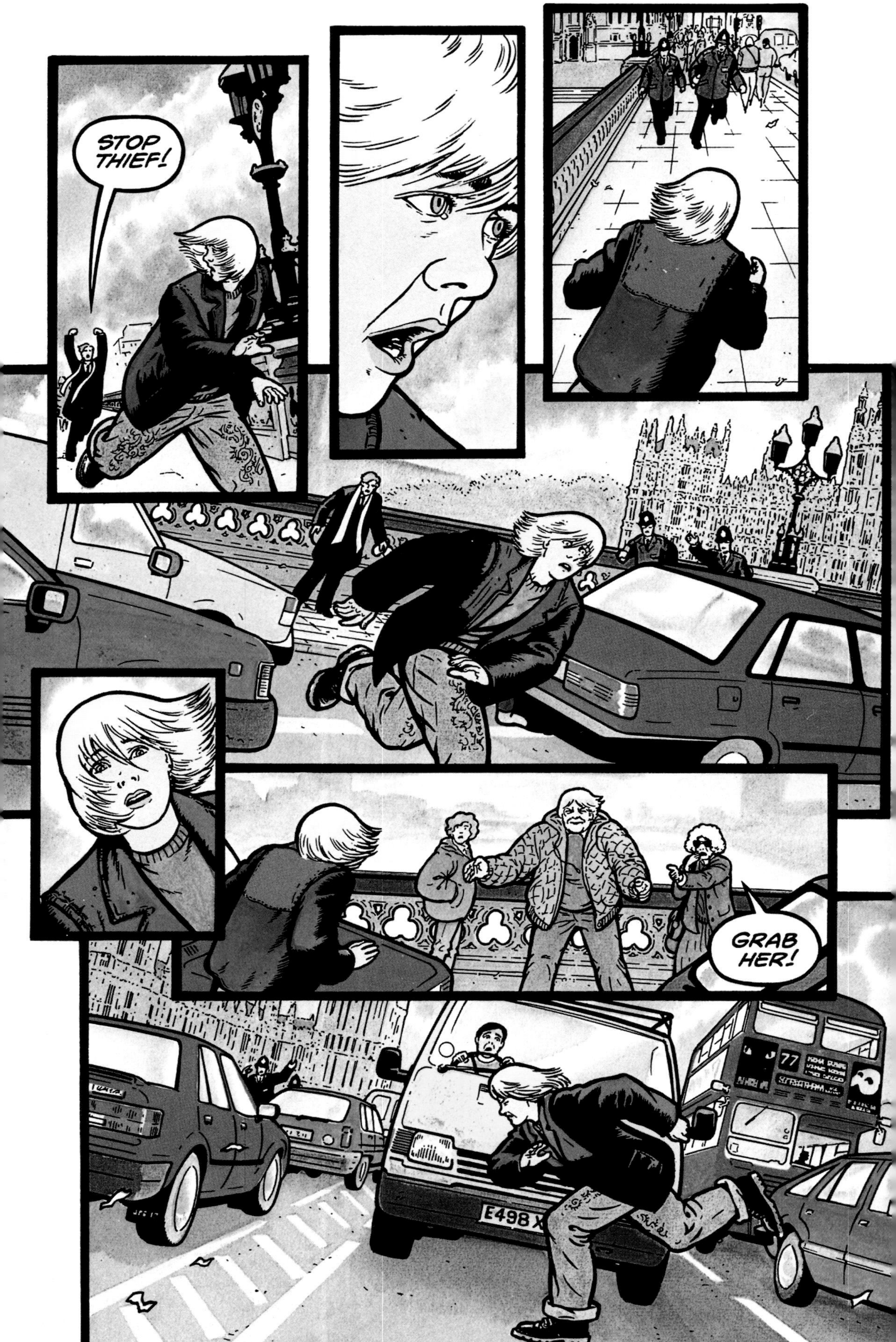
STOP THIEF!
GRAB HER!
77
E498 X

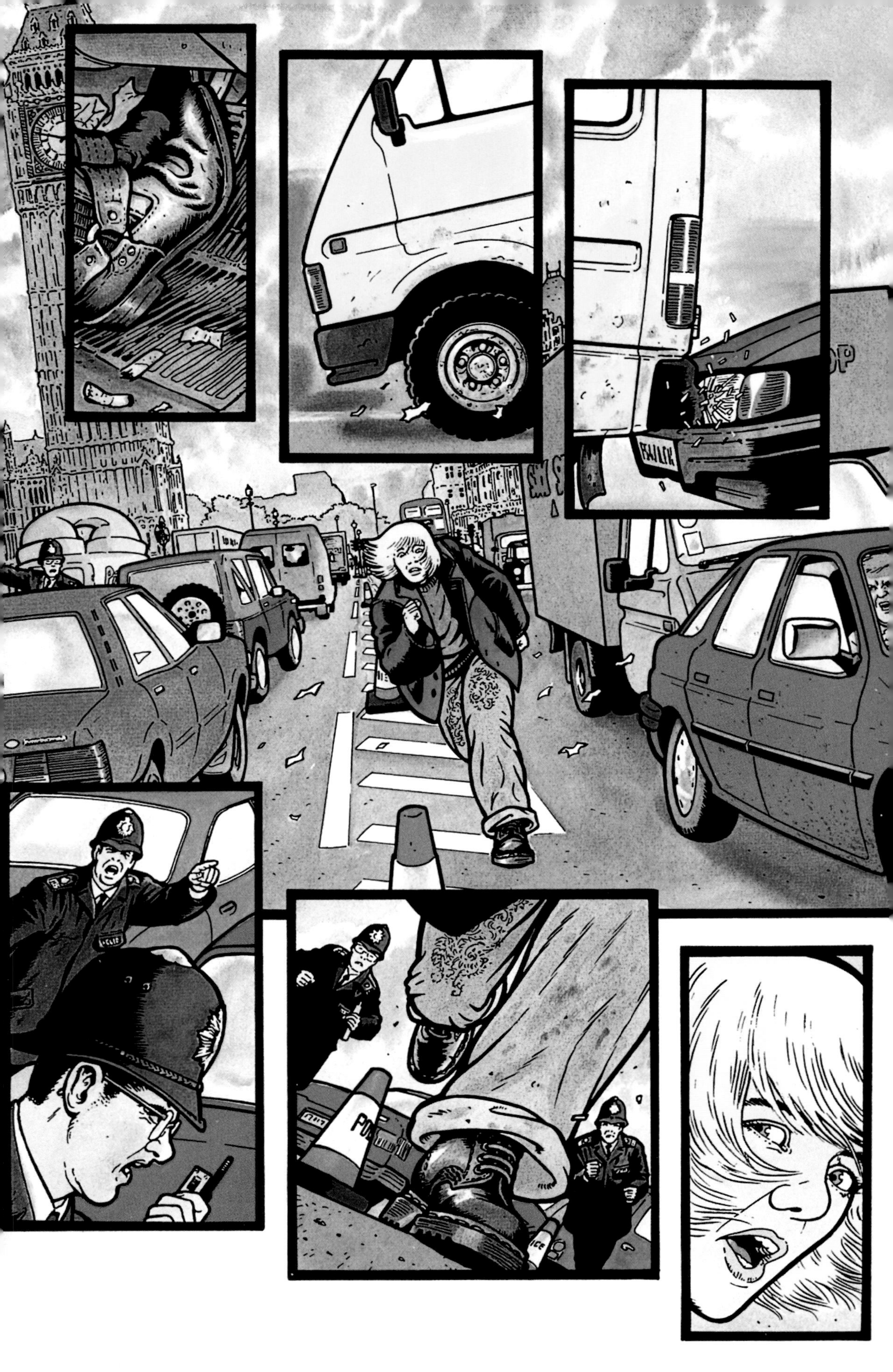

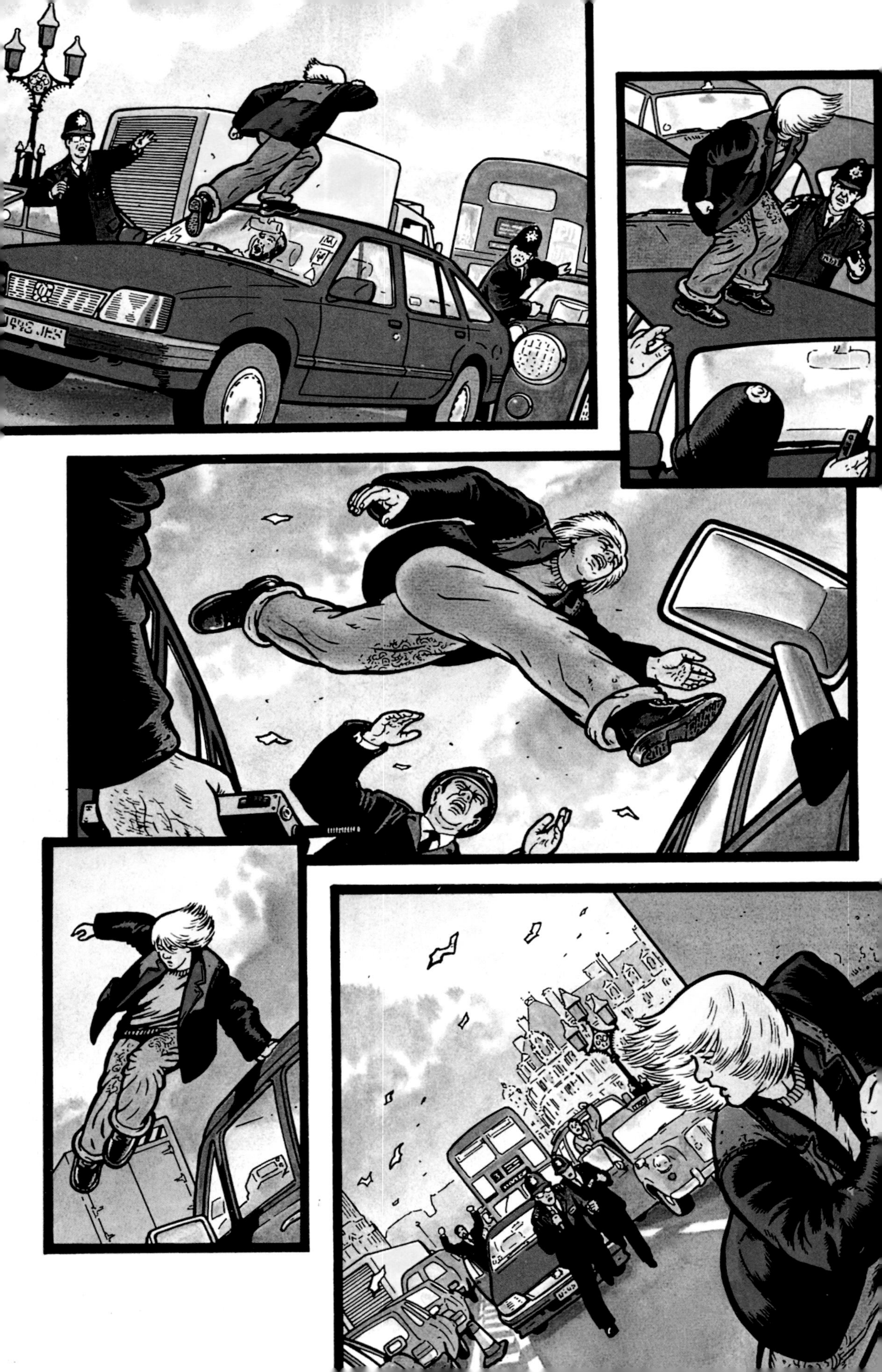

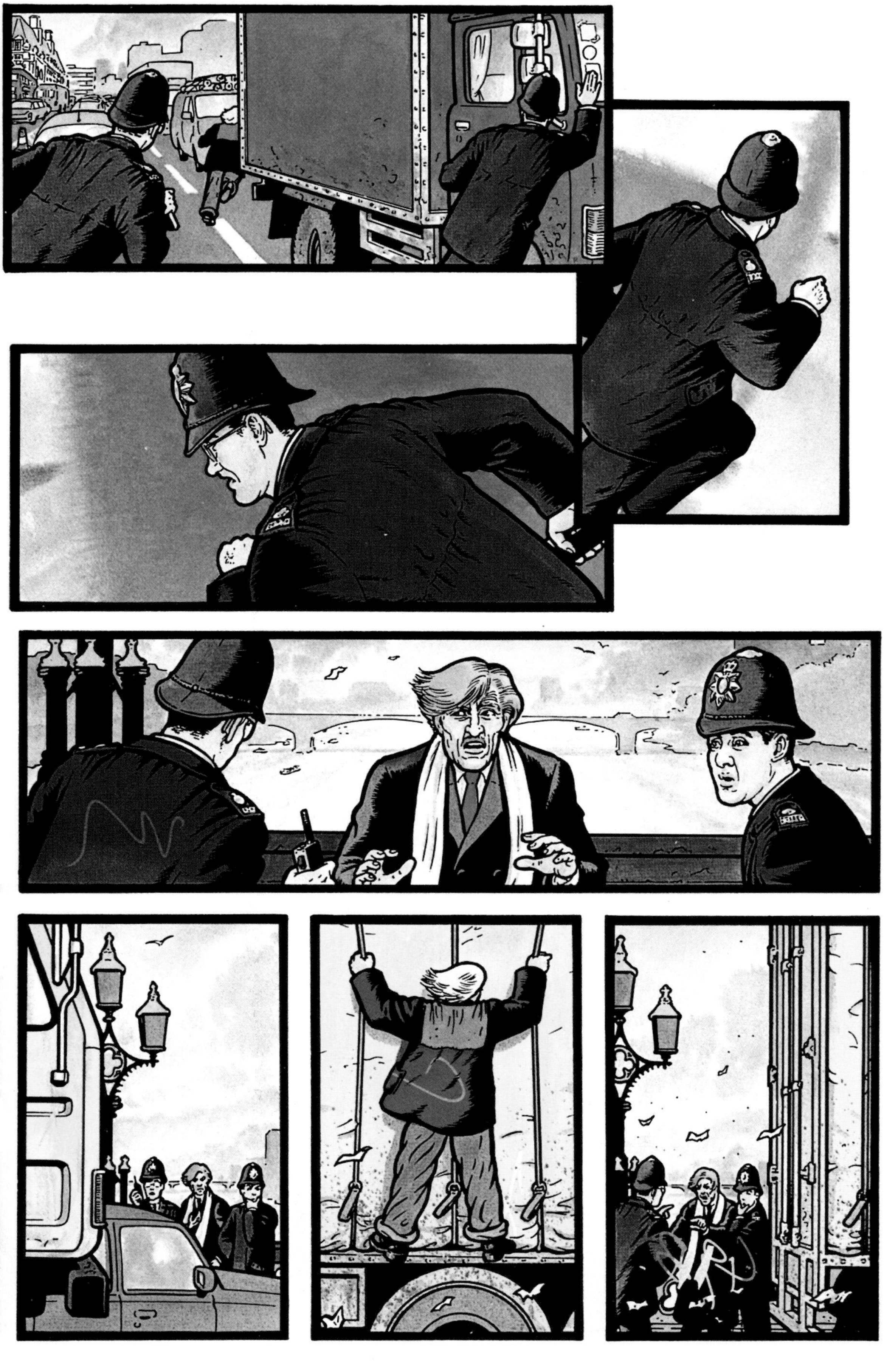

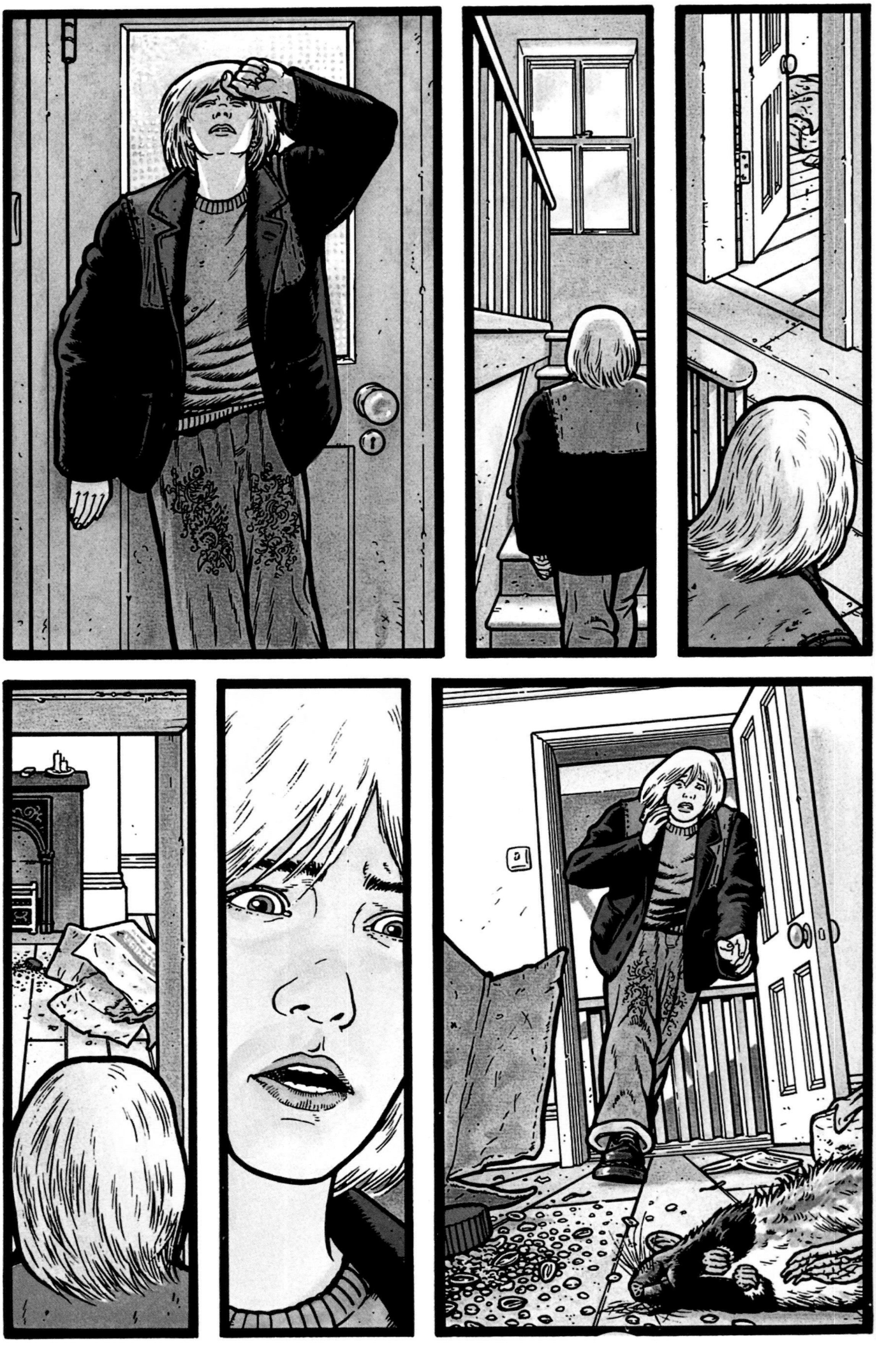

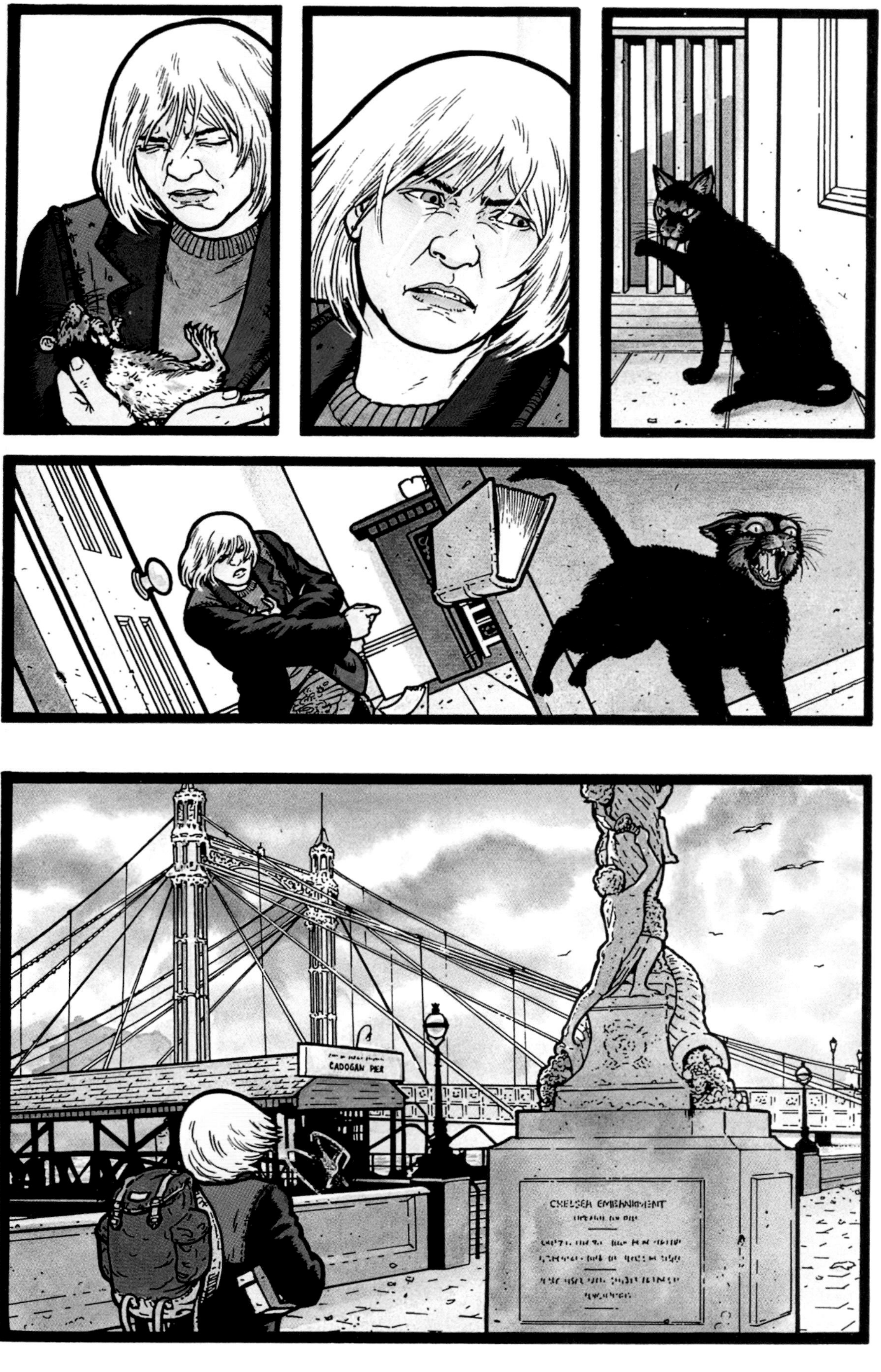
CADOGAN PIER
CHELSEA EMBANKMENT

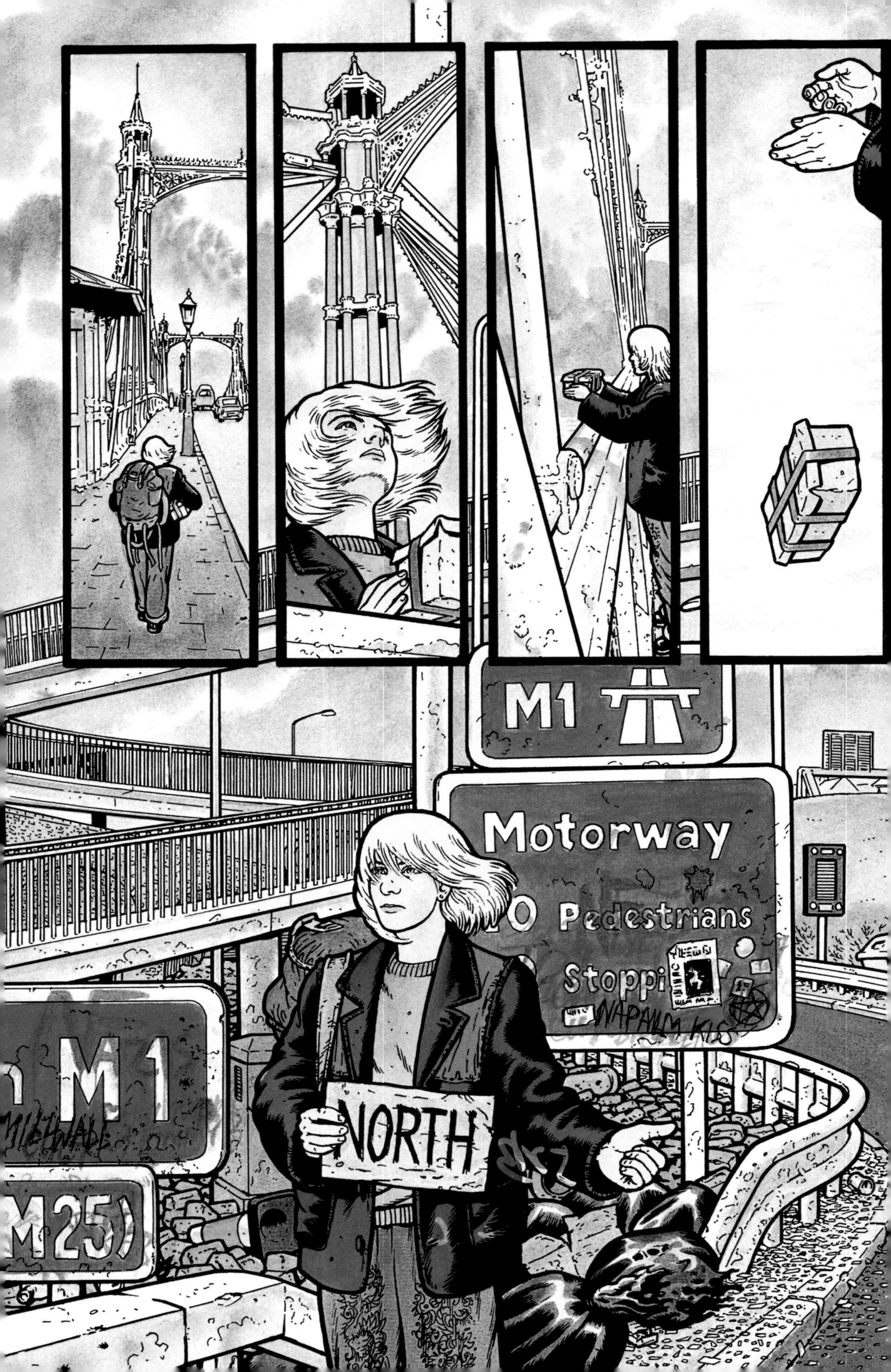
M1
Motorway
O Pedestrians
Stoppi
M1
M25)
NORTH

ROAD

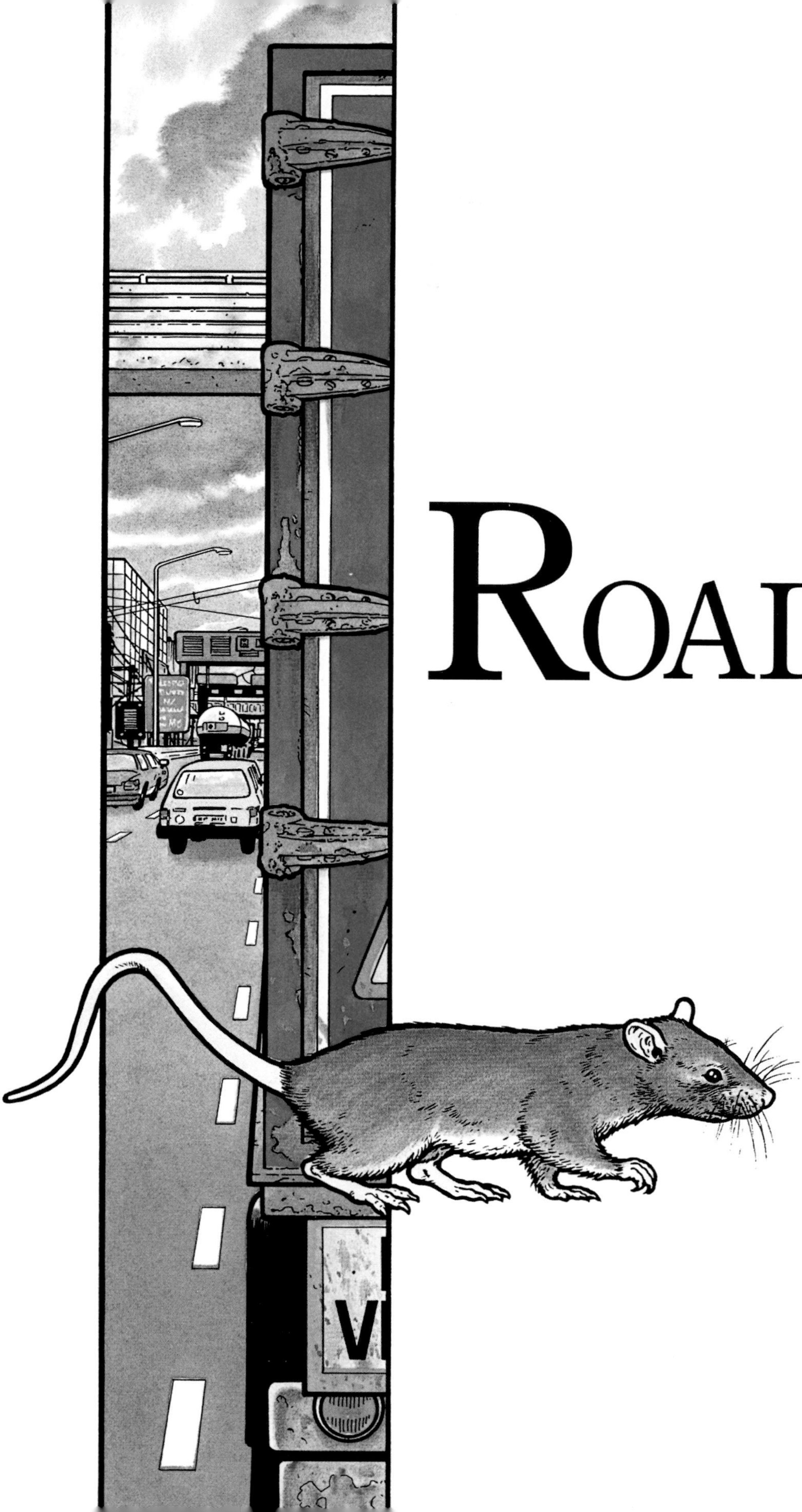

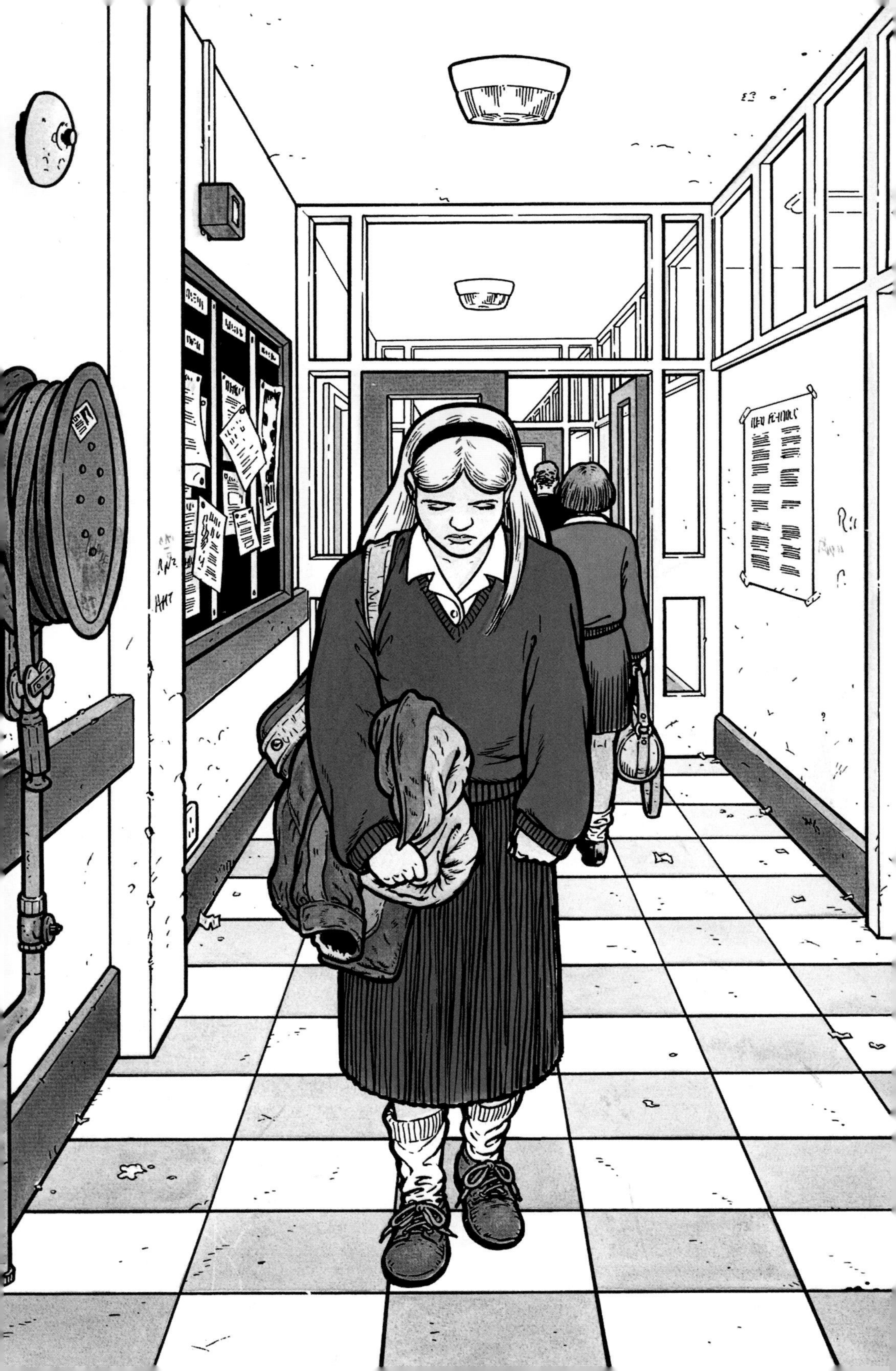

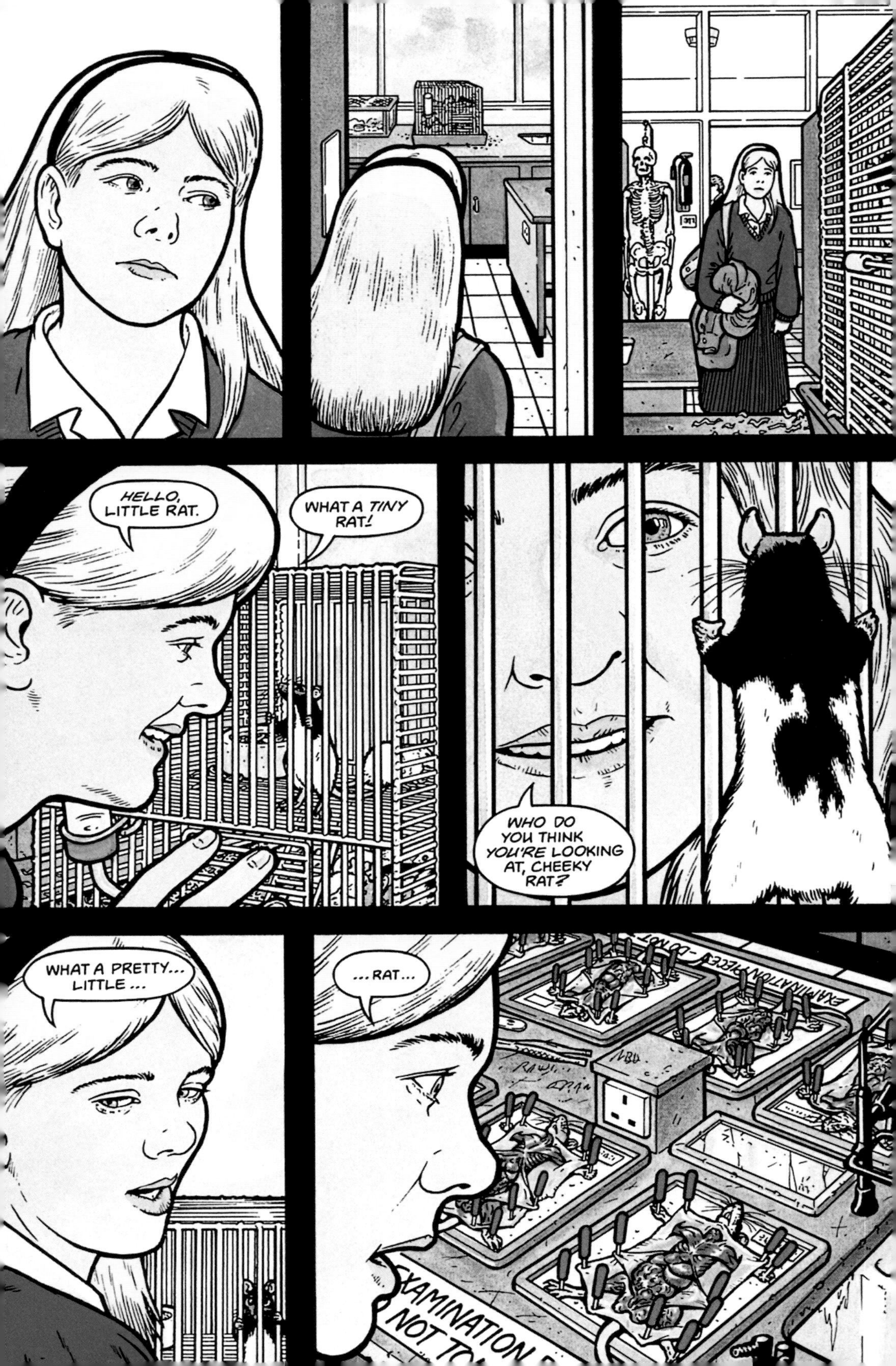
HELLO, LITTLE RAT.
WHAT A *TINY* RAT!
WHO DO YOU THINK *YOU'RE* LOOKING AT, CHEEKY RAT?
WHAT A PRETTY... LITTLE ...
...RAT...

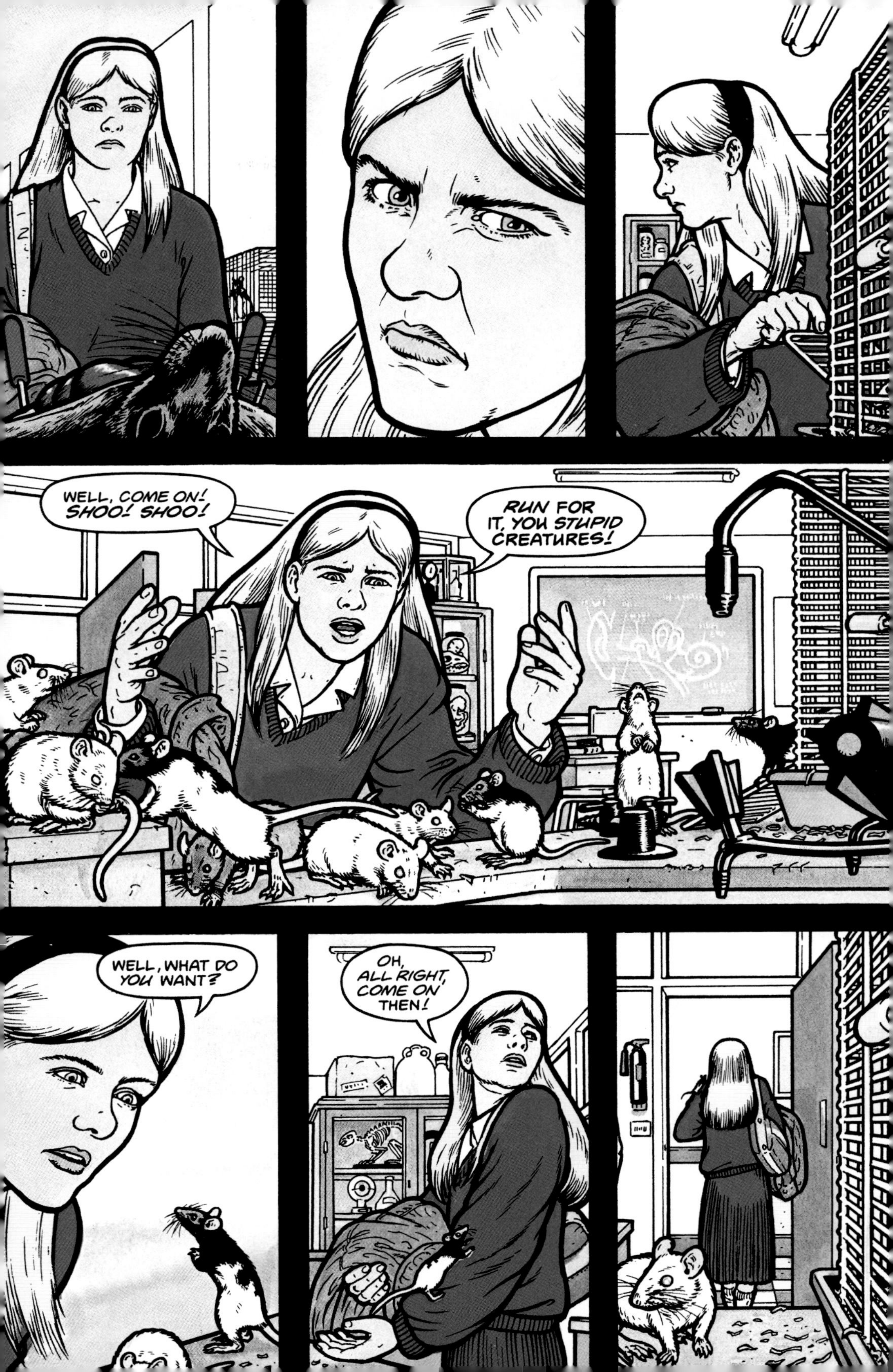
WELL, COME ON! SHOO! SHOO!
RUN FOR IT, YOU STUPID CREATURES!
WELL, WHAT DO YOU WANT?
OH, ALL RIGHT, COME ON THEN!

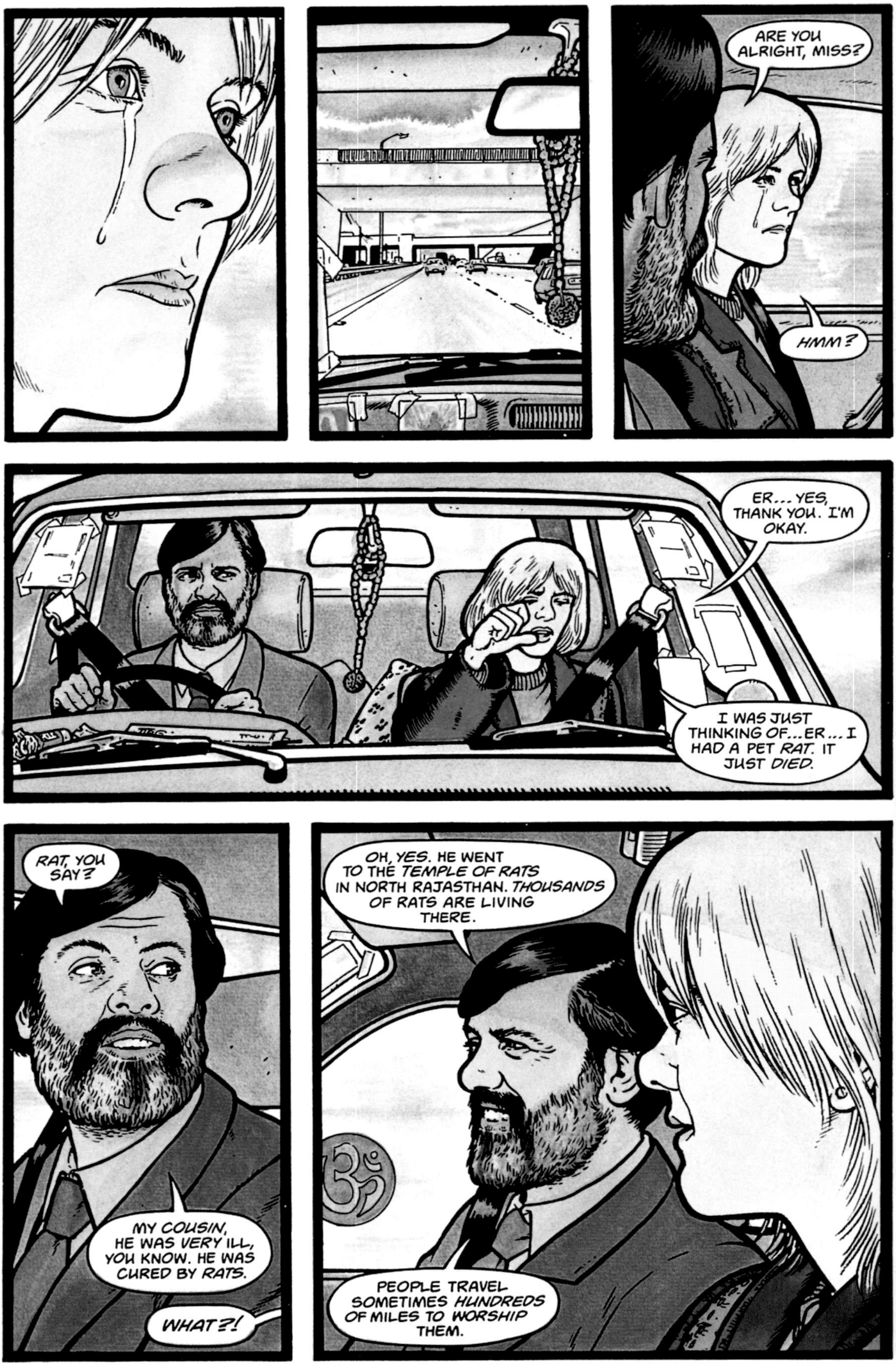
ARE YOU ALRIGHT, MISS?
HMM?
ER... YES, THANK YOU. I'M OKAY.
I WAS JUST THINKING OF...ER... I HAD A PET RAT. IT JUST DIED.
RAT, YOU SAY?
MY COUSIN, HE WAS VERY ILL, YOU KNOW. HE WAS CURED BY RATS.
WHAT?!
OH, YES. HE WENT TO THE TEMPLE OF RATS IN NORTH RAJASTHAN. THOUSANDS OF RATS ARE LIVING THERE.
PEOPLE TRAVEL SOMETIMES HUNDREDS OF MILES TO WORSHIP THEM.

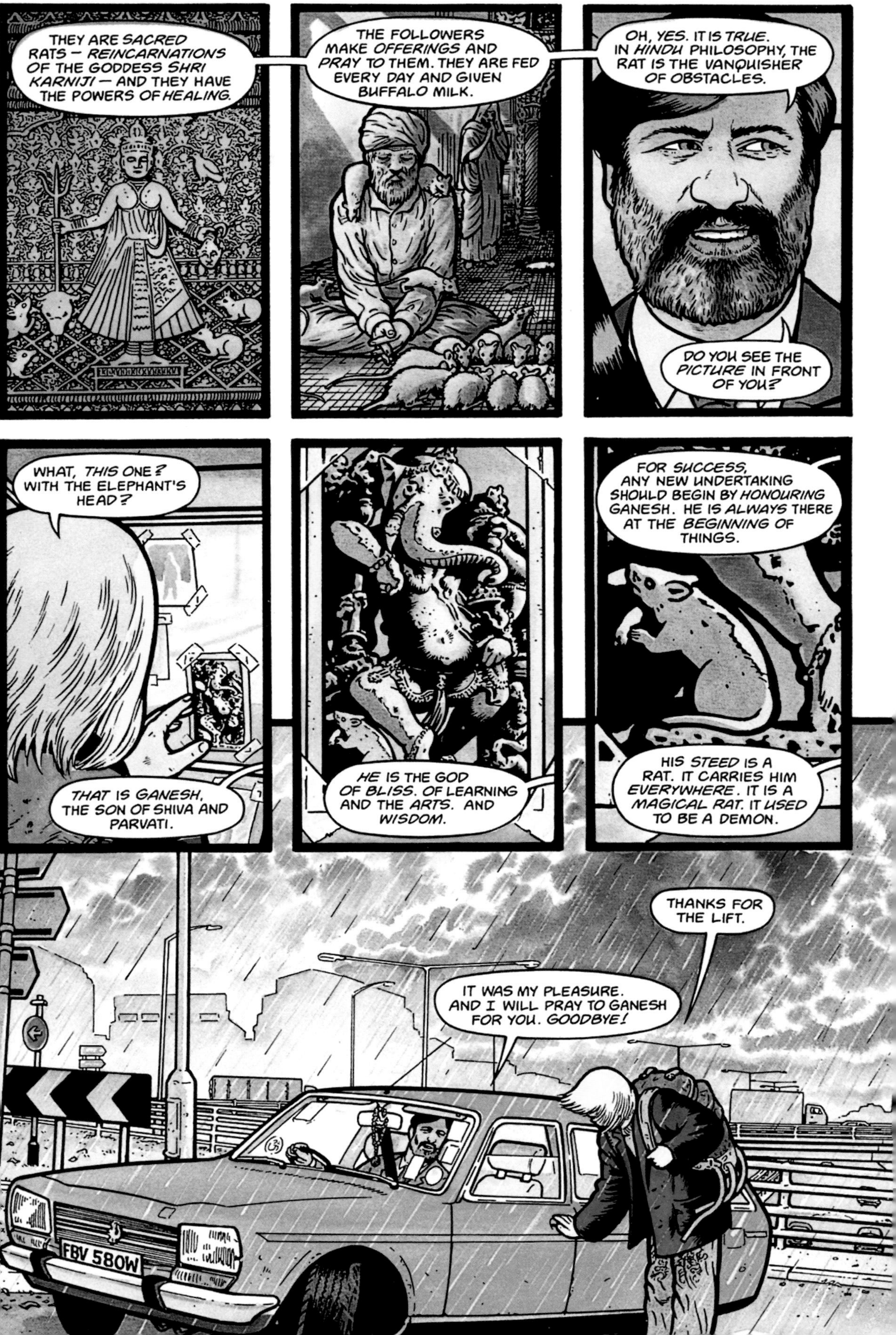
THEY ARE SACRED RATS — REINCARNATIONS OF THE GODDESS SHRI KARNIJI — AND THEY HAVE THE POWERS OF HEALING.
THE FOLLOWERS MAKE OFFERINGS AND PRAY TO THEM. THEY ARE FED EVERY DAY AND GIVEN BUFFALO MILK.
OH, YES. IT IS TRUE. IN HINDU PHILOSOPHY, THE RAT IS THE VANQUISHER OF OBSTACLES.
DO YOU SEE THE PICTURE IN FRONT OF YOU?
WHAT, THIS ONE? WITH THE ELEPHANT'S HEAD?
THAT IS GANESH, THE SON OF SHIVA AND PARVATI.
HE IS THE GOD OF BLISS. OF LEARNING AND THE ARTS. AND WISDOM.
FOR SUCCESS, ANY NEW UNDERTAKING SHOULD BEGIN BY HONOURING GANESH. HE IS ALWAYS THERE AT THE BEGINNING OF THINGS.
HIS STEED IS A RAT. IT CARRIES HIM EVERYWHERE. IT IS A MAGICAL RAT. IT USED TO BE A DEMON.
THANKS FOR THE LIFT.
IT WAS MY PLEASURE. AND I WILL PRAY TO GANESH FOR YOU. GOODBYE!
FBV 580W

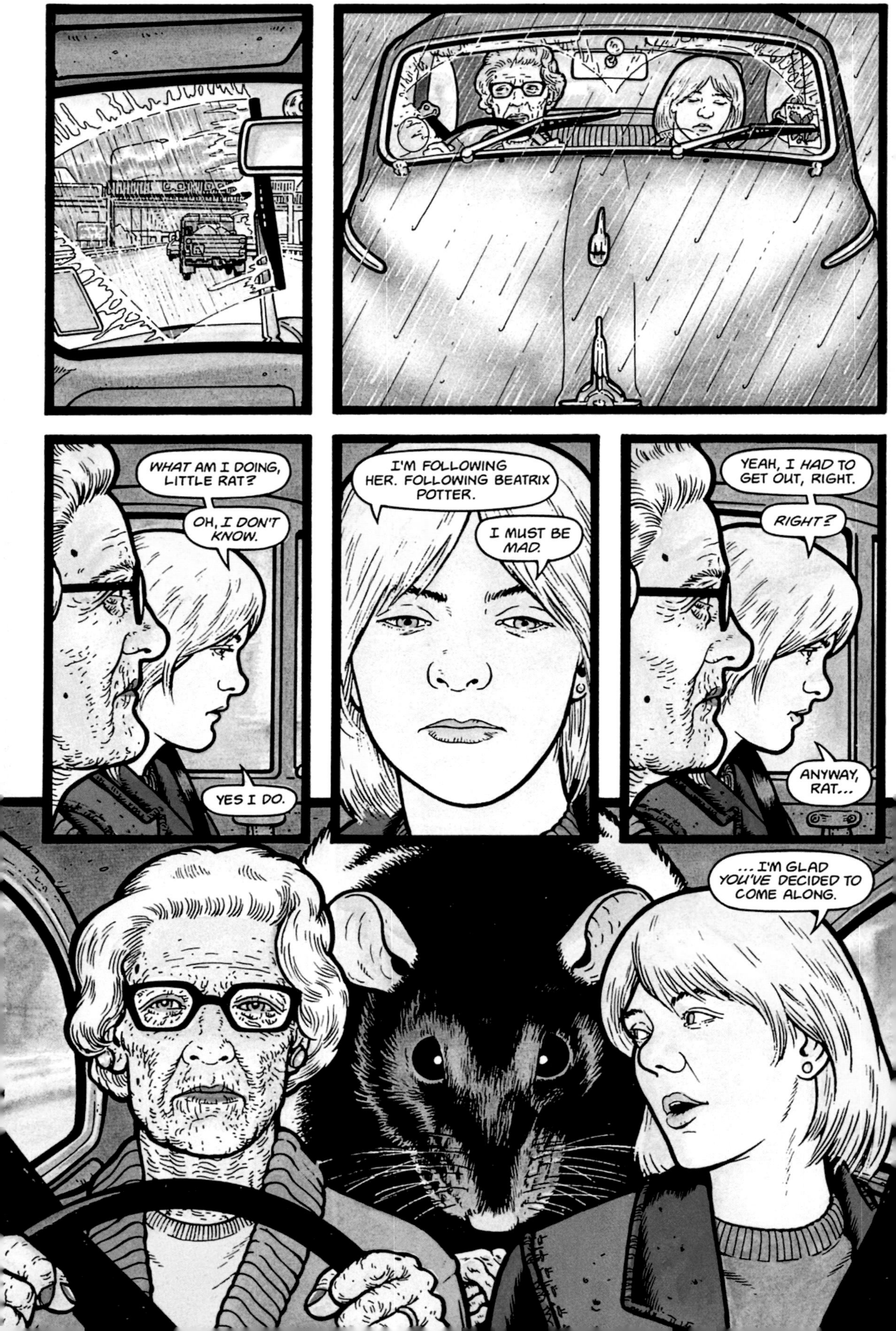

WHAT AM I DOING, LITTLE RAT?
OH, I DON'T KNOW.
YES I DO.
I'M FOLLOWING HER. FOLLOWING BEATRIX POTTER.
I MUST BE MAD.
YEAH, I HAD TO GET OUT, RIGHT.
RIGHT?
ANYWAY, RAT...
... I'M GLAD YOU'VE DECIDED TO COME ALONG.

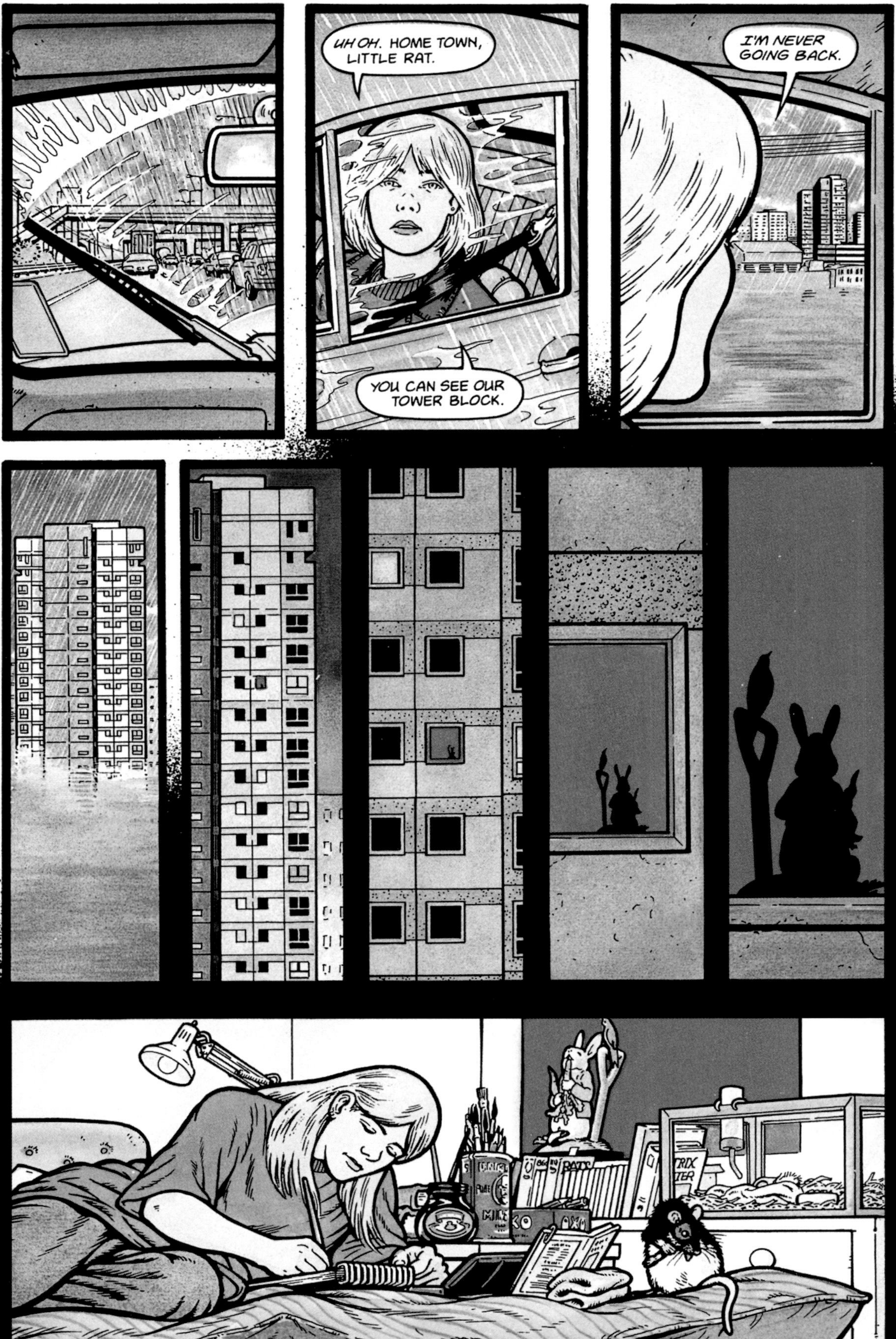
UH OH. HOME TOWN, LITTLE RAT.
YOU CAN SEE OUR TOWER BLOCK.
I'M NEVER GOING BACK.

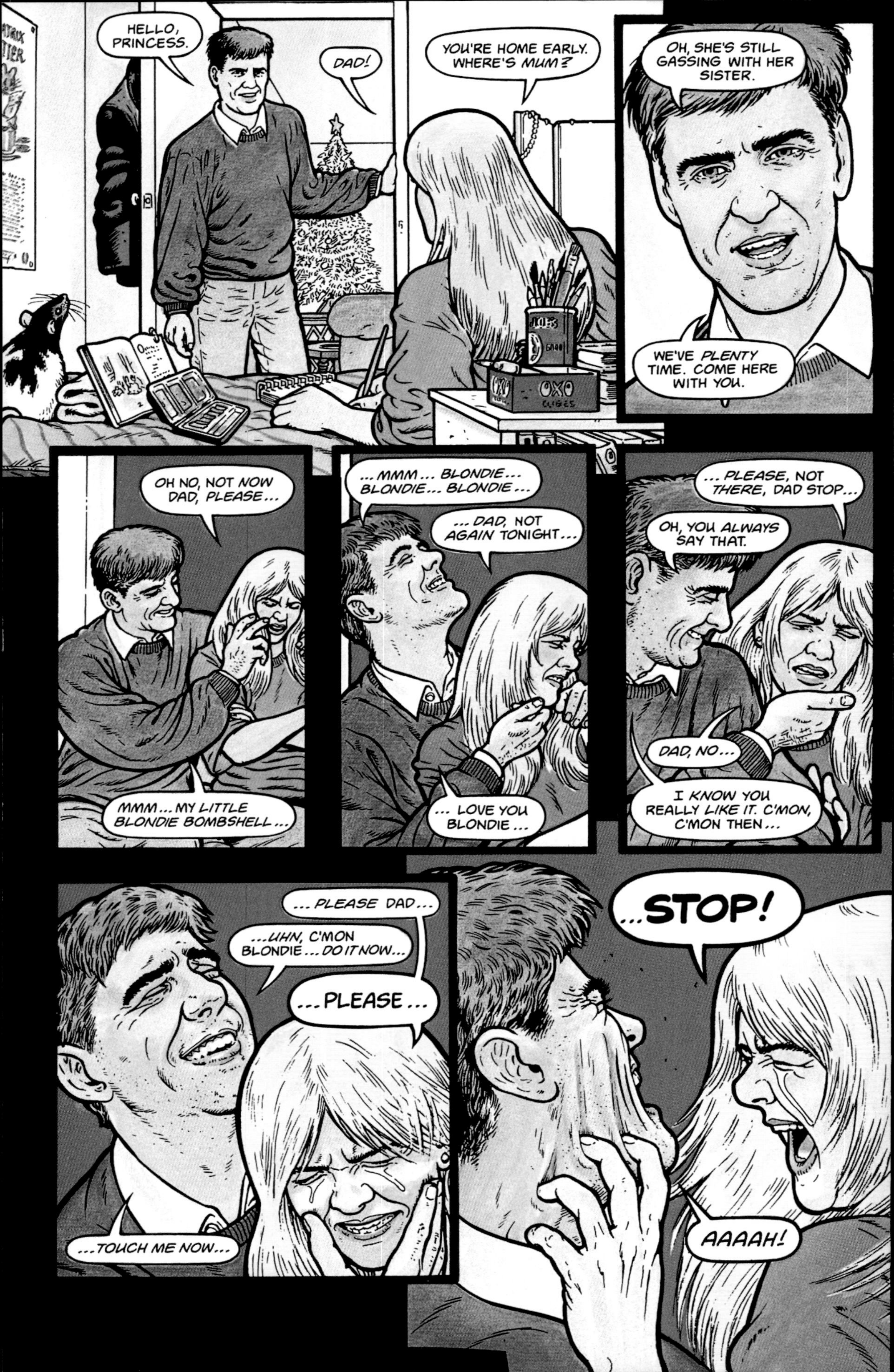
HELLO, PRINCESS.
DAD!
YOU'RE HOME EARLY. WHERE'S MUM?
OH, SHE'S STILL GASSING WITH HER SISTER.
WE'VE PLENTY TIME. COME HERE WITH YOU.
OH NO, NOT NOW DAD, PLEASE...
MMM... MY LITTLE BLONDIE BOMBSHELL...
...MMM... BLONDIE... BLONDIE... BLONDIE...
...DAD, NOT AGAIN TONIGHT...
... LOVE YOU BLONDIE...
...PLEASE, NOT THERE, DAD STOP...
OH, YOU ALWAYS SAY THAT.
DAD, NO...
I KNOW YOU REALLY LIKE IT. C'MON, C'MON THEN...
...PLEASE DAD...
...UHN, C'MON BLONDIE... DO IT NOW...
...PLEASE...
...TOUCH ME NOW...
...STOP!
AAAAH!

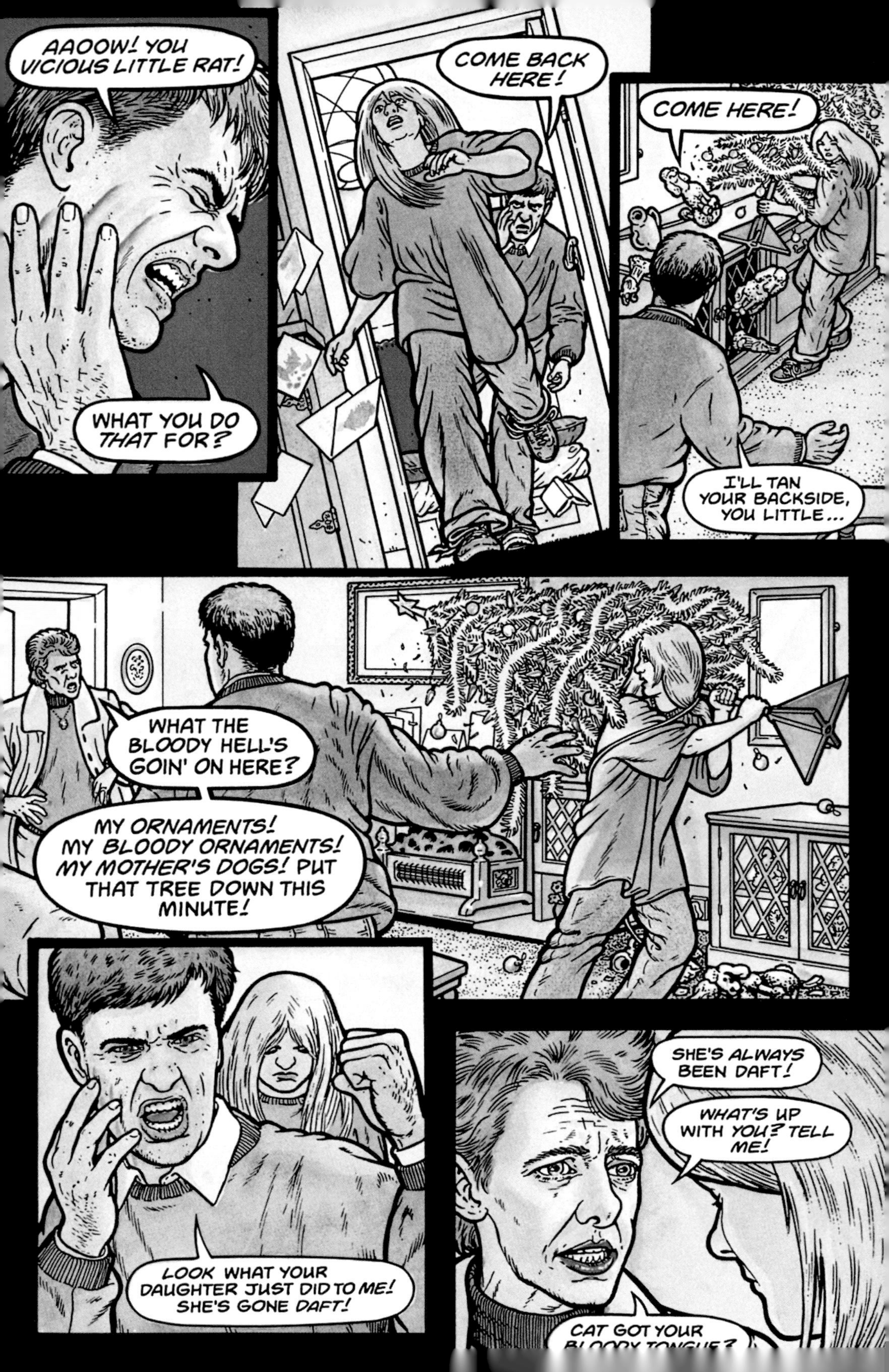
AAOOW! YOU VICIOUS LITTLE RAT!
WHAT YOU DO THAT FOR?
COME BACK HERE!
COME HERE!
I'LL TAN YOUR BACKSIDE, YOU LITTLE...
WHAT THE BLOODY HELL'S GOIN' ON HERE?
MY ORNAMENTS! MY BLOODY ORNAMENTS! MY MOTHER'S DOGS! PUT THAT TREE DOWN THIS MINUTE!
LOOK WHAT YOUR DAUGHTER JUST DID TO ME! SHE'S GONE DAFT!
SHE'S ALWAYS BEEN DAFT!
WHAT'S UP WITH YOU? TELL ME!
CAT GOT YOUR

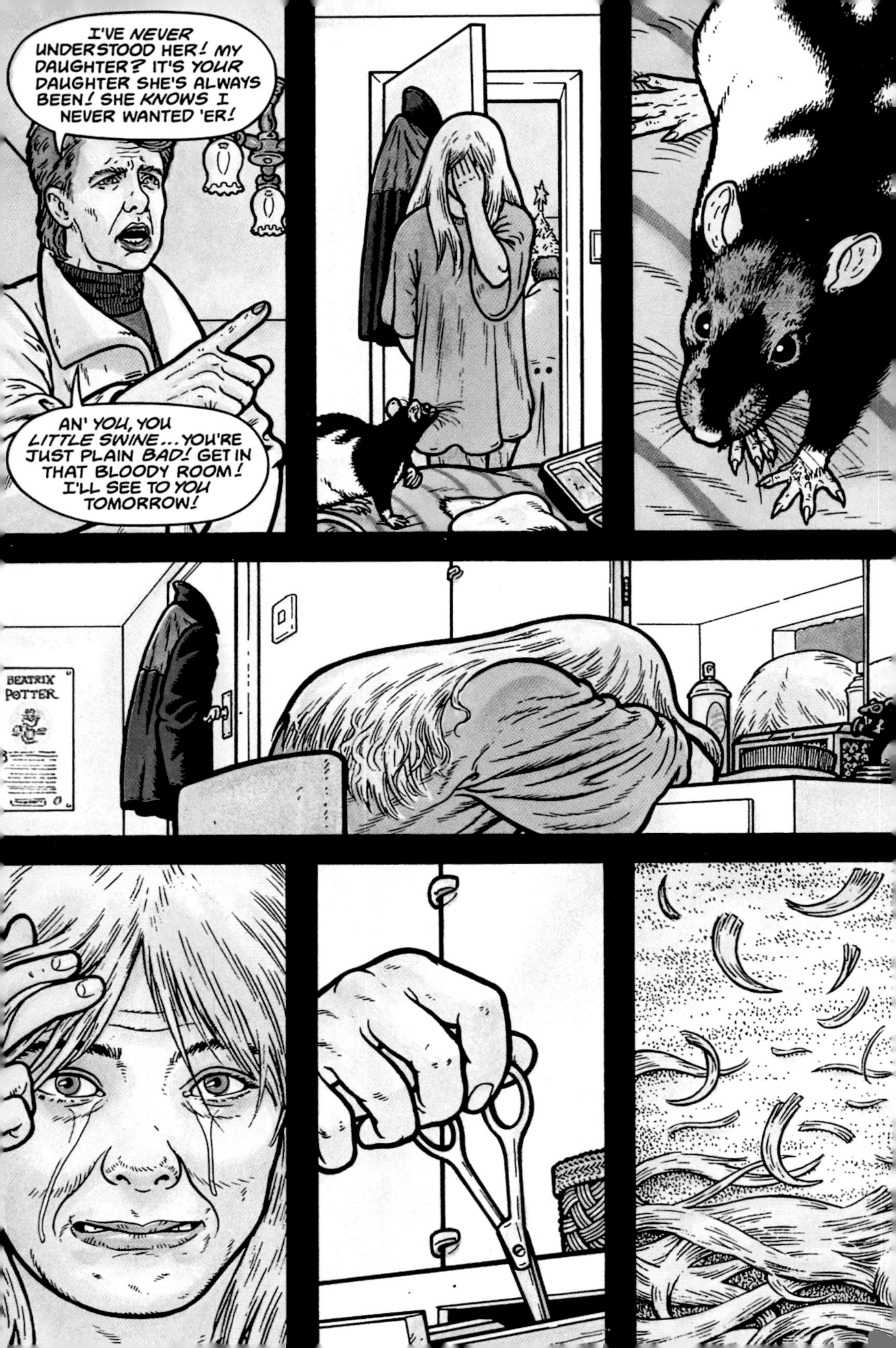
I'VE NEVER UNDERSTOOD HER! MY DAUGHTER? IT'S YOUR DAUGHTER SHE'S ALWAYS BEEN! SHE KNOWS I NEVER WANTED 'ER!
AN' YOU, YOU LITTLE SWINE... YOU'RE JUST PLAIN BAD! GET IN THAT BLOODY ROOM! I'LL SEE TO YOU TOMORROW!
BEATRIX POTTER

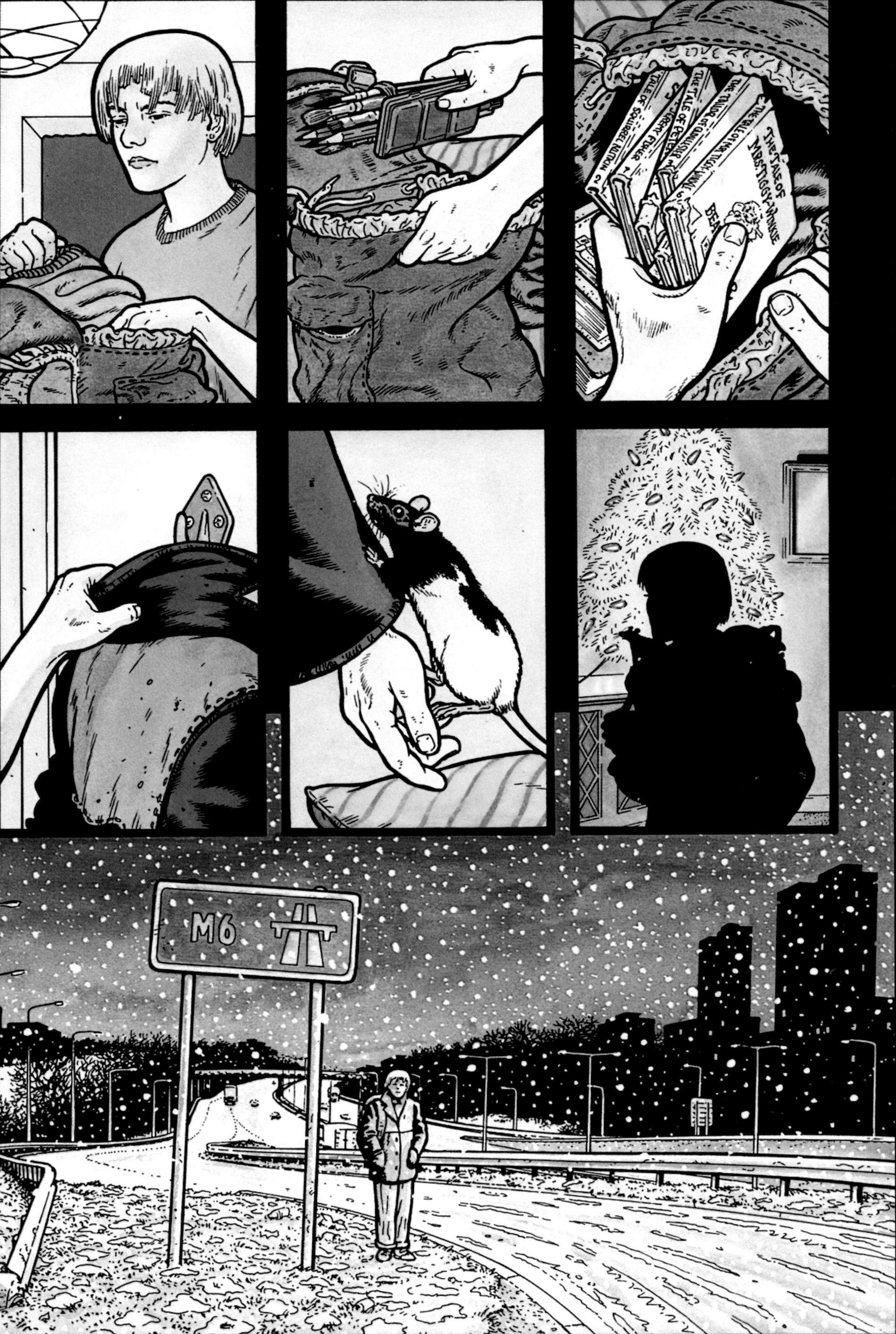
THE TALE OF MRS. TIGGY-WINKLE
M6

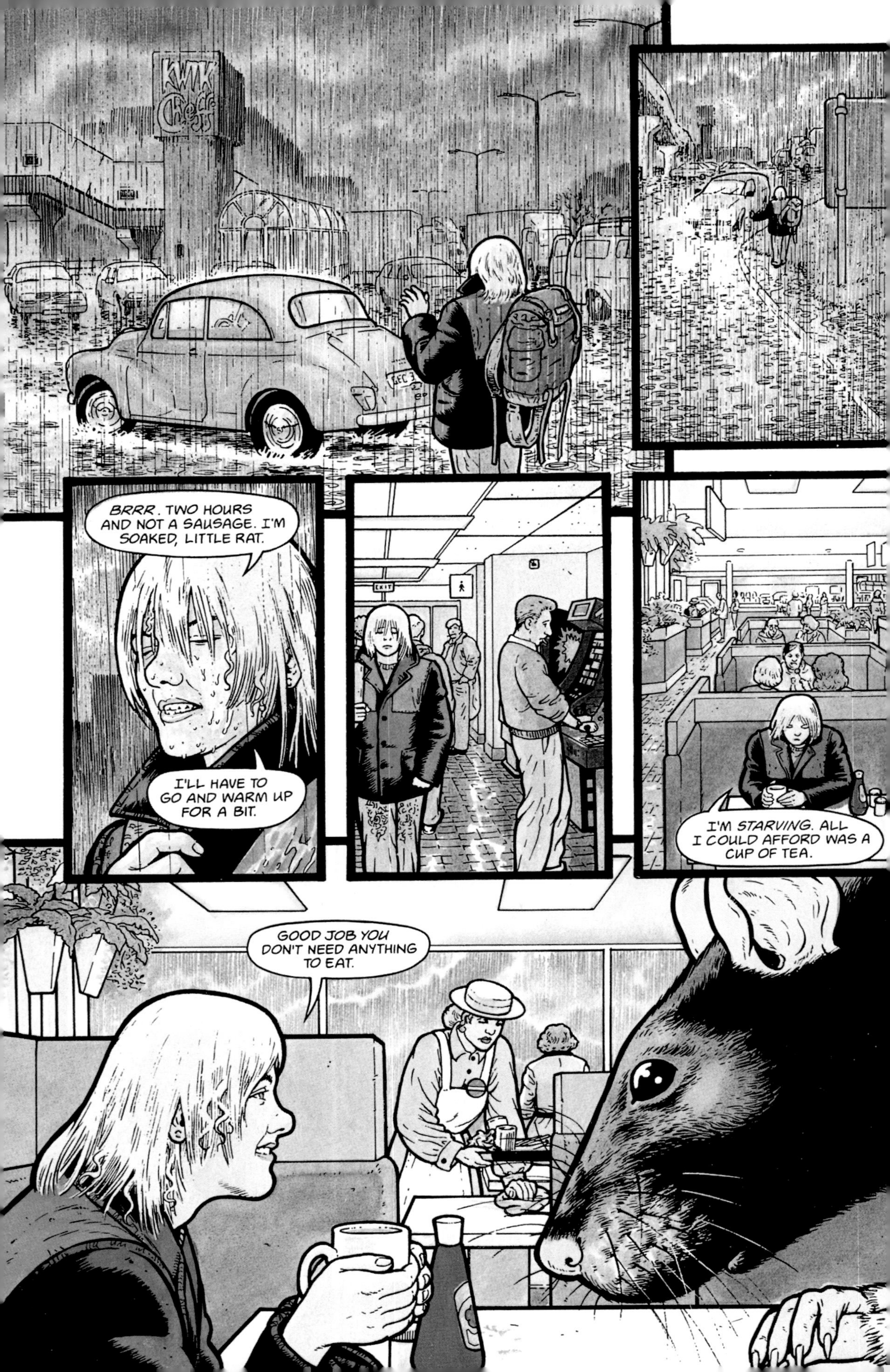
KWIK Chefs
BRRR. TWO HOURS AND NOT A SAUSAGE. I'M SOAKED, LITTLE RAT.
I'LL HAVE TO GO AND WARM UP FOR A BIT.
EXIT
I'M *STARVING*. ALL I COULD AFFORD WAS A CUP OF TEA.
GOOD JOB YOU DON'T NEED ANYTHING TO EAT.

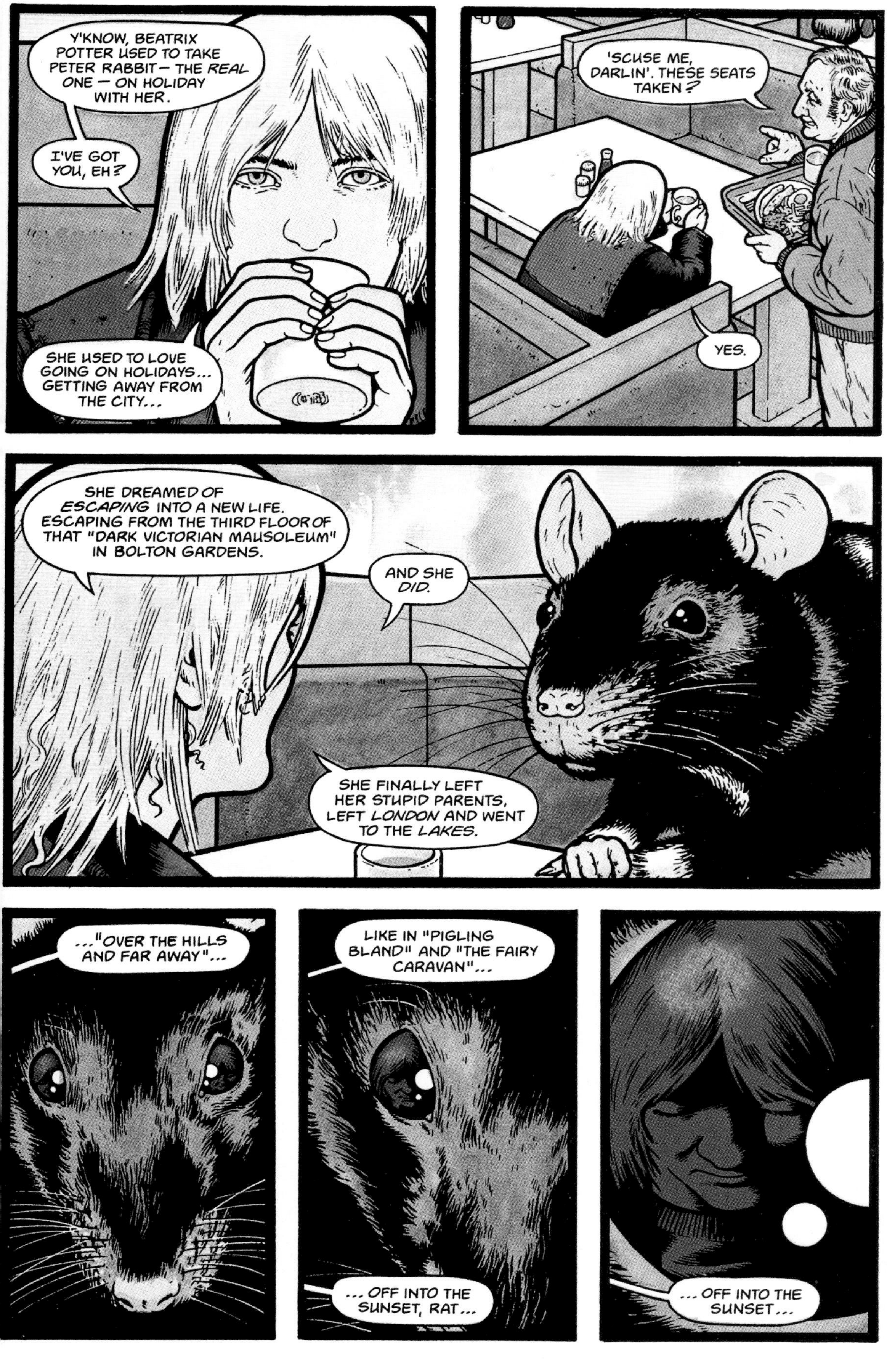
Y'KNOW, BEATRIX POTTER USED TO TAKE PETER RABBIT — THE *REAL* ONE — ON HOLIDAY WITH HER.
I'VE GOT YOU, EH?
SHE USED TO LOVE GOING ON HOLIDAYS... GETTING AWAY FROM THE CITY...
'SCUSE ME, DARLIN'. THESE SEATS TAKEN?
YES.
SHE DREAMED OF *ESCAPING* INTO A NEW LIFE. ESCAPING FROM THE THIRD FLOOR OF THAT "DARK VICTORIAN MAUSOLEUM" IN BOLTON GARDENS.
AND SHE *DID*.
SHE FINALLY LEFT HER STUPID PARENTS, LEFT *LONDON* AND WENT TO THE *LAKES*.
..."OVER THE HILLS AND FAR AWAY"...
LIKE IN "PIGLING BLAND" AND "THE FAIRY CARAVAN"...
... OFF INTO THE SUNSET, RAT...
... OFF INTO THE SUNSET...

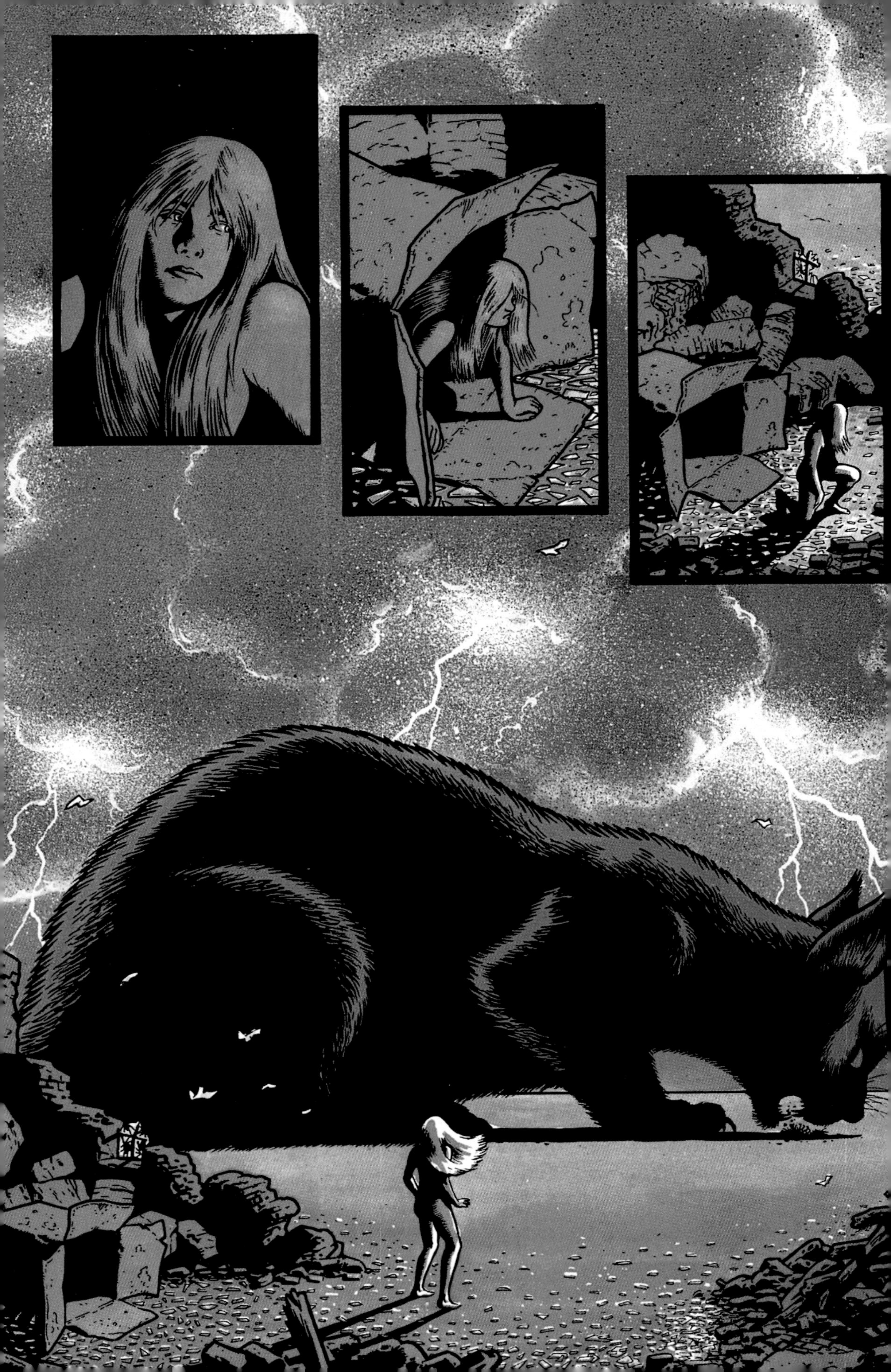

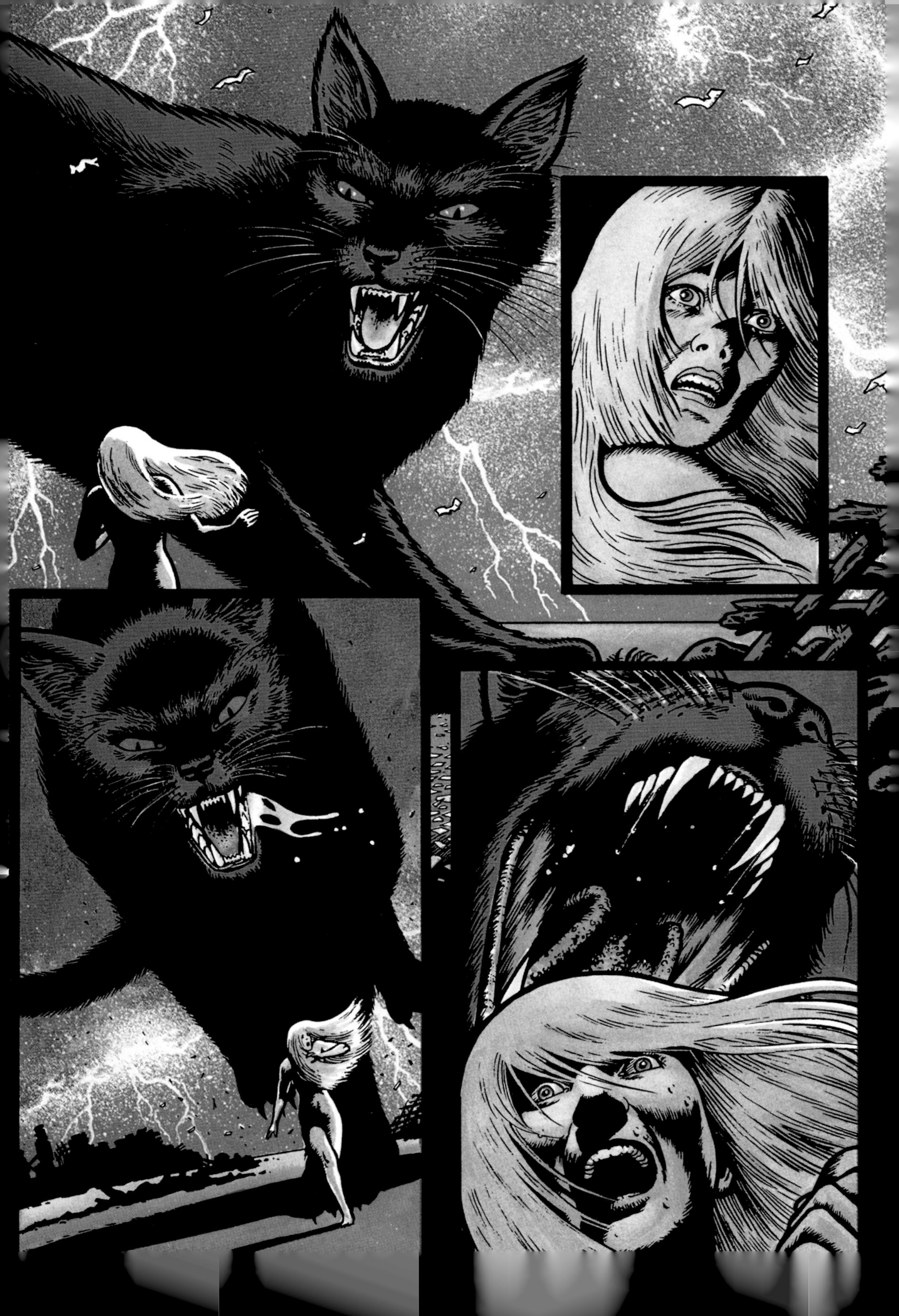

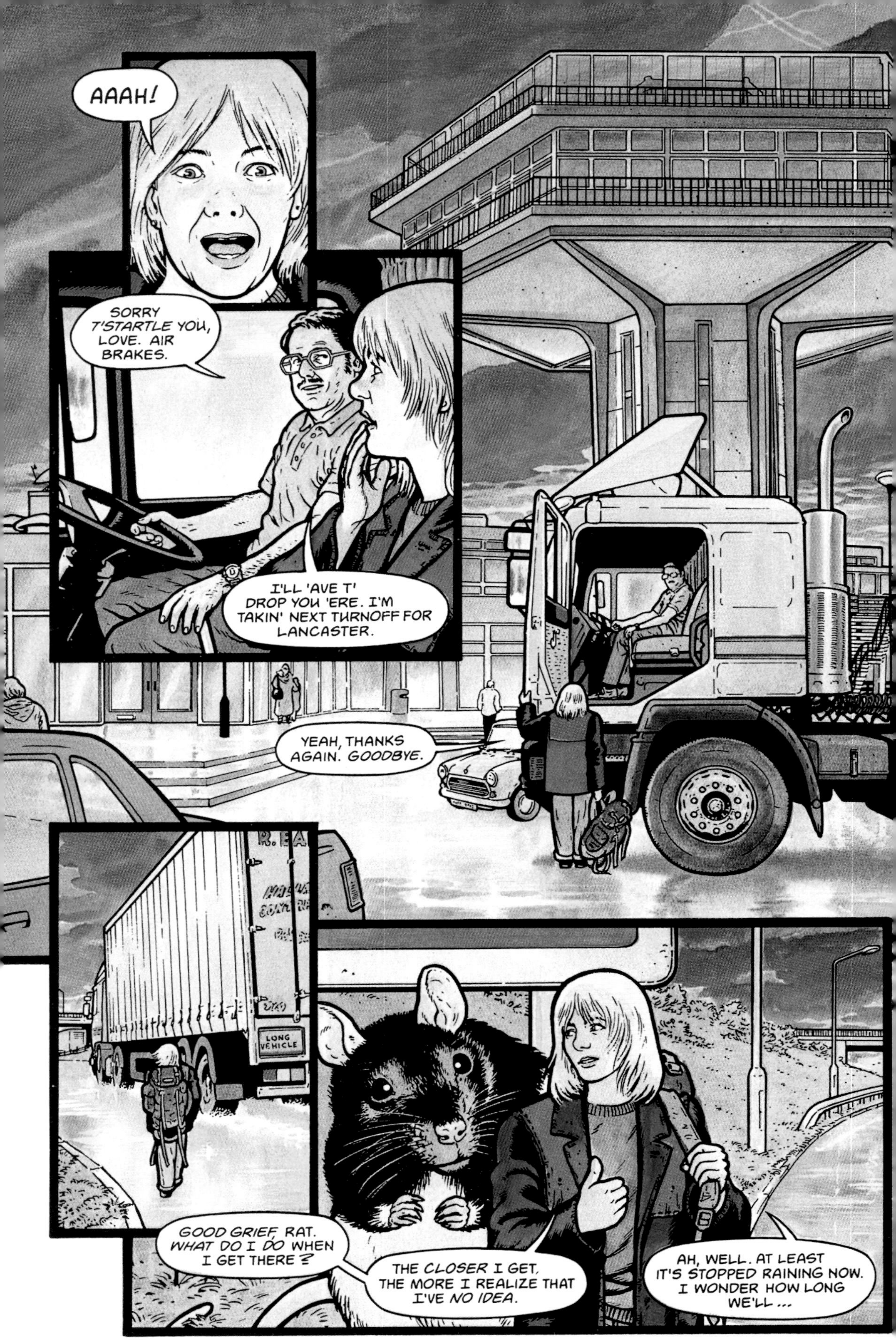
AAAH!
SORRY T'STARTLE YOU, LOVE. AIR BRAKES.
I'LL 'AVE T' DROP YOU 'ERE. I'M TAKIN' NEXT TURNOFF FOR LANCASTER.
YEAH, THANKS AGAIN. GOODBYE.
LONG VEHICLE
GOOD GRIEF, RAT. WHAT DO I DO WHEN I GET THERE?
THE CLOSER I GET, THE MORE I REALIZE THAT I'VE NO IDEA.
AH, WELL. AT LEAST IT'S STOPPED RAINING NOW. I WONDER HOW LONG WE'LL ...

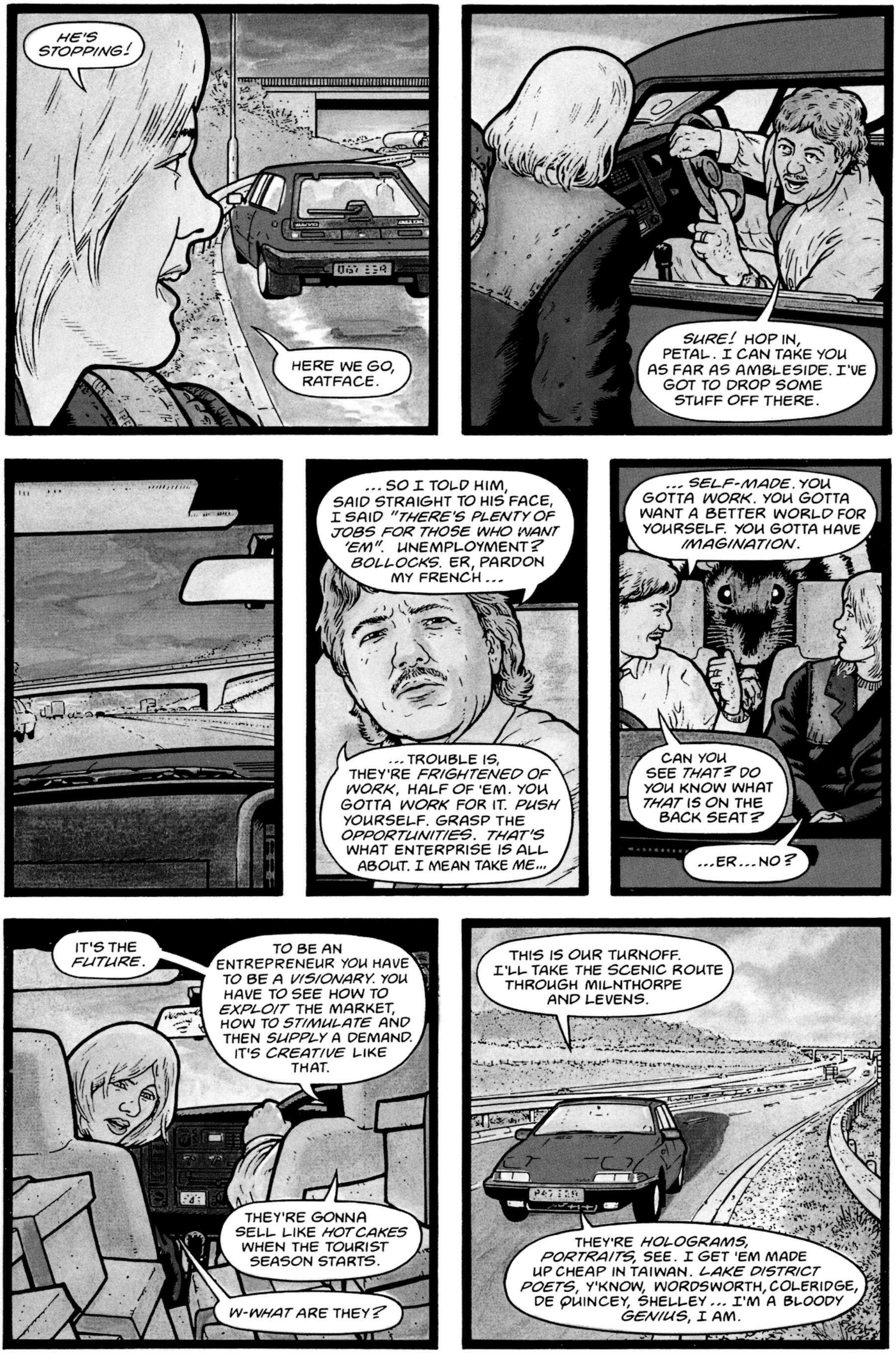
HE'S STOPPING!
HERE WE GO, RATFACE.
SURE! HOP IN, PETAL. I CAN TAKE YOU AS FAR AS AMBLESIDE. I'VE GOT TO DROP SOME STUFF OFF THERE.
...SO I TOLD HIM, SAID STRAIGHT TO HIS FACE, I SAID "THERE'S PLENTY OF JOBS FOR THOSE WHO WANT 'EM". UNEMPLOYMENT? BOLLOCKS. ER, PARDON MY FRENCH...
...TROUBLE IS, THEY'RE FRIGHTENED OF WORK, HALF OF 'EM. YOU GOTTA WORK FOR IT. PUSH YOURSELF. GRASP THE OPPORTUNITIES. THAT'S WHAT ENTERPRISE IS ALL ABOUT. I MEAN TAKE ME...
...SELF-MADE. YOU GOTTA WORK. YOU GOTTA WANT A BETTER WORLD FOR YOURSELF. YOU GOTTA HAVE IMAGINATION.
CAN YOU SEE THAT? DO YOU KNOW WHAT THAT IS ON THE BACK SEAT?
...ER...NO?
IT'S THE FUTURE.
TO BE AN ENTREPRENEUR YOU HAVE TO BE A VISIONARY. YOU HAVE TO SEE HOW TO EXPLOIT THE MARKET, HOW TO STIMULATE AND THEN SUPPLY A DEMAND. IT'S CREATIVE LIKE THAT.
THEY'RE GONNA SELL LIKE HOT CAKES WHEN THE TOURIST SEASON STARTS.
W-WHAT ARE THEY?
THIS IS OUR TURNOFF. I'LL TAKE THE SCENIC ROUTE THROUGH MILNTHORPE AND LEVENS.
THEY'RE HOLOGRAMS, PORTRAITS, SEE. I GET 'EM MADE UP CHEAP IN TAIWAN. LAKE DISTRICT POETS, Y'KNOW, WORDSWORTH, COLERIDGE, DE QUINCEY, SHELLEY... I'M A BLOODY GENIUS, I AM.

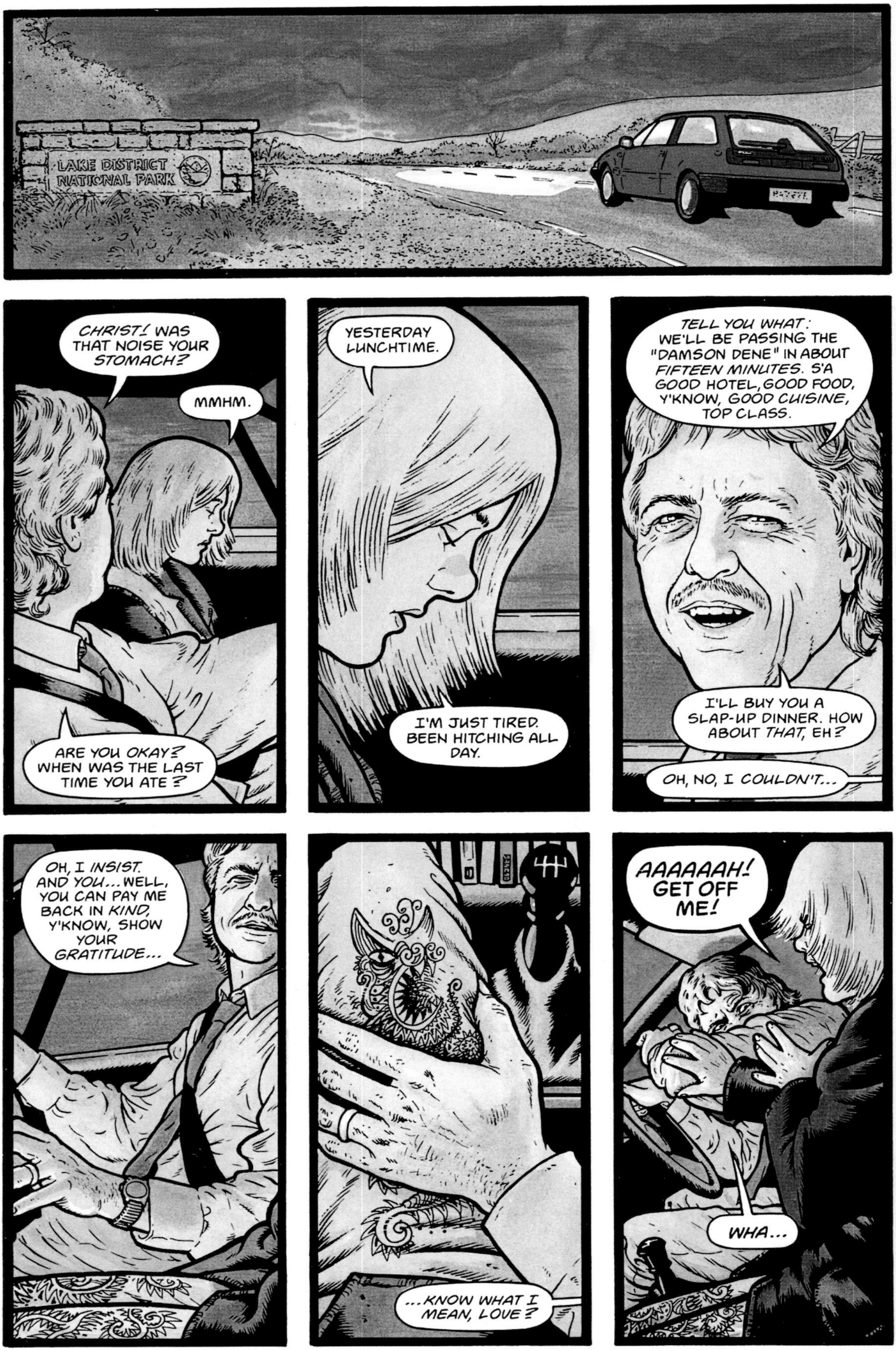
LAKE DISTRICT
NATIONAL PARK
CHRIST! WAS THAT NOISE YOUR STOMACH?
MMHM.
ARE YOU OKAY? WHEN WAS THE LAST TIME YOU ATE?
YESTERDAY LUNCHTIME.
I'M JUST TIRED. BEEN HITCHING ALL DAY.
TELL YOU WHAT: WE'LL BE PASSING THE "DAMSON DENE" IN ABOUT FIFTEEN MINUTES. S'A GOOD HOTEL, GOOD FOOD, Y'KNOW, GOOD CUISINE, TOP CLASS.
I'LL BUY YOU A SLAP-UP DINNER. HOW ABOUT THAT, EH?
OH, NO, I COULDN'T...
OH, I INSIST. AND YOU... WELL, YOU CAN PAY ME BACK IN KIND, Y'KNOW, SHOW YOUR GRATITUDE...
...KNOW WHAT I MEAN, LOVE?
AAAAAAH! GET OFF ME!
WHA...

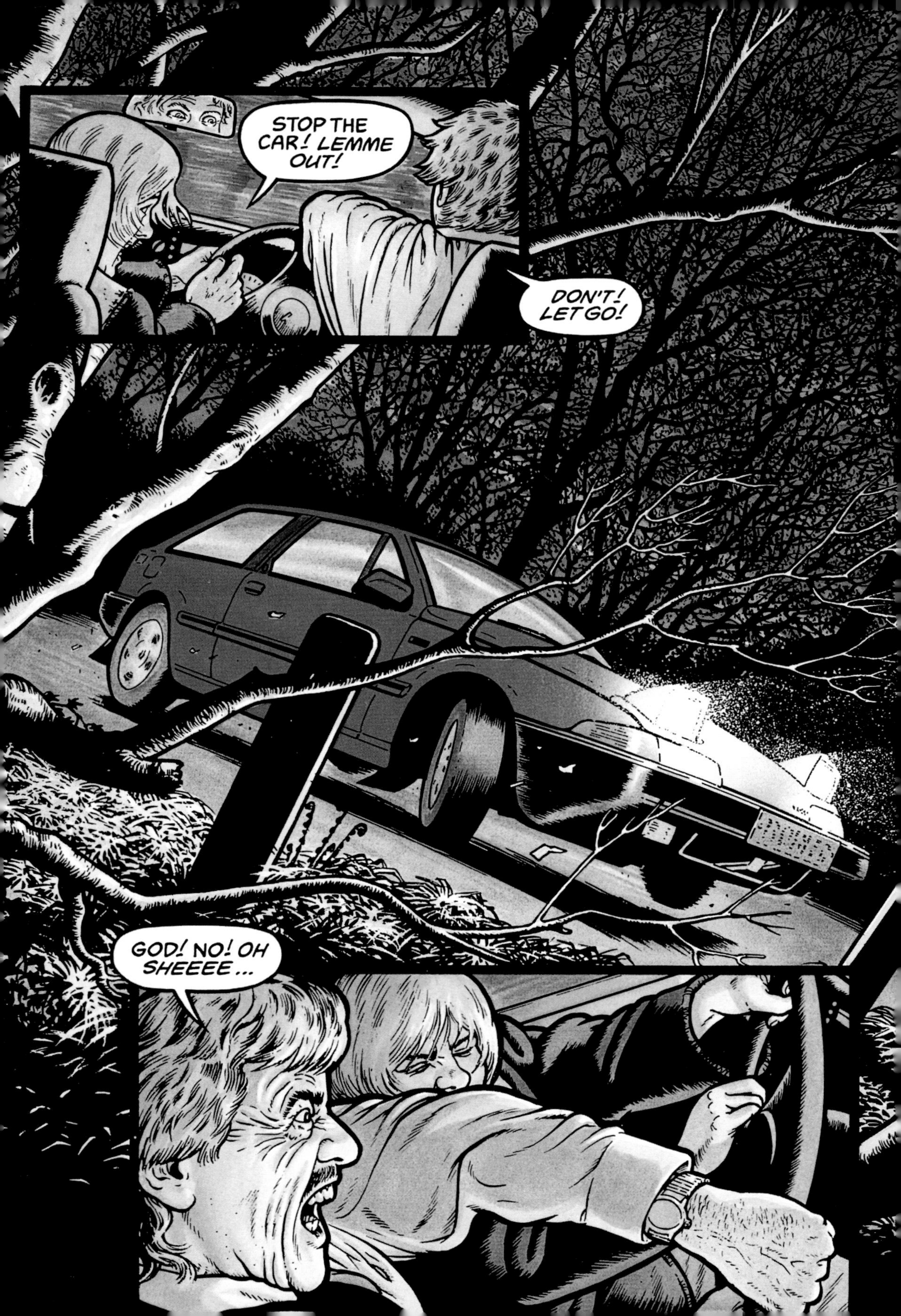
STOP THE CAR! LEMME OUT!
DON'T! LET GO!
GOD! NO! OH SHEEEE ...

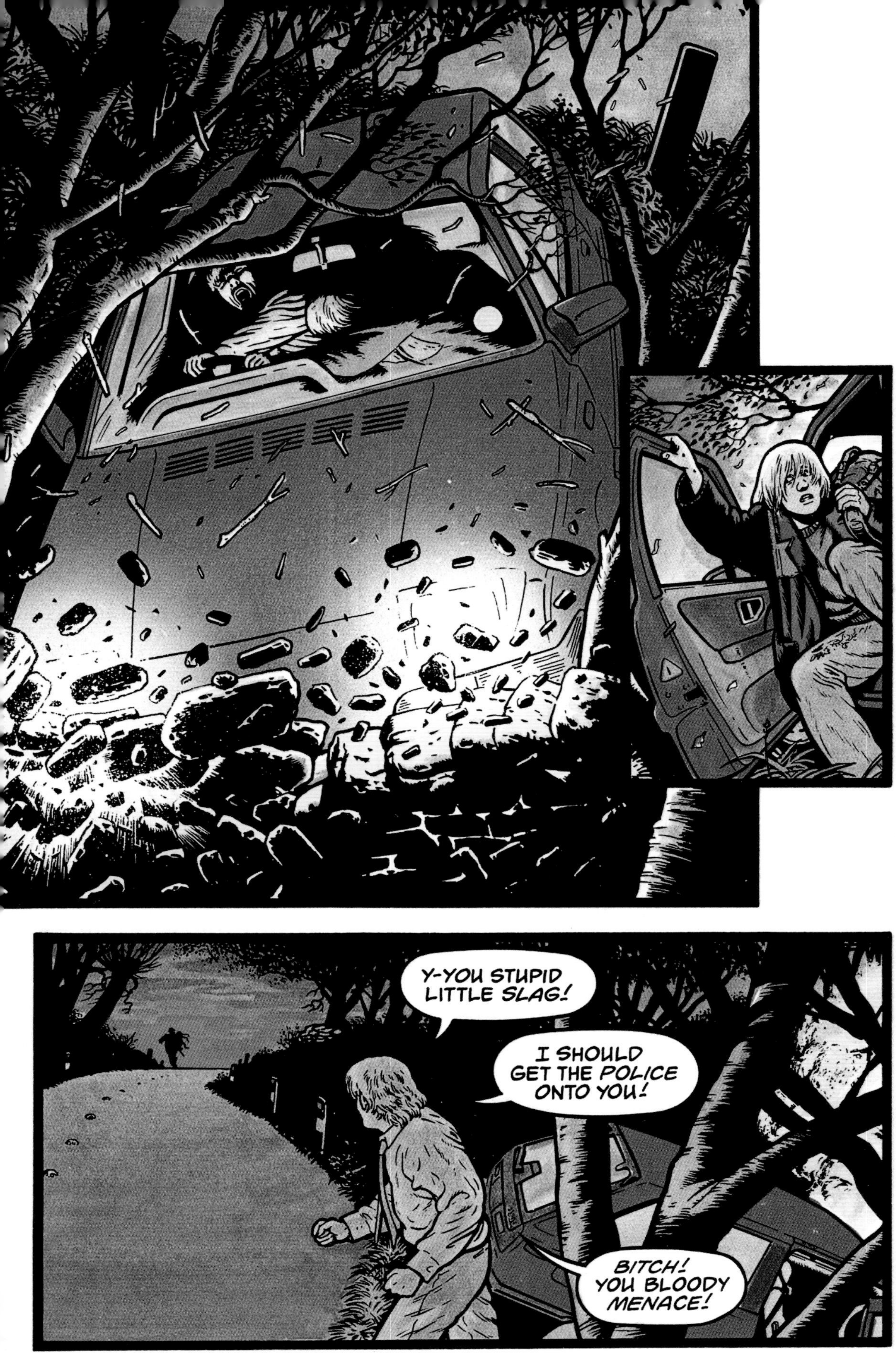
Y-YOU STUPID LITTLE SLAG!
I SHOULD GET THE POLICE ONTO YOU!
BITCH! YOU BLOODY MENACE!

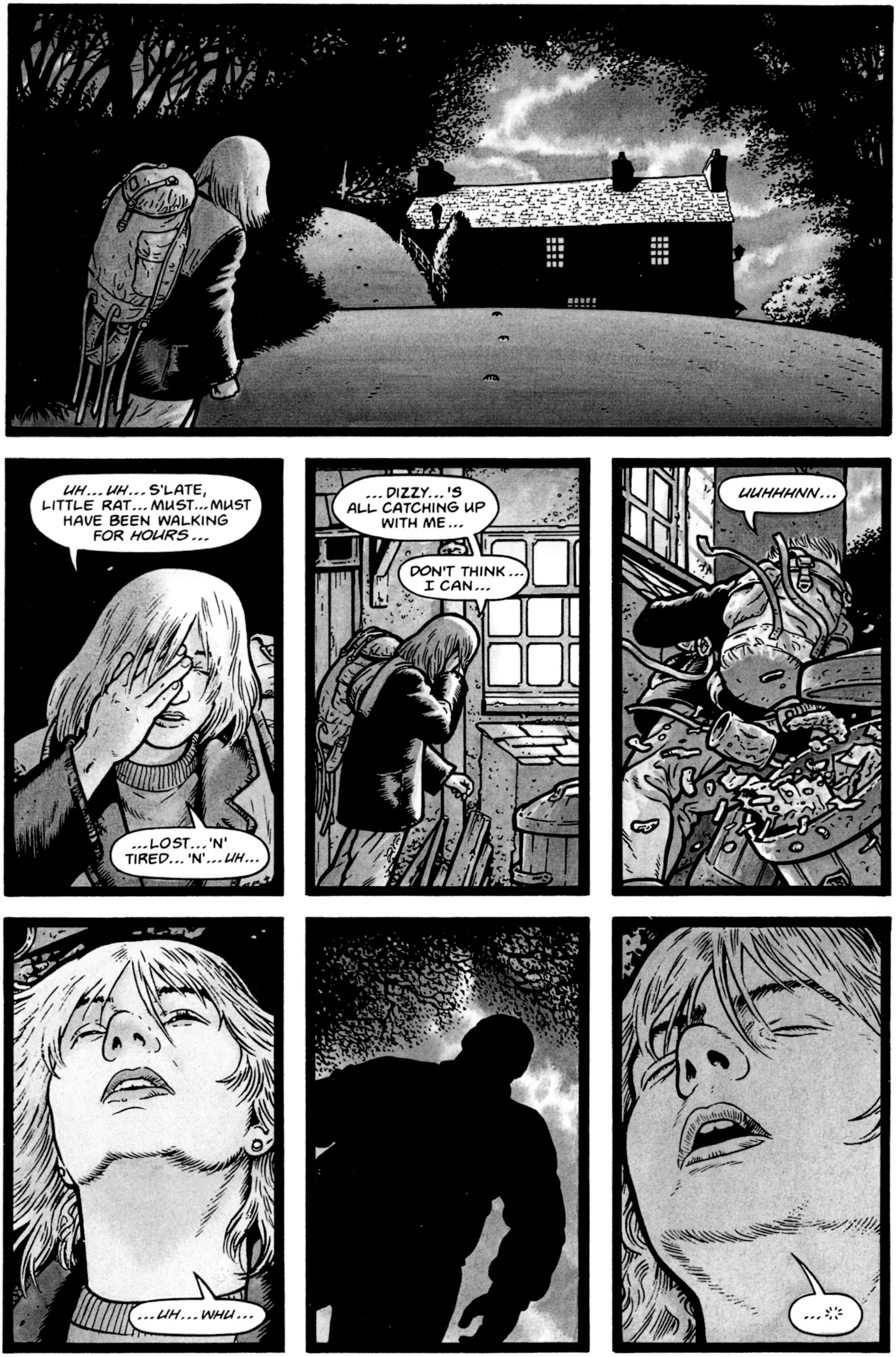
UH... UH... S'LATE, LITTLE RAT... MUST... MUST HAVE BEEN WALKING FOR HOURS...
...LOST... 'N' TIRED... 'N'... UH...
...DIZZY... 'S ALL CATCHING UP WITH ME...
DON'T THINK... I CAN...
UUHHHNN...
...UH... WHU...

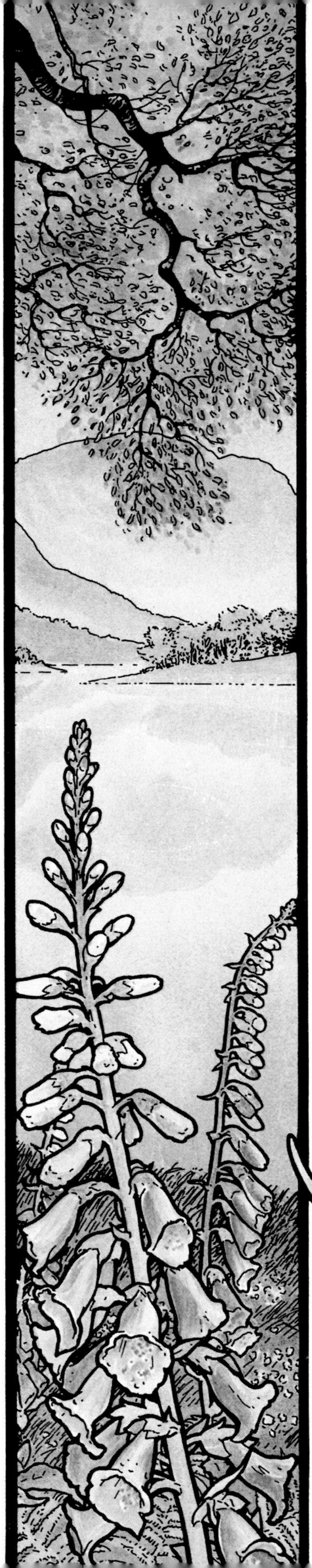

COUNTRY

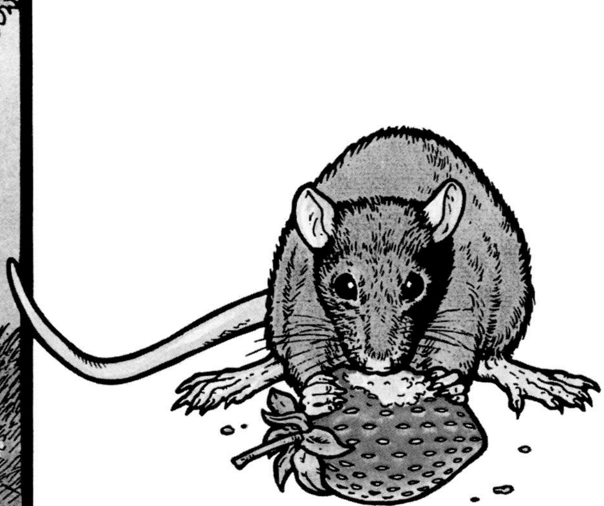

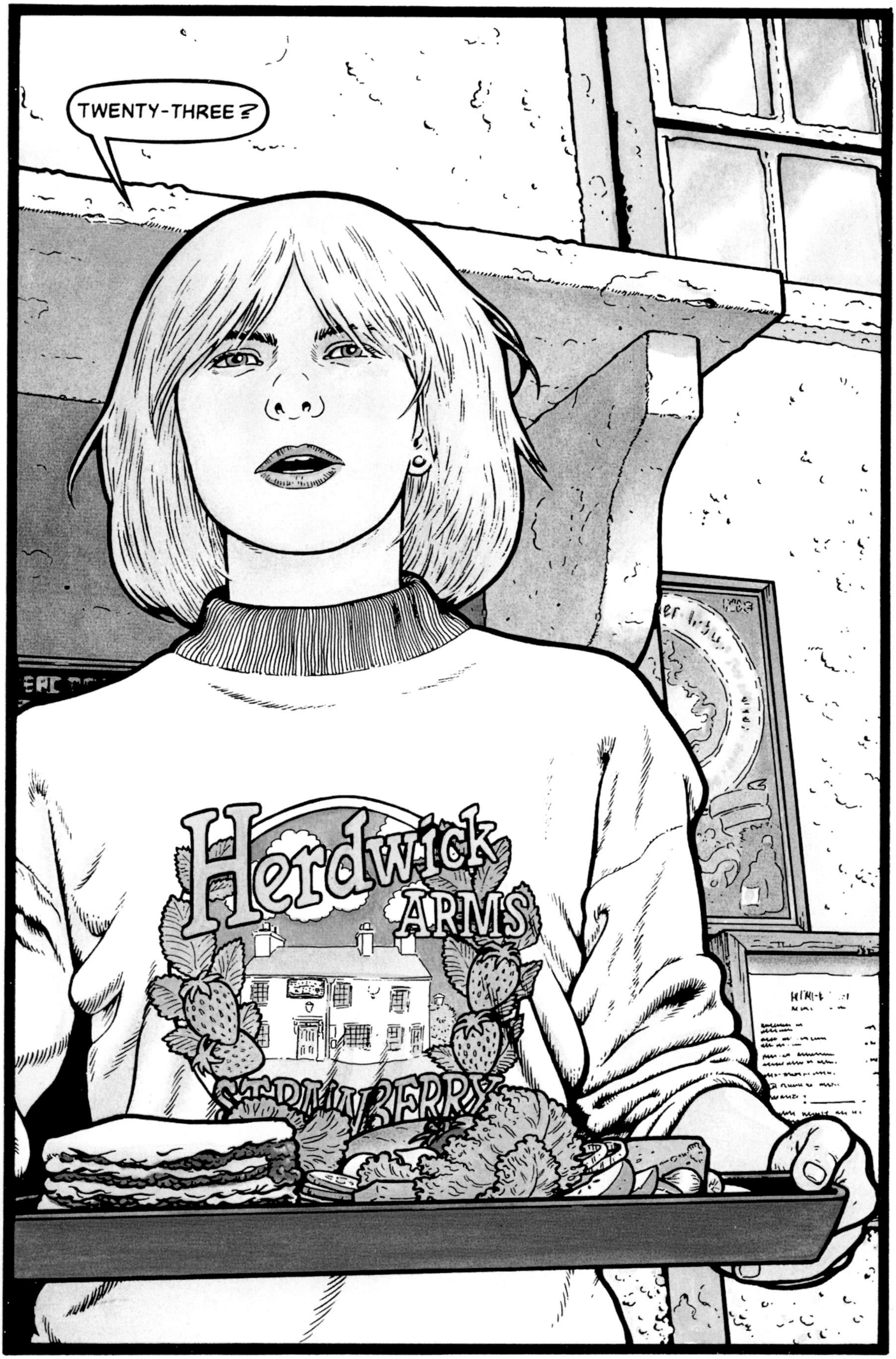
TWENTY-THREE?
Herdwick ARMS
STRAWBERRY

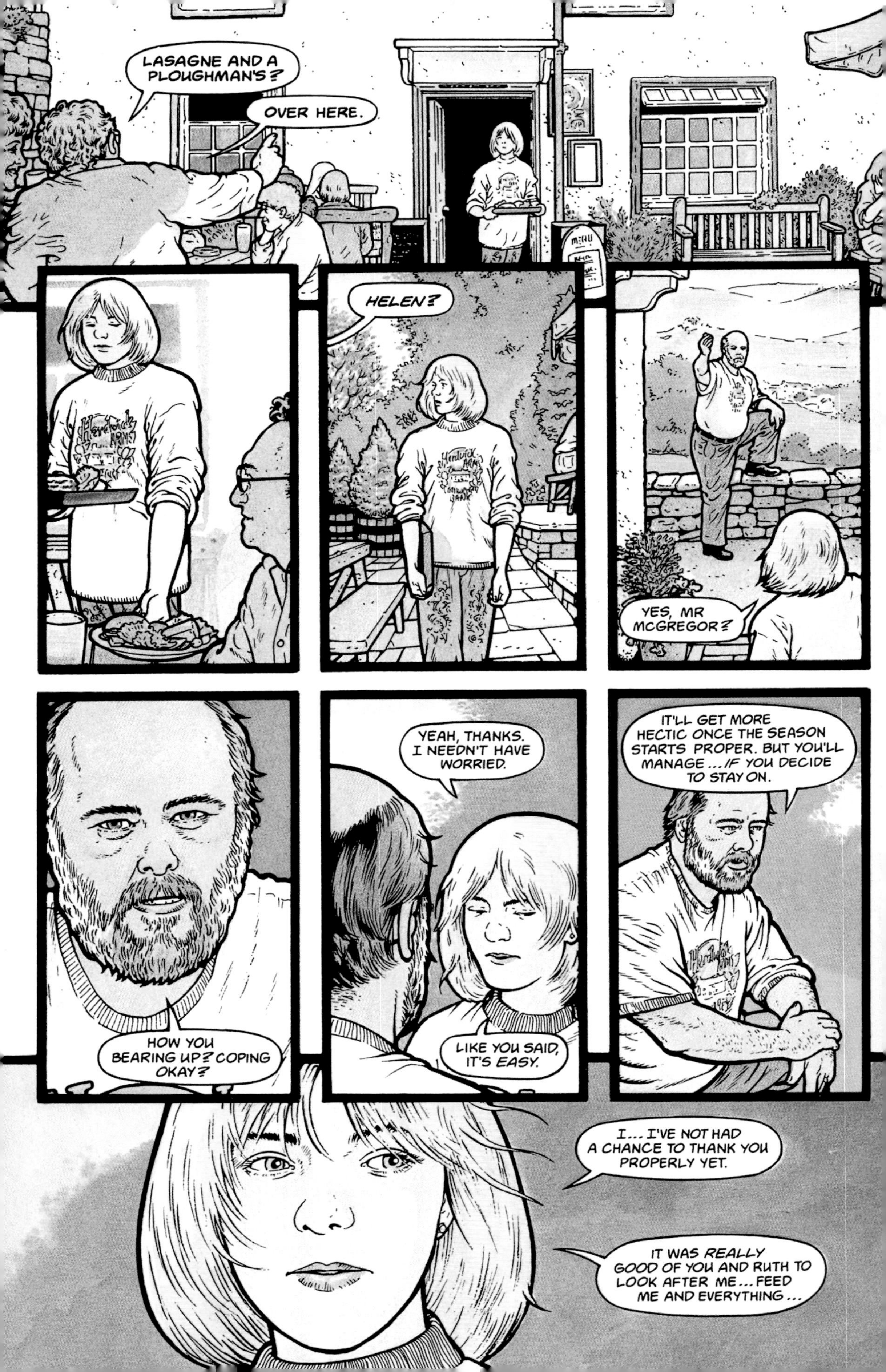
LASAGNE AND A PLOUGHMAN'S?
OVER HERE.
HELEN?
YES, MR McGREGOR?
HOW YOU BEARING UP? COPING OKAY?
YEAH, THANKS. I NEEDN'T HAVE WORRIED.
LIKE YOU SAID, IT'S *EASY*.
IT'LL GET MORE HECTIC ONCE THE SEASON STARTS PROPER. BUT YOU'LL MANAGE ... *IF* YOU DECIDE TO STAY ON.
I... I'VE NOT HAD A CHANCE TO THANK YOU PROPERLY YET.
IT WAS *REALLY* GOOD OF YOU AND RUTH TO LOOK AFTER ME... FEED ME AND EVERYTHING...

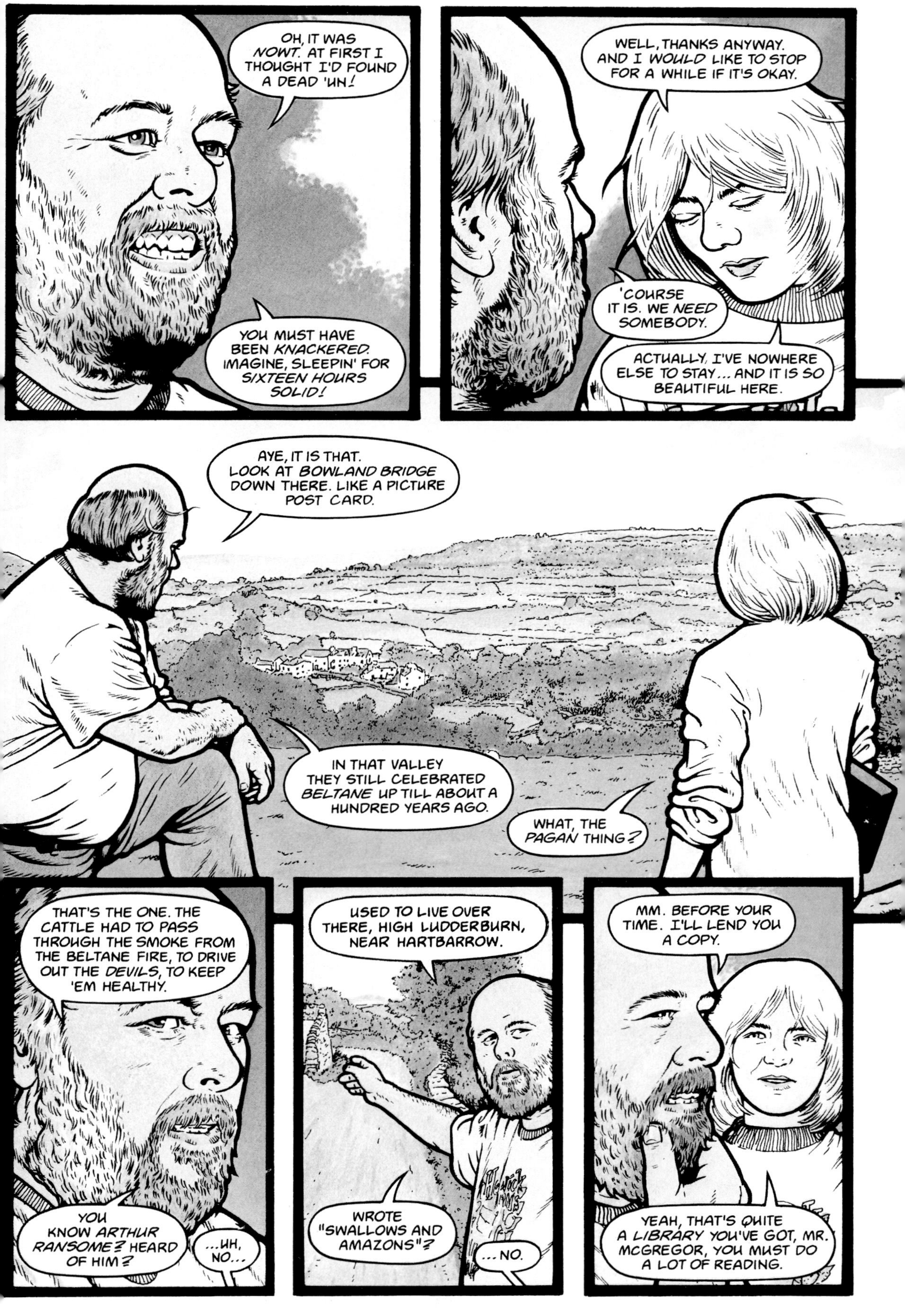
OH, IT WAS NOWT. AT FIRST I THOUGHT I'D FOUND A DEAD 'UN!
YOU MUST HAVE BEEN KNACKERED. IMAGINE, SLEEPIN' FOR SIXTEEN HOURS SOLID!
WELL, THANKS ANYWAY. AND I WOULD LIKE TO STOP FOR A WHILE IF IT'S OKAY.
'COURSE IT IS. WE NEED SOMEBODY.
ACTUALLY, I'VE NOWHERE ELSE TO STAY... AND IT IS SO BEAUTIFUL HERE.
AYE, IT IS THAT. LOOK AT BOWLAND BRIDGE DOWN THERE. LIKE A PICTURE POST CARD.
IN THAT VALLEY THEY STILL CELEBRATED BELTANE UP TILL ABOUT A HUNDRED YEARS AGO.
WHAT, THE PAGAN THING?
THAT'S THE ONE. THE CATTLE HAD TO PASS THROUGH THE SMOKE FROM THE BELTANE FIRE, TO DRIVE OUT THE DEVILS, TO KEEP 'EM HEALTHY.
YOU KNOW ARTHUR RANSOME? HEARD OF HIM?
...UH, NO...
USED TO LIVE OVER THERE, HIGH LUDDERBURN, NEAR HARTBARROW.
WROTE "SWALLOWS AND AMAZONS"?
...NO.
MM. BEFORE YOUR TIME. I'LL LEND YOU A COPY.
YEAH, THAT'S QUITE A LIBRARY YOU'VE GOT, MR. MCGREGOR, YOU MUST DO A LOT OF READING.

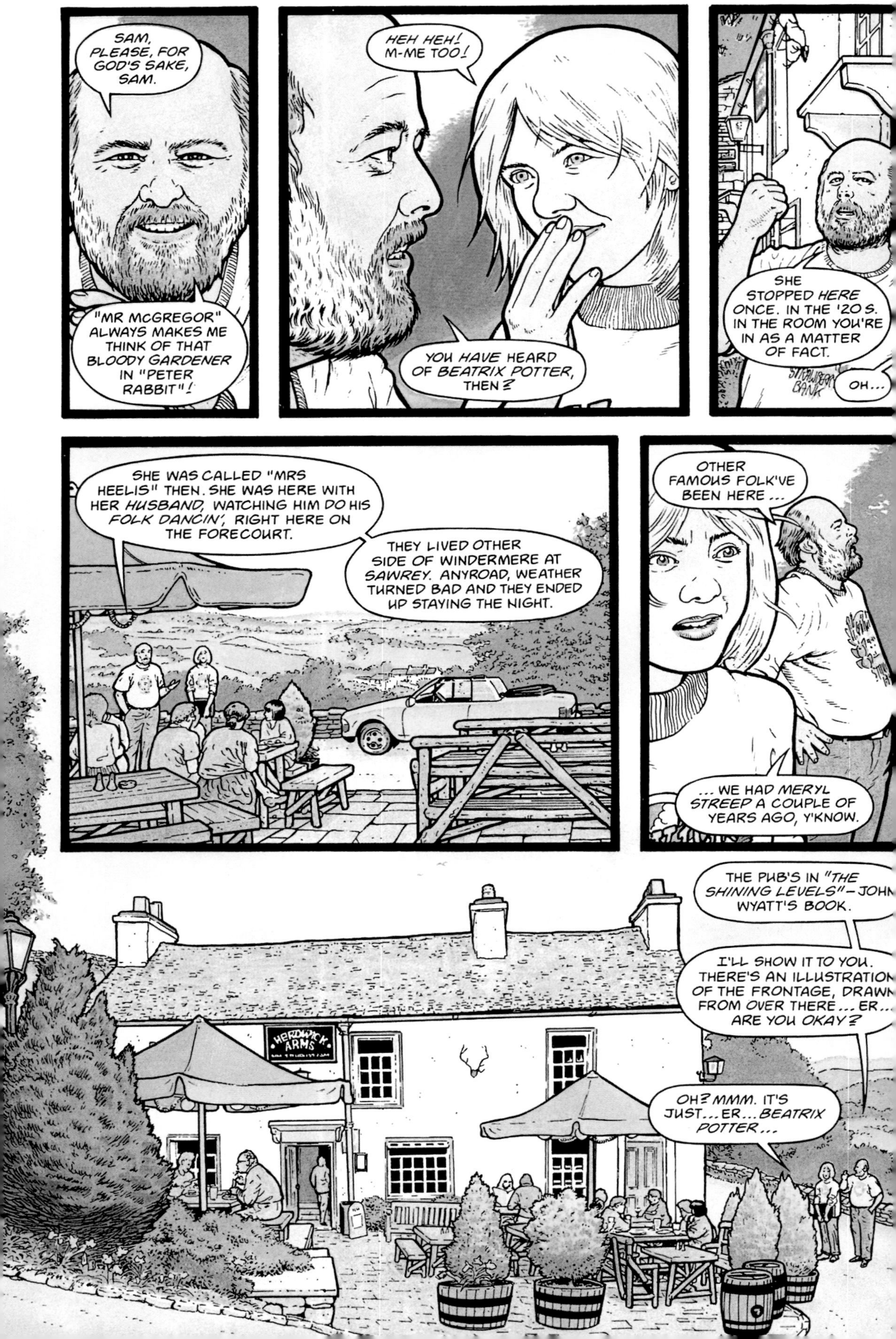
SAM, PLEASE, FOR GOD'S SAKE, SAM.
"MR MCGREGOR" ALWAYS MAKES ME THINK OF THAT BLOODY GARDENER IN "PETER RABBIT"!
HEH HEH! M-ME TOO!
YOU HAVE HEARD OF BEATRIX POTTER, THEN?
SHE STOPPED HERE ONCE. IN THE '20 S. IN THE ROOM YOU'RE IN AS A MATTER OF FACT.
OH...
SHE WAS CALLED "MRS HEELIS" THEN. SHE WAS HERE WITH HER HUSBAND, WATCHING HIM DO HIS FOLK DANCIN', RIGHT HERE ON THE FORECOURT.
THEY LIVED OTHER SIDE OF WINDERMERE AT SAWREY. ANYROAD, WEATHER TURNED BAD AND THEY ENDED UP STAYING THE NIGHT.
OTHER FAMOUS FOLK'VE BEEN HERE...
...WE HAD MERYL STREEP A COUPLE OF YEARS AGO, Y'KNOW.
THE PUB'S IN "THE SHINING LEVELS" – JOHN WYATT'S BOOK.
I'LL SHOW IT TO YOU. THERE'S AN ILLUSTRATION OF THE FRONTAGE, DRAWN FROM OVER THERE... ER... ARE YOU OKAY?
OH? MMM. IT'S JUST... ER... BEATRIX POTTER...
HERDWICK ARMS

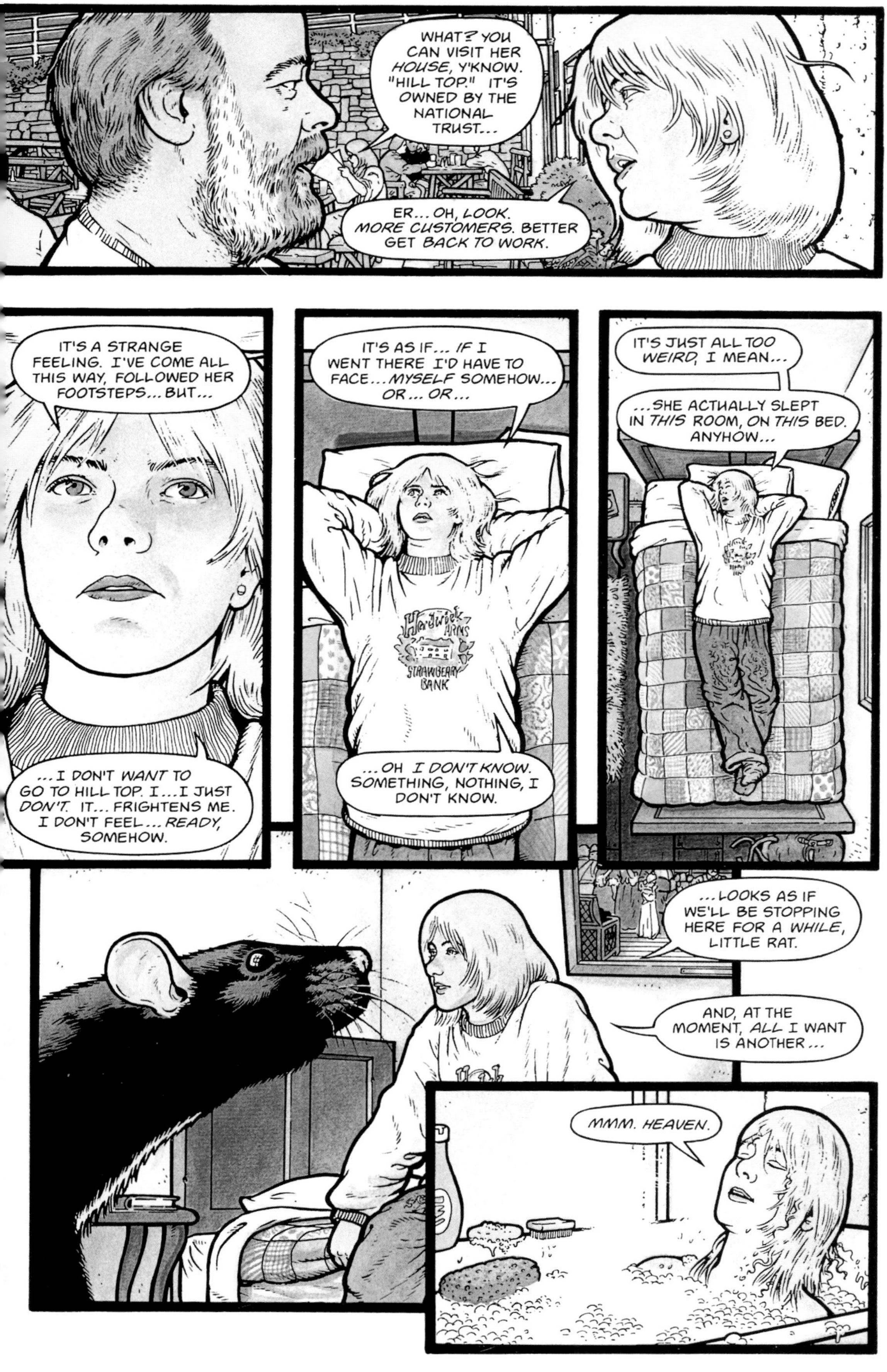
WHAT? YOU CAN VISIT HER HOUSE, Y'KNOW. "HILL TOP." IT'S OWNED BY THE NATIONAL TRUST...
ER... OH, LOOK. MORE CUSTOMERS. BETTER GET BACK TO WORK.
IT'S A STRANGE FEELING. I'VE COME ALL THIS WAY, FOLLOWED HER FOOTSTEPS... BUT...
...I DON'T WANT TO GO TO HILL TOP. I... I JUST DON'T. IT... FRIGHTENS ME. I DON'T FEEL... READY, SOMEHOW.
IT'S AS IF... IF I WENT THERE I'D HAVE TO FACE... MYSELF SOMEHOW... OR... OR...
...OH I DON'T KNOW. SOMETHING, NOTHING, I DON'T KNOW.
IT'S JUST ALL TOO WEIRD, I MEAN...
...SHE ACTUALLY SLEPT IN THIS ROOM, ON THIS BED. ANYHOW...
...LOOKS AS IF WE'LL BE STOPPING HERE FOR A WHILE, LITTLE RAT.
AND, AT THE MOMENT, ALL I WANT IS ANOTHER...
MMM. HEAVEN.

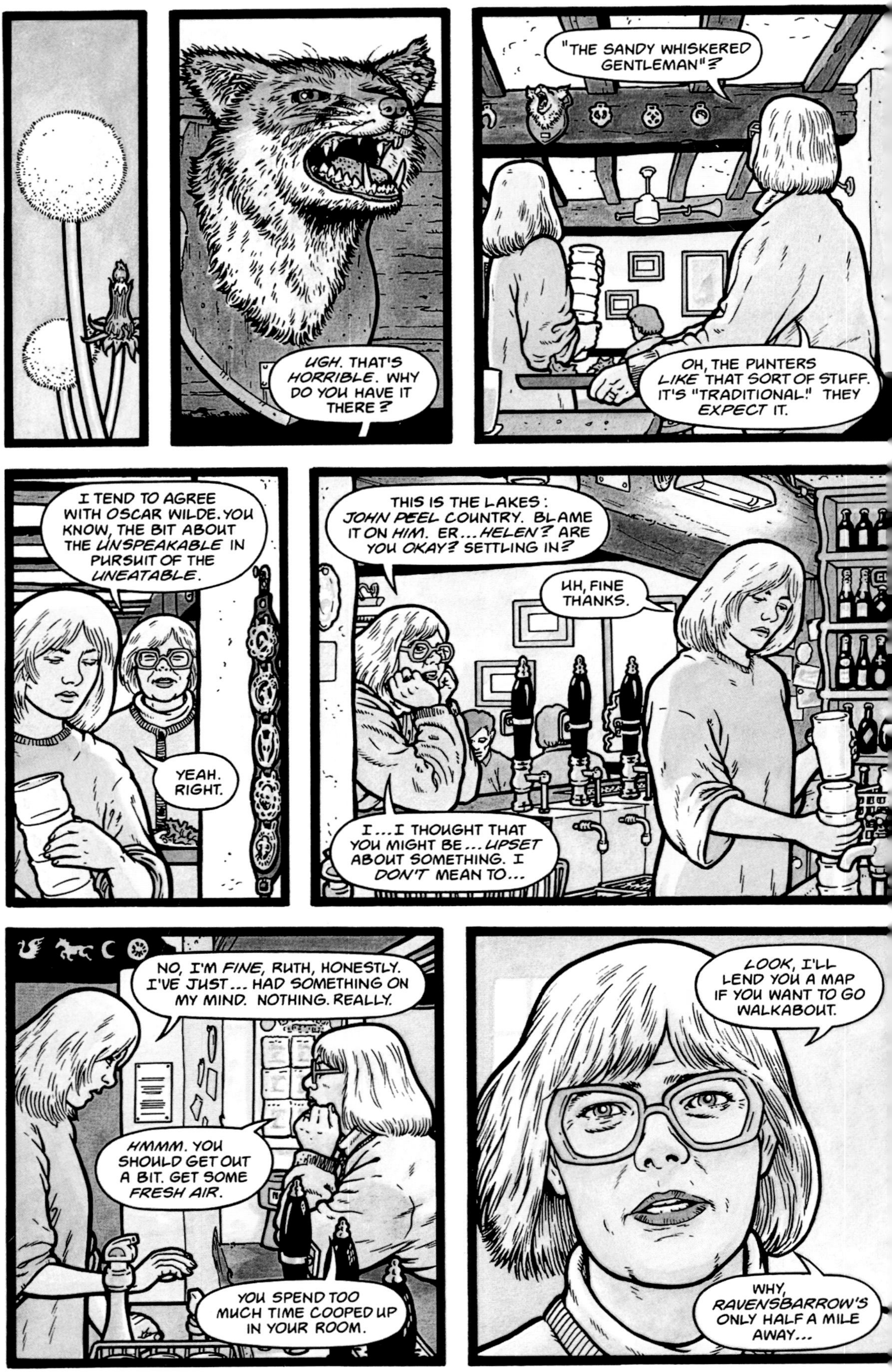
UGH. THAT'S HORRIBLE. WHY DO YOU HAVE IT THERE?
"THE SANDY WHISKERED GENTLEMAN"?
OH, THE PUNTERS LIKE THAT SORT OF STUFF. IT'S "TRADITIONAL." THEY EXPECT IT.
I TEND TO AGREE WITH OSCAR WILDE. YOU KNOW, THE BIT ABOUT THE UNSPEAKABLE IN PURSUIT OF THE UNEATABLE.
YEAH. RIGHT.
THIS IS THE LAKES: JOHN PEEL COUNTRY. BLAME IT ON HIM. ER... HELEN? ARE YOU OKAY? SETTLING IN?
UH, FINE THANKS.
I... I THOUGHT THAT YOU MIGHT BE... UPSET ABOUT SOMETHING. I DON'T MEAN TO...
NO, I'M FINE, RUTH, HONESTLY. I'VE JUST... HAD SOMETHING ON MY MIND. NOTHING. REALLY.
HMMM. YOU SHOULD GET OUT A BIT. GET SOME FRESH AIR.
YOU SPEND TOO MUCH TIME COOPED UP IN YOUR ROOM.
LOOK, I'LL LEND YOU A MAP IF YOU WANT TO GO WALKABOUT.
WHY, RAVENSBARROW'S ONLY HALF A MILE AWAY...

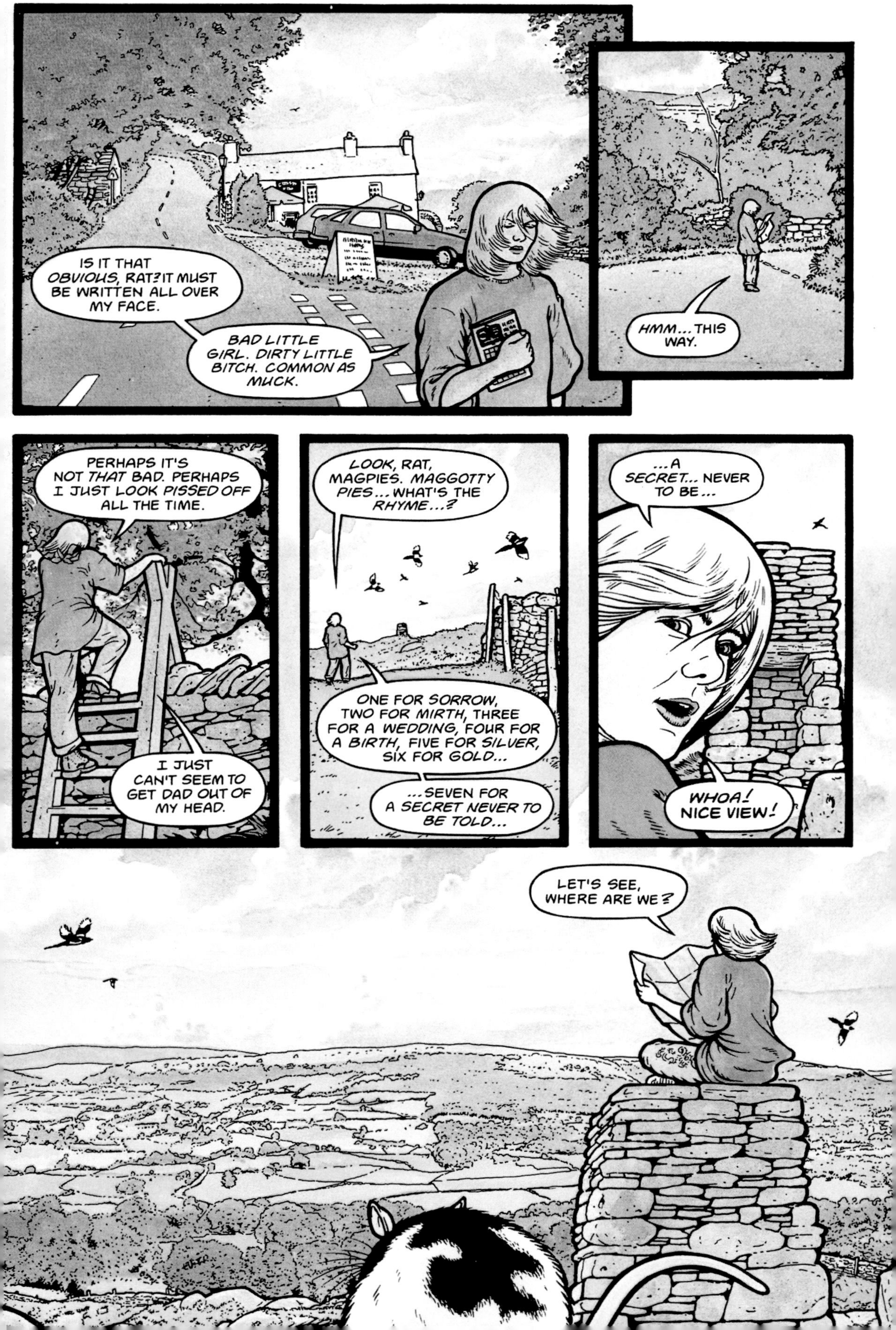
IS IT THAT OBVIOUS, RAT? IT MUST BE WRITTEN ALL OVER MY FACE.
BAD LITTLE GIRL. DIRTY LITTLE BITCH. COMMON AS MUCK.
HMM... THIS WAY.
PERHAPS IT'S NOT THAT BAD. PERHAPS I JUST LOOK PISSED OFF ALL THE TIME.
I JUST CAN'T SEEM TO GET DAD OUT OF MY HEAD.
LOOK, RAT, MAGPIES. MAGGOTTY PIES... WHAT'S THE RHYME...?
ONE FOR SORROW, TWO FOR MIRTH, THREE FOR A WEDDING, FOUR FOR A BIRTH, FIVE FOR SILVER, SIX FOR GOLD...
...SEVEN FOR A SECRET NEVER TO BE TOLD...
...A SECRET... NEVER TO BE...
WHOA! NICE VIEW!
LET'S SEE, WHERE ARE WE?

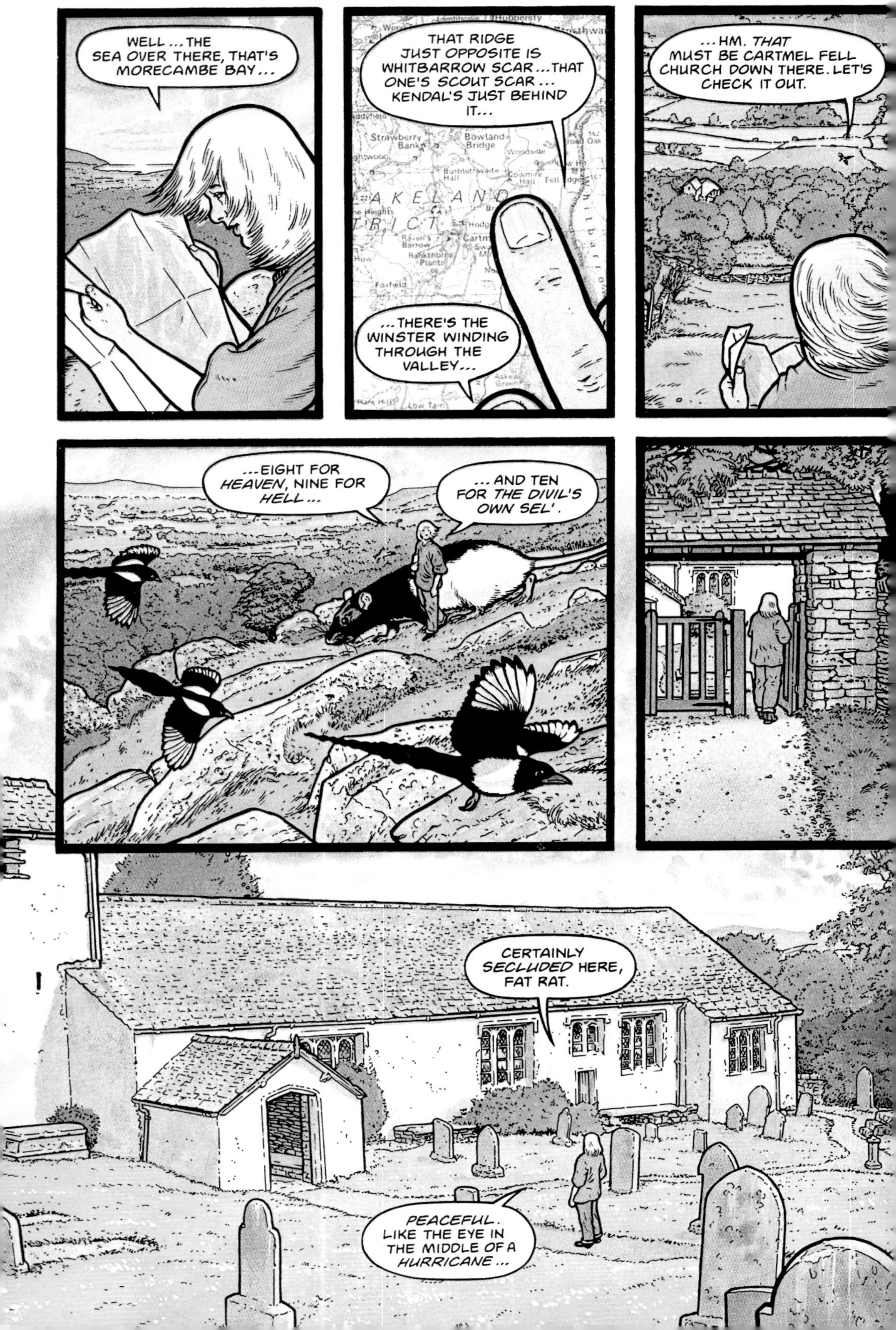
WELL ... THE SEA OVER THERE, THAT'S MORECAMBE BAY ...
THAT RIDGE JUST OPPOSITE IS WHITBARROW SCAR ... THAT ONE'S SCOUT SCAR ... KENDAL'S JUST BEHIND IT ...
Strawberry Bank
Bowland Bridge
Woodside
Burblethwaite Hall
Cowmire Hall
Foxfield
... THERE'S THE WINSTER WINDING THROUGH THE VALLEY ...
... HM. *THAT* MUST BE CARTMEL FELL CHURCH DOWN THERE. LET'S CHECK IT OUT.
... EIGHT FOR *HEAVEN*, NINE FOR *HELL* ...
... AND TEN FOR *THE DIVIL'S OWN SEL'*.
CERTAINLY *SECLUDED* HERE, FAT RAT.
PEACEFUL. LIKE THE EYE IN THE MIDDLE OF A *HURRICANE* ...

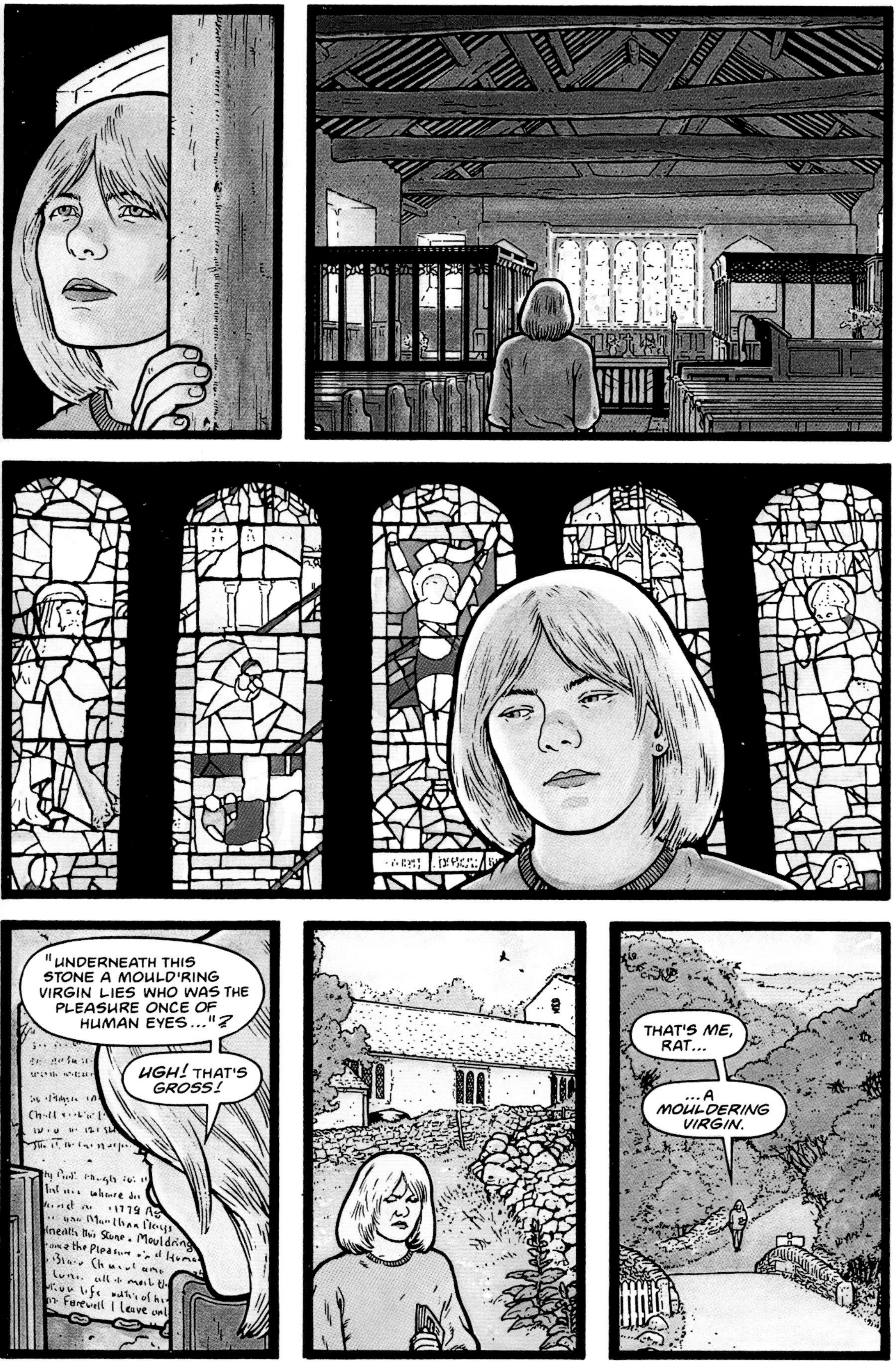
"UNDERNEATH THIS STONE A MOULD'RING VIRGIN LIES WHO WAS THE PLEASURE ONCE OF HUMAN EYES..."?
UGH! THAT'S GROSS!
THAT'S ME, RAT...
...A MOULDERING VIRGIN.

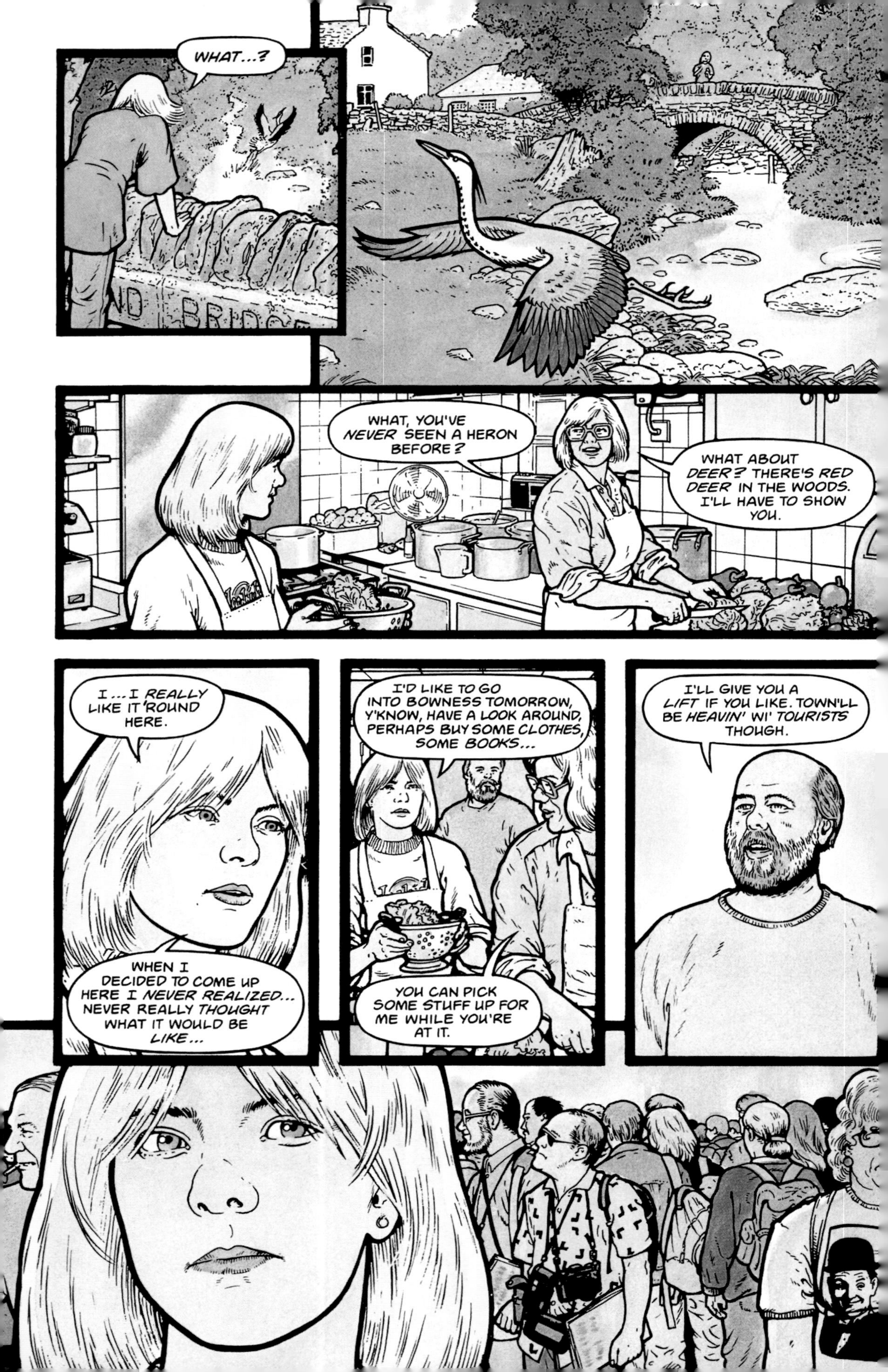
WHAT...?
WHAT, YOU'VE NEVER SEEN A HERON BEFORE?
WHAT ABOUT DEER? THERE'S RED DEER IN THE WOODS. I'LL HAVE TO SHOW YOU.
I... I REALLY LIKE IT 'ROUND HERE.
WHEN I DECIDED TO COME UP HERE I NEVER REALIZED... NEVER REALLY THOUGHT WHAT IT WOULD BE LIKE...
I'D LIKE TO GO INTO BOWNESS TOMORROW, Y'KNOW, HAVE A LOOK AROUND, PERHAPS BUY SOME CLOTHES, SOME BOOKS...
YOU CAN PICK SOME STUFF UP FOR ME WHILE YOU'RE AT IT.
I'LL GIVE YOU A LIFT IF YOU LIKE. TOWN'LL BE HEAVIN' WI' TOURISTS THOUGH.

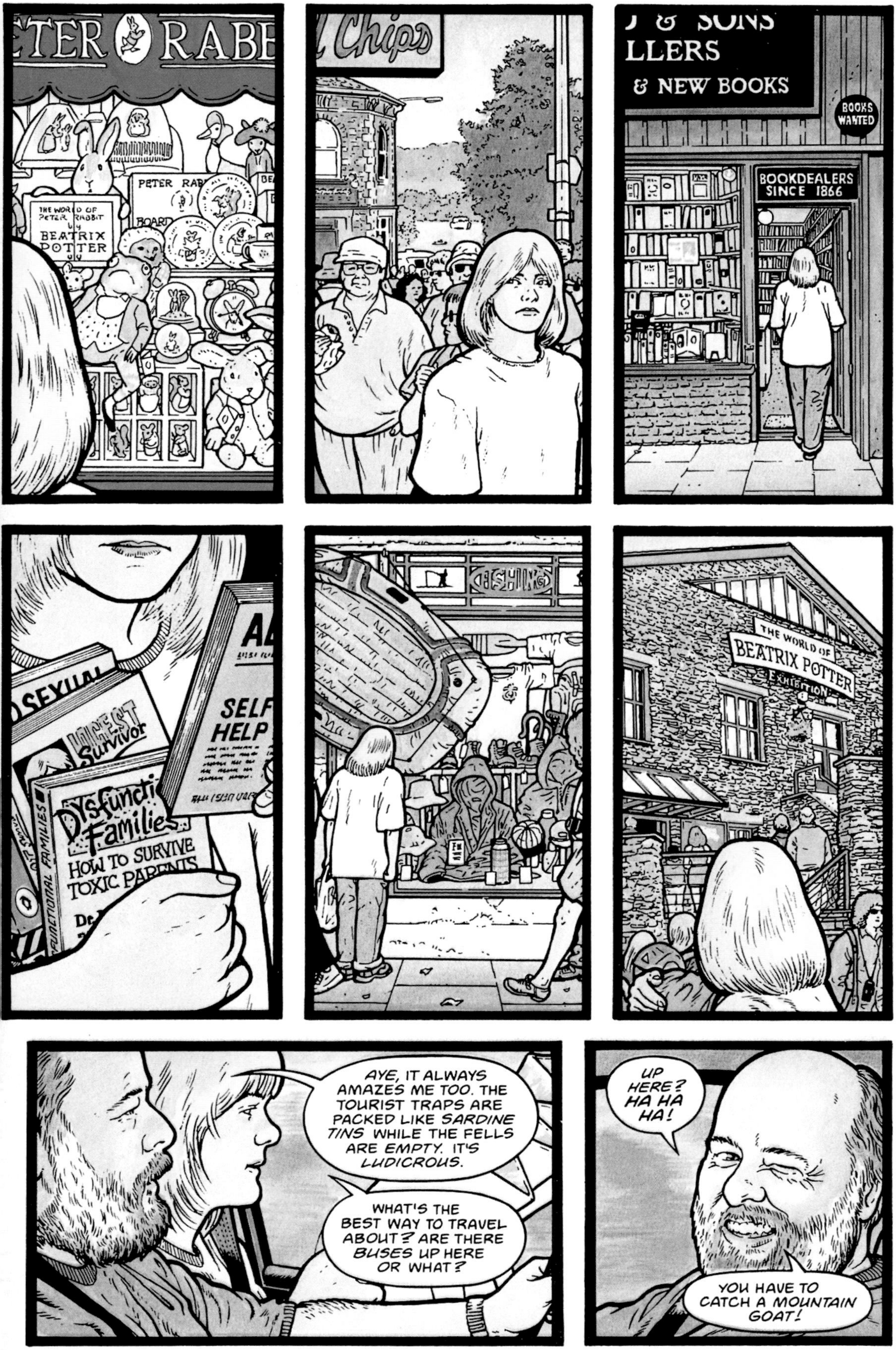
THE WORLD OF PETER RABBIT BY BEATRIX POTTER
PETER RAB
Chips
& SONS
LLERS
& NEW BOOKS
BOOKS WANTED
BOOKDEALERS SINCE 1866
SELF HELP
Survivor
Dysfuncti Families
HOW TO SURVIVE TOXIC PARENTS
THE WORLD OF BEATRIX POTTER EXHIBITION
AYE, IT ALWAYS AMAZES ME TOO. THE TOURIST TRAPS ARE PACKED LIKE SARDINE TINS WHILE THE FELLS ARE EMPTY. IT'S LUDICROUS.
WHAT'S THE BEST WAY TO TRAVEL ABOUT? ARE THERE BUSES UP HERE OR WHAT?
UP HERE? HA HA HA!
YOU HAVE TO CATCH A MOUNTAIN GOAT!

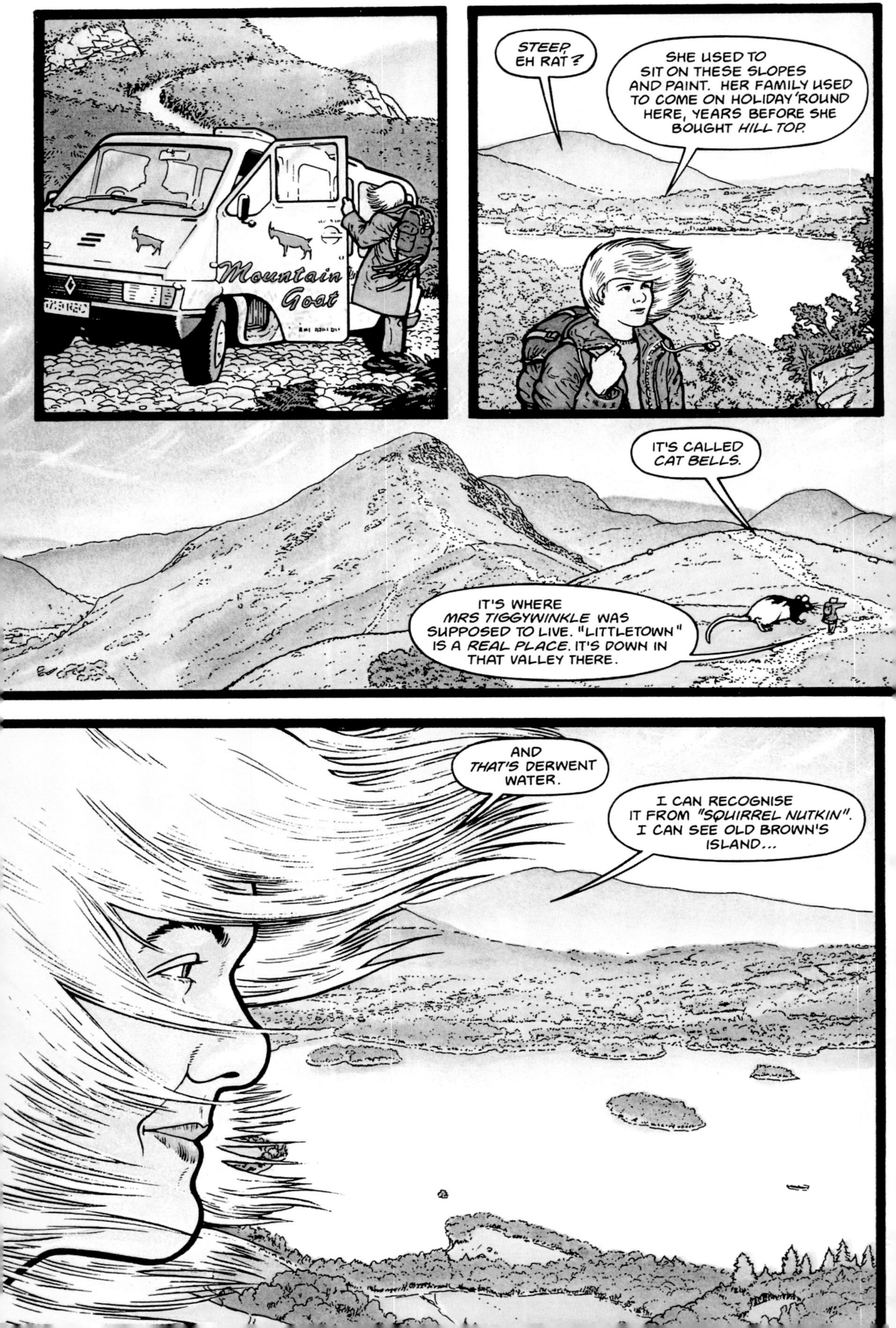
Mountain Goat
STEEP, EH RAT?
SHE USED TO SIT ON THESE SLOPES AND PAINT. HER FAMILY USED TO COME ON HOLIDAY 'ROUND HERE, YEARS BEFORE SHE BOUGHT *HILL TOP*.
IT'S CALLED *CAT BELLS*.
IT'S WHERE *MRS TIGGYWINKLE* WAS SUPPOSED TO LIVE. "LITTLETOWN" IS A *REAL PLACE*. IT'S DOWN IN THAT VALLEY THERE.
AND *THAT'S* DERWENT WATER.
I CAN RECOGNISE IT FROM *"SQUIRREL NUTKIN"*. I CAN SEE OLD BROWN'S ISLAND...

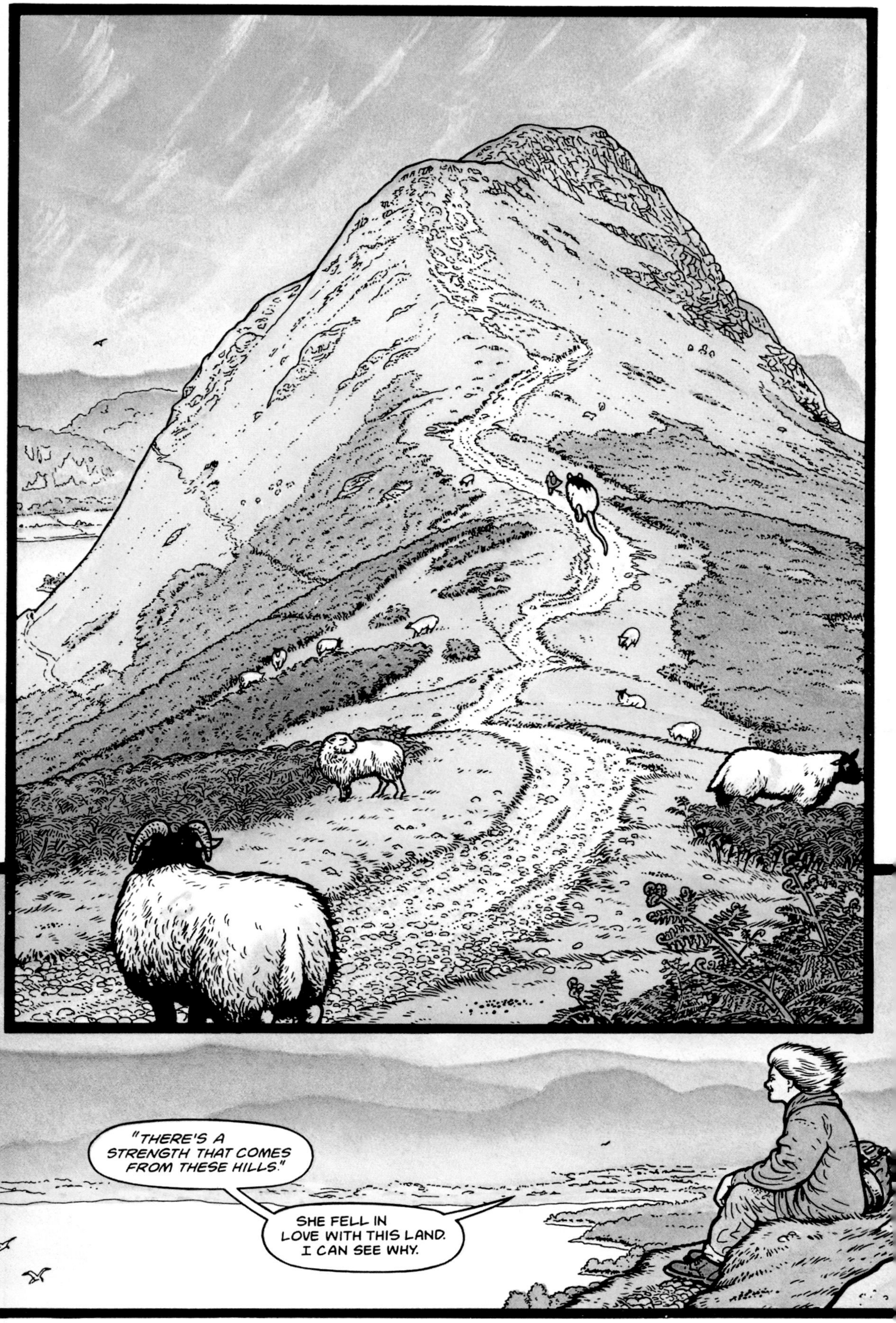
"THERE'S A STRENGTH THAT COMES FROM THESE HILLS."
SHE FELL IN LOVE WITH THIS LAND. I CAN SEE WHY.

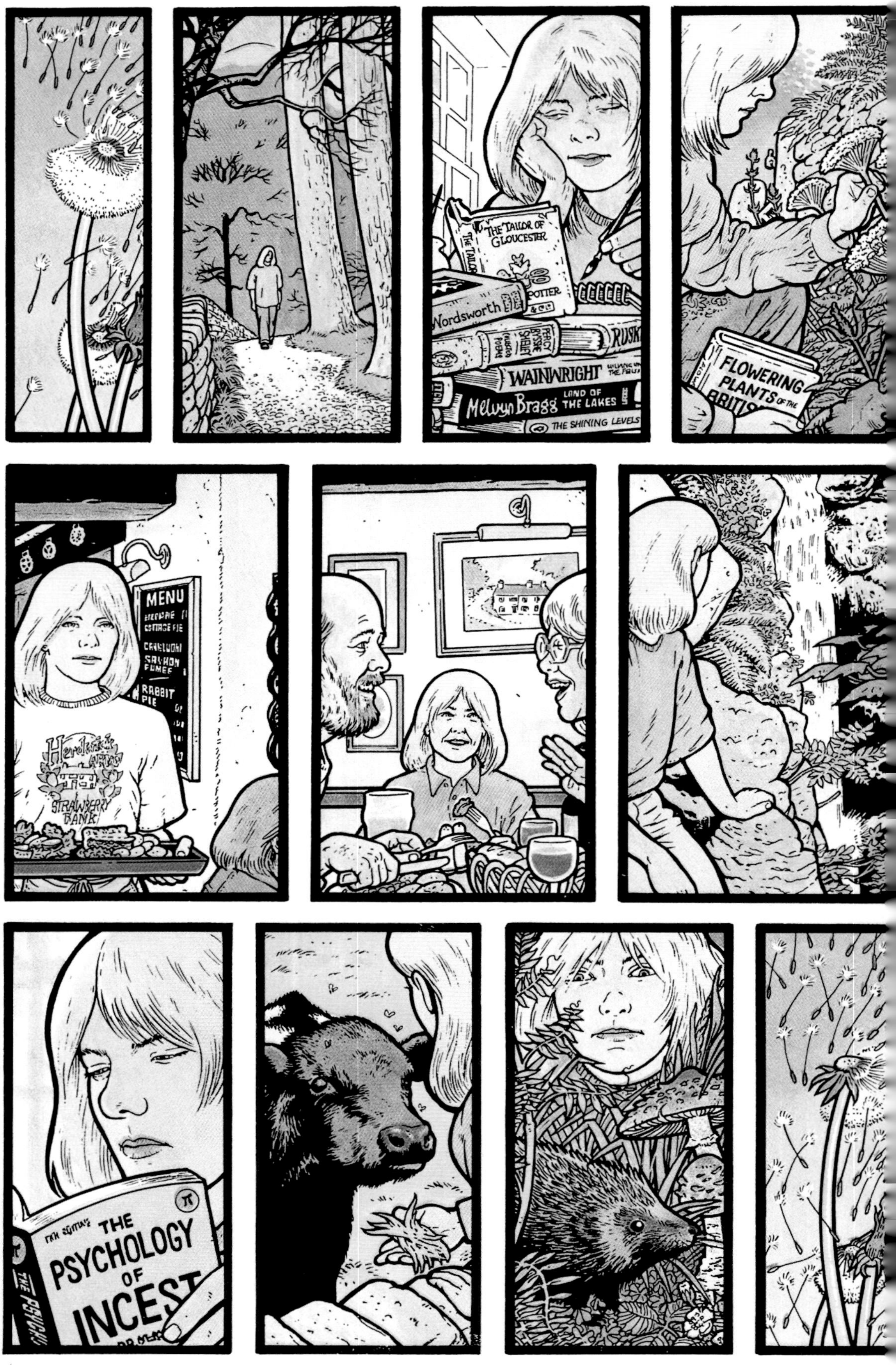
THE TAILOR OF GLOUCESTER
POTTER
Wordsworth
RUSK
WAINWRIGHT
Melvyn Bragg
LAND OF THE LAKES
THE SHINING LEVELS
FLOWERING PLANTS OF THE BRITIS
MENU
RABBIT PIE
STRAWBERRY BANK
THE PSYCHOLOGY OF INCEST

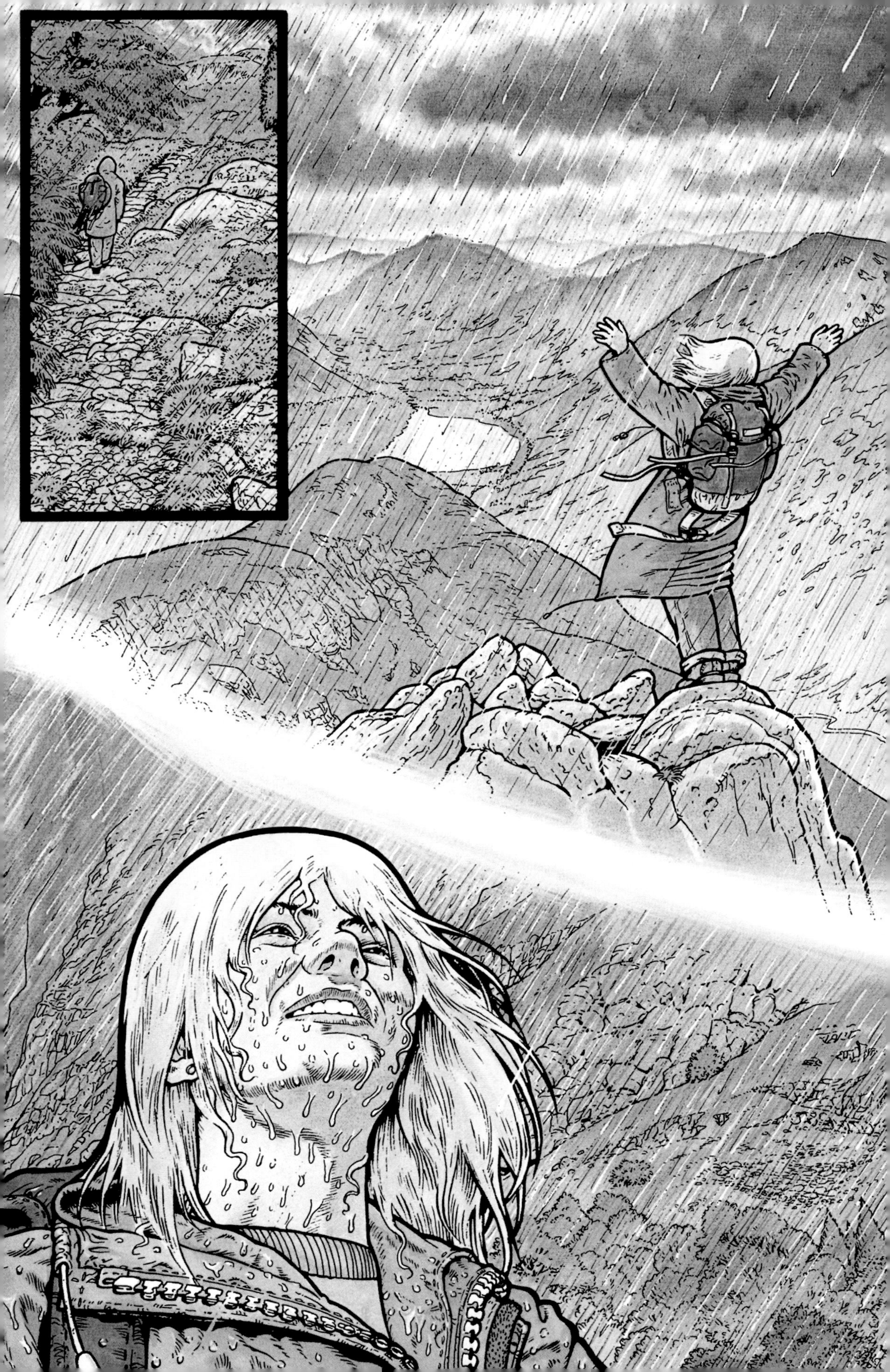

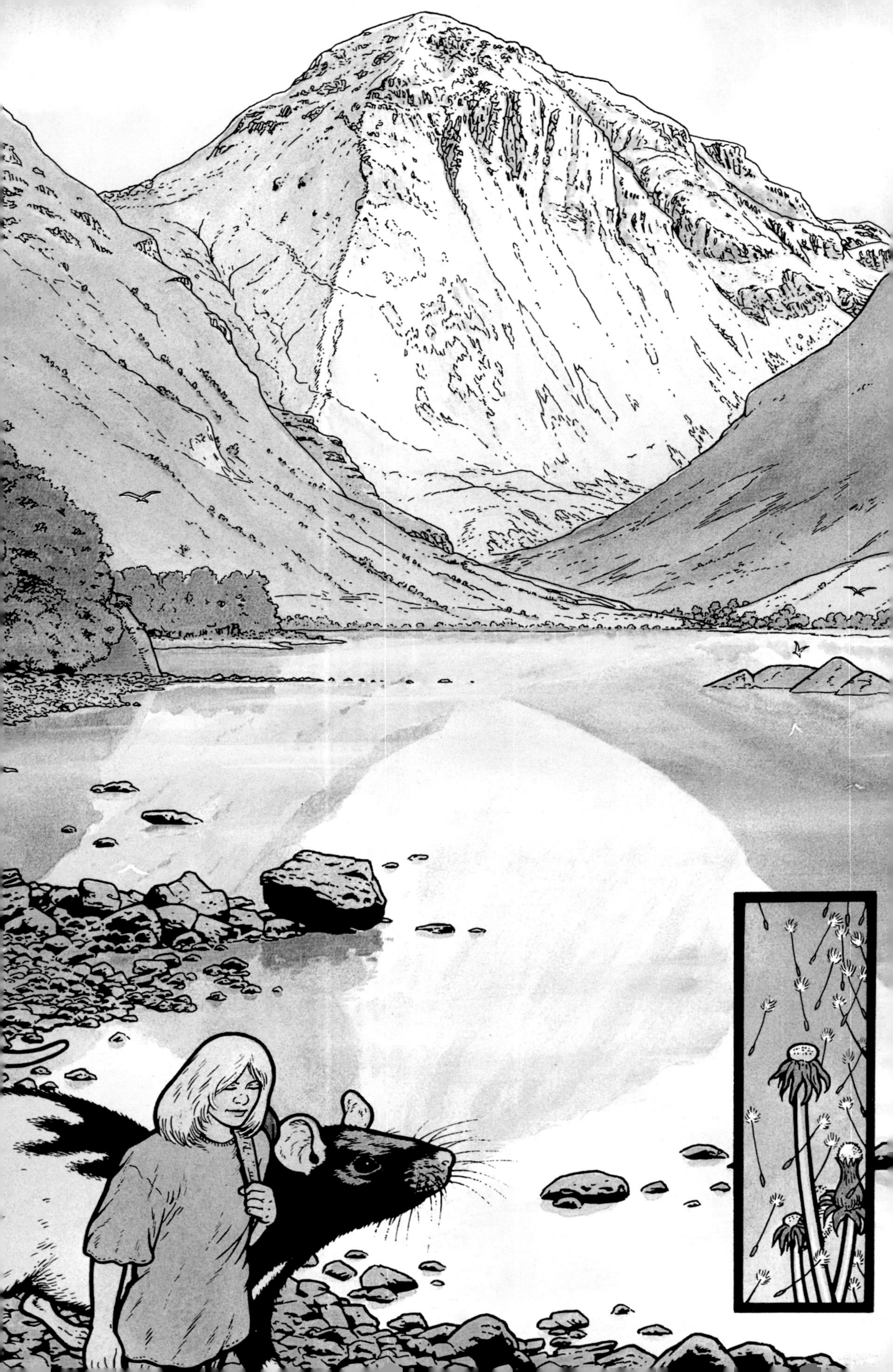

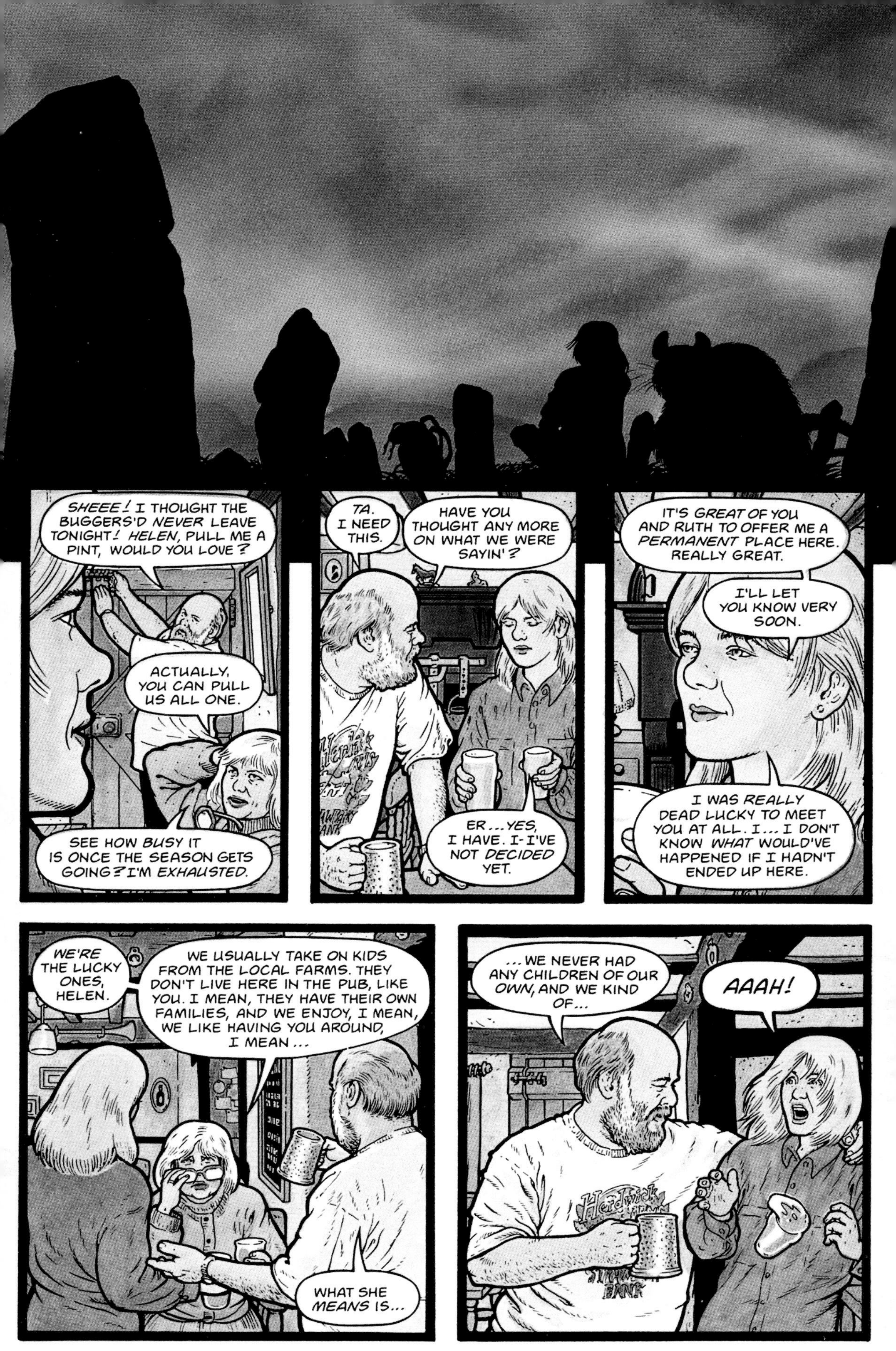
SHEEE! I THOUGHT THE BUGGERS'D NEVER LEAVE TONIGHT! HELEN, PULL ME A PINT, WOULD YOU LOVE?
ACTUALLY, YOU CAN PULL US ALL ONE.
SEE HOW BUSY IT IS ONCE THE SEASON GETS GOING? I'M EXHAUSTED.
TA. I NEED THIS.
HAVE YOU THOUGHT ANY MORE ON WHAT WE WERE SAYIN'?
ER... YES, I HAVE. I-I'VE NOT DECIDED YET.
IT'S GREAT OF YOU AND RUTH TO OFFER ME A PERMANENT PLACE HERE. REALLY GREAT.
I'LL LET YOU KNOW VERY SOON.
I WAS REALLY DEAD LUCKY TO MEET YOU AT ALL. I... I DON'T KNOW WHAT WOULD'VE HAPPENED IF I HADN'T ENDED UP HERE.
WE'RE THE LUCKY ONES, HELEN.
WE USUALLY TAKE ON KIDS FROM THE LOCAL FARMS. THEY DON'T LIVE HERE IN THE PUB, LIKE YOU. I MEAN, THEY HAVE THEIR OWN FAMILIES, AND WE ENJOY, I MEAN, WE LIKE HAVING YOU AROUND, I MEAN...
WHAT SHE MEANS IS...
...WE NEVER HAD ANY CHILDREN OF OUR OWN, AND WE KIND OF...
AAAH!

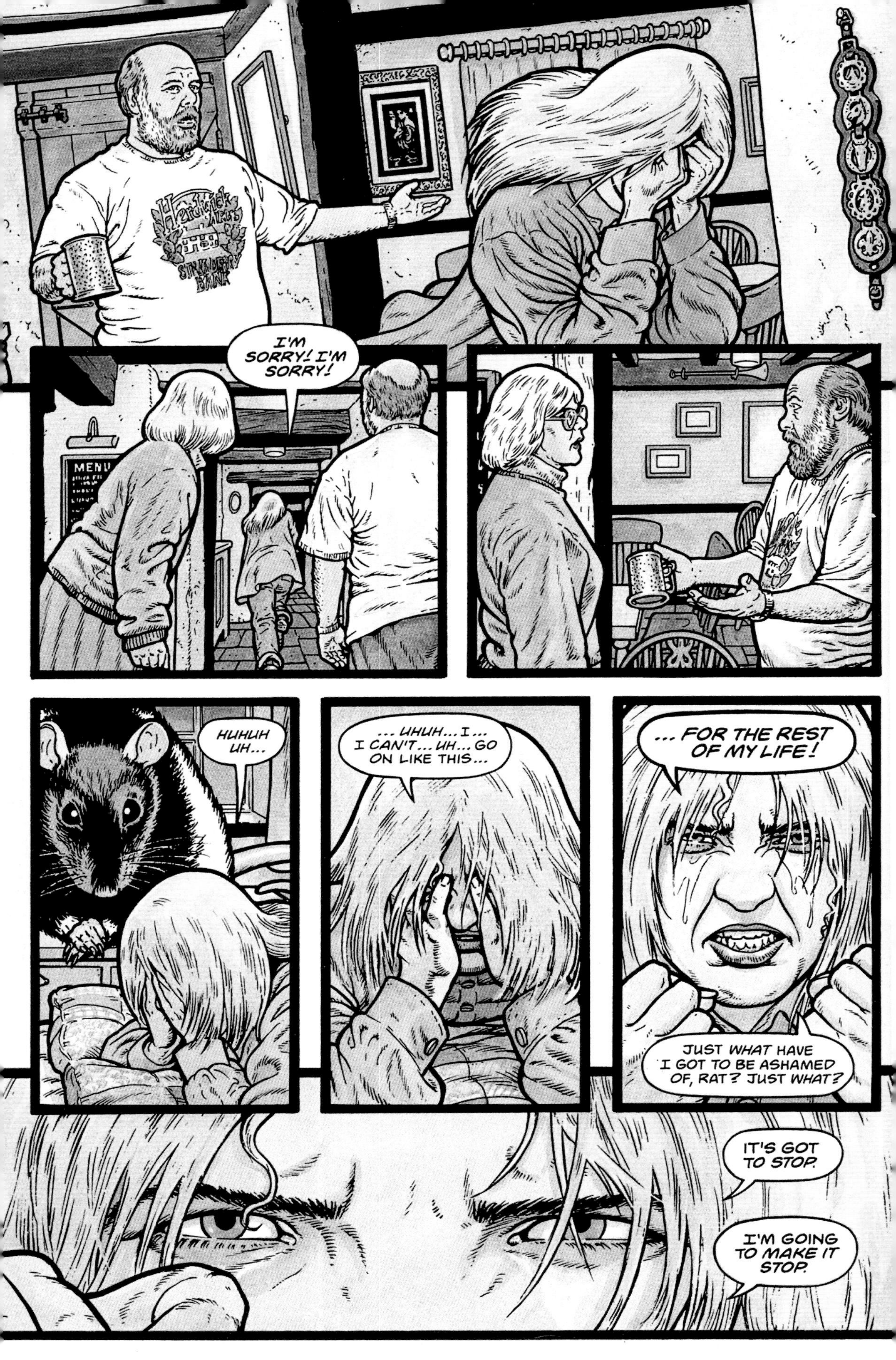
I'M SORRY! I'M SORRY!
HUHUH UH...
... UHUH... I... I CAN'T... UH... GO ON LIKE THIS...
... FOR THE REST OF MY LIFE!
JUST WHAT HAVE I GOT TO BE ASHAMED OF, RAT? JUST WHAT?
IT'S GOT TO STOP.
I'M GOING TO MAKE IT STOP.

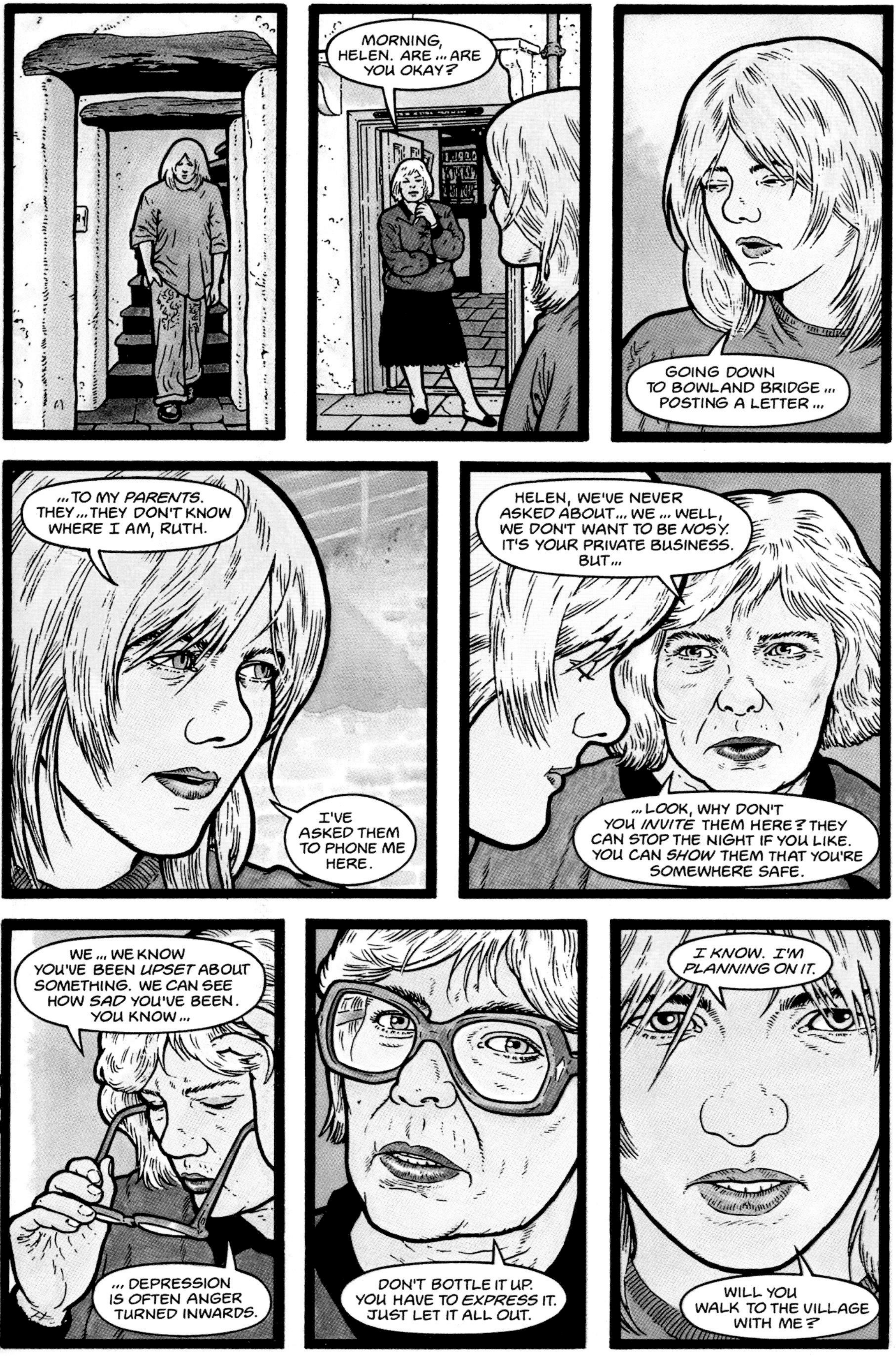
MORNING, HELEN. ARE ... ARE YOU OKAY?
GOING DOWN TO BOWLAND BRIDGE ... POSTING A LETTER ...
... TO MY PARENTS. THEY ... THEY DON'T KNOW WHERE I AM, RUTH.
I'VE ASKED THEM TO PHONE ME HERE.
HELEN, WE'VE NEVER ASKED ABOUT ... WE ... WELL, WE DON'T WANT TO BE NOSY. IT'S YOUR PRIVATE BUSINESS. BUT ...
... LOOK, WHY DON'T YOU INVITE THEM HERE? THEY CAN STOP THE NIGHT IF YOU LIKE. YOU CAN SHOW THEM THAT YOU'RE SOMEWHERE SAFE.
WE ... WE KNOW YOU'VE BEEN UPSET ABOUT SOMETHING. WE CAN SEE HOW SAD YOU'VE BEEN. YOU KNOW ...
... DEPRESSION IS OFTEN ANGER TURNED INWARDS.
DON'T BOTTLE IT UP. YOU HAVE TO EXPRESS IT. JUST LET IT ALL OUT.
I KNOW. I'M PLANNING ON IT.
WILL YOU WALK TO THE VILLAGE WITH ME?

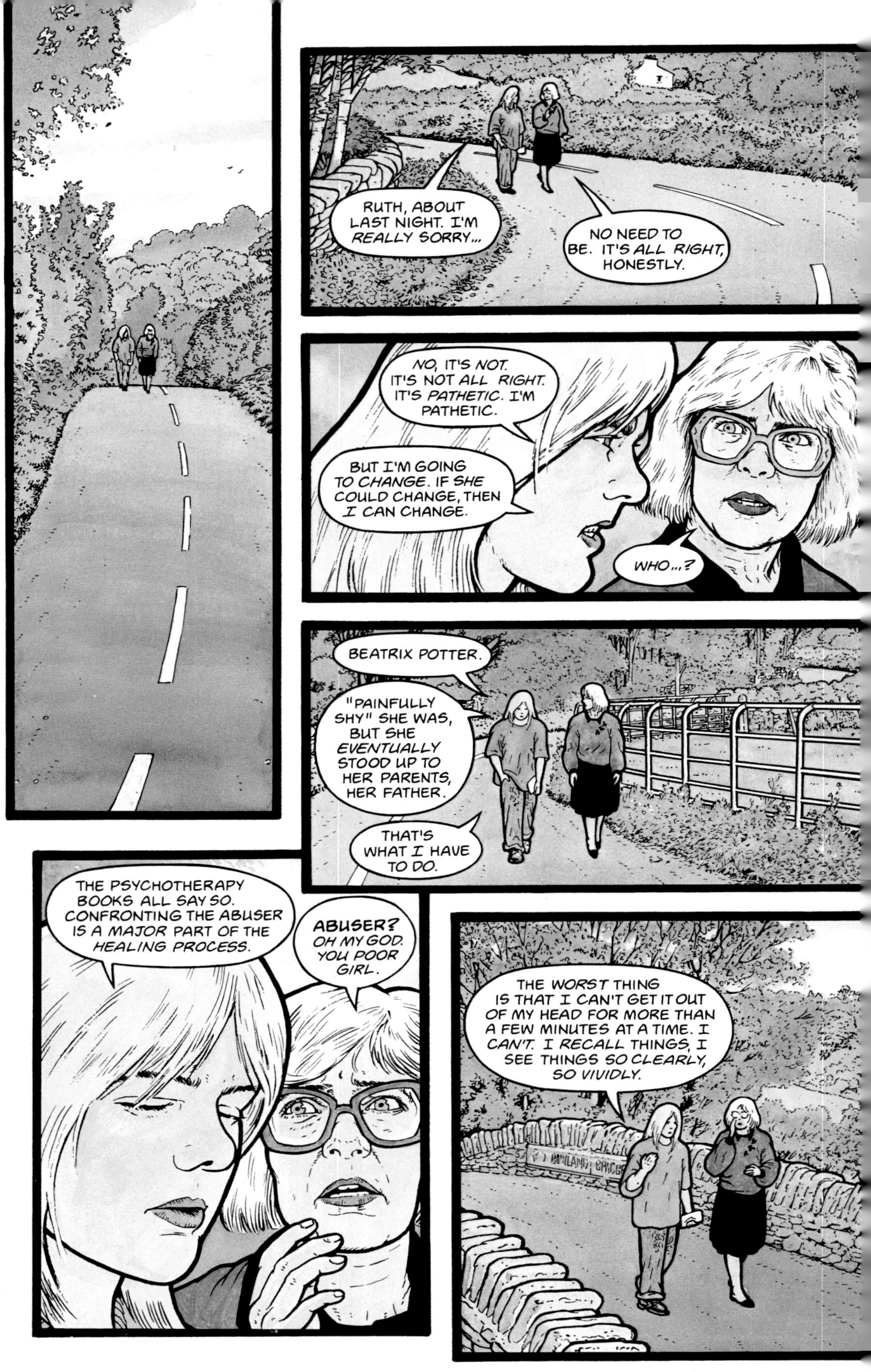
RUTH, ABOUT LAST NIGHT. I'M REALLY SORRY...
NO NEED TO BE. IT'S ALL RIGHT, HONESTLY.
NO, IT'S NOT. IT'S NOT ALL RIGHT. IT'S PATHETIC. I'M PATHETIC.
BUT I'M GOING TO CHANGE. IF SHE COULD CHANGE, THEN I CAN CHANGE.
WHO...?
BEATRIX POTTER.
"PAINFULLY SHY" SHE WAS, BUT SHE EVENTUALLY STOOD UP TO HER PARENTS, HER FATHER.
THAT'S WHAT I HAVE TO DO.
THE PSYCHOTHERAPY BOOKS ALL SAY SO. CONFRONTING THE ABUSER IS A MAJOR PART OF THE HEALING PROCESS.
ABUSER? OH MY GOD. YOU POOR GIRL.
THE WORST THING IS THAT I CAN'T GET IT OUT OF MY HEAD FOR MORE THAN A FEW MINUTES AT A TIME. I CAN'T. I RECALL THINGS, I SEE THINGS SO CLEARLY, SO VIVIDLY.

IT'S A CURSE. RUTH ...

YES?

...I DO NEED SOME HELP WITH THIS.

I NEED TO TALK IT THROUGH. I NEED SOMEONE TO *LISTEN.*

YOU DON'T HAVE TO ASK. I'M HERE, HELEN. WE HAVE A FEW DAYS AT LEAST.

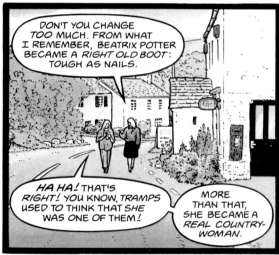

DON'T YOU CHANGE *TOO* MUCH. FROM WHAT I REMEMBER, BEATRIX POTTER BECAME A *RIGHT OLD BOOT:* TOUGH AS NAILS.

HA HA! THAT'S *RIGHT!* YOU KNOW, *TRAMPS* USED TO THINK THAT *SHE* WAS ONE OF THEM!

MORE THAN THAT, SHE BECAME A *REAL COUNTRY-WOMAN.*

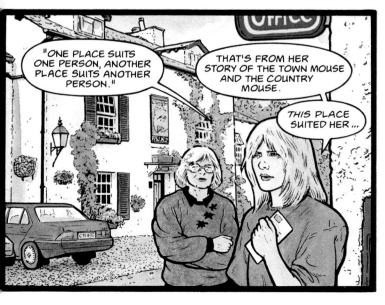

"ONE PLACE SUITS ONE PERSON, ANOTHER PLACE SUITS ANOTHER PERSON."

THAT'S FROM HER STORY OF THE TOWN MOUSE AND THE COUNTRY MOUSE.

THIS PLACE SUITED HER ...

...SUITS ME TOO.

AND *NOBODY'S* GOING TO TAKE IT AWAY FROM ME.

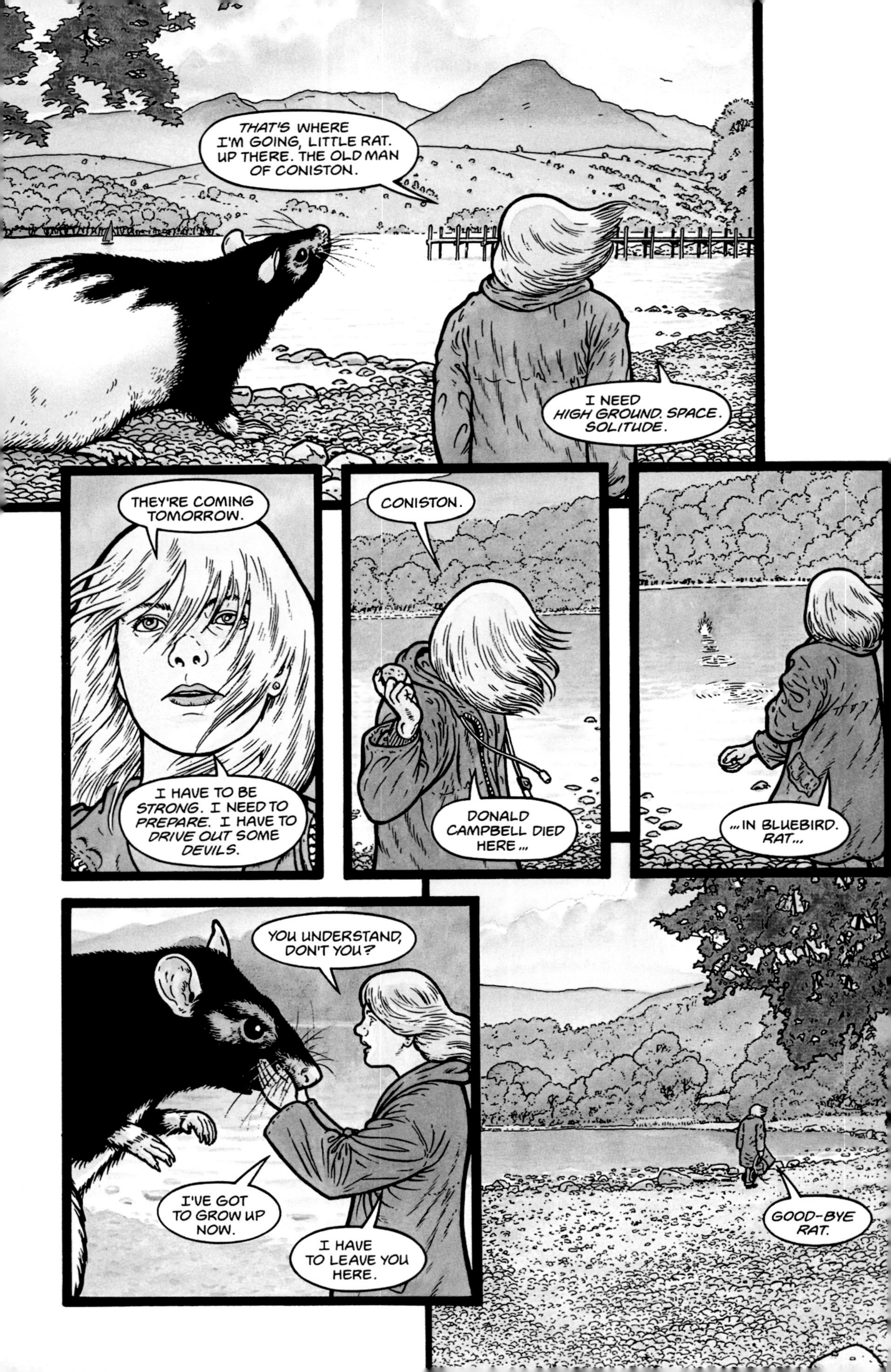
THAT'S WHERE I'M GOING, LITTLE RAT. UP THERE. THE OLD MAN OF CONISTON.
I NEED HIGH GROUND. SPACE. SOLITUDE.
THEY'RE COMING TOMORROW.
I HAVE TO BE STRONG. I NEED TO PREPARE. I HAVE TO DRIVE OUT SOME DEVILS.
CONISTON.
DONALD CAMPBELL DIED HERE...
...IN BLUEBIRD. RAT...
YOU UNDERSTAND, DON'T YOU?
I'VE GOT TO GROW UP NOW.
I HAVE TO LEAVE YOU HERE.
GOOD-BYE RAT.

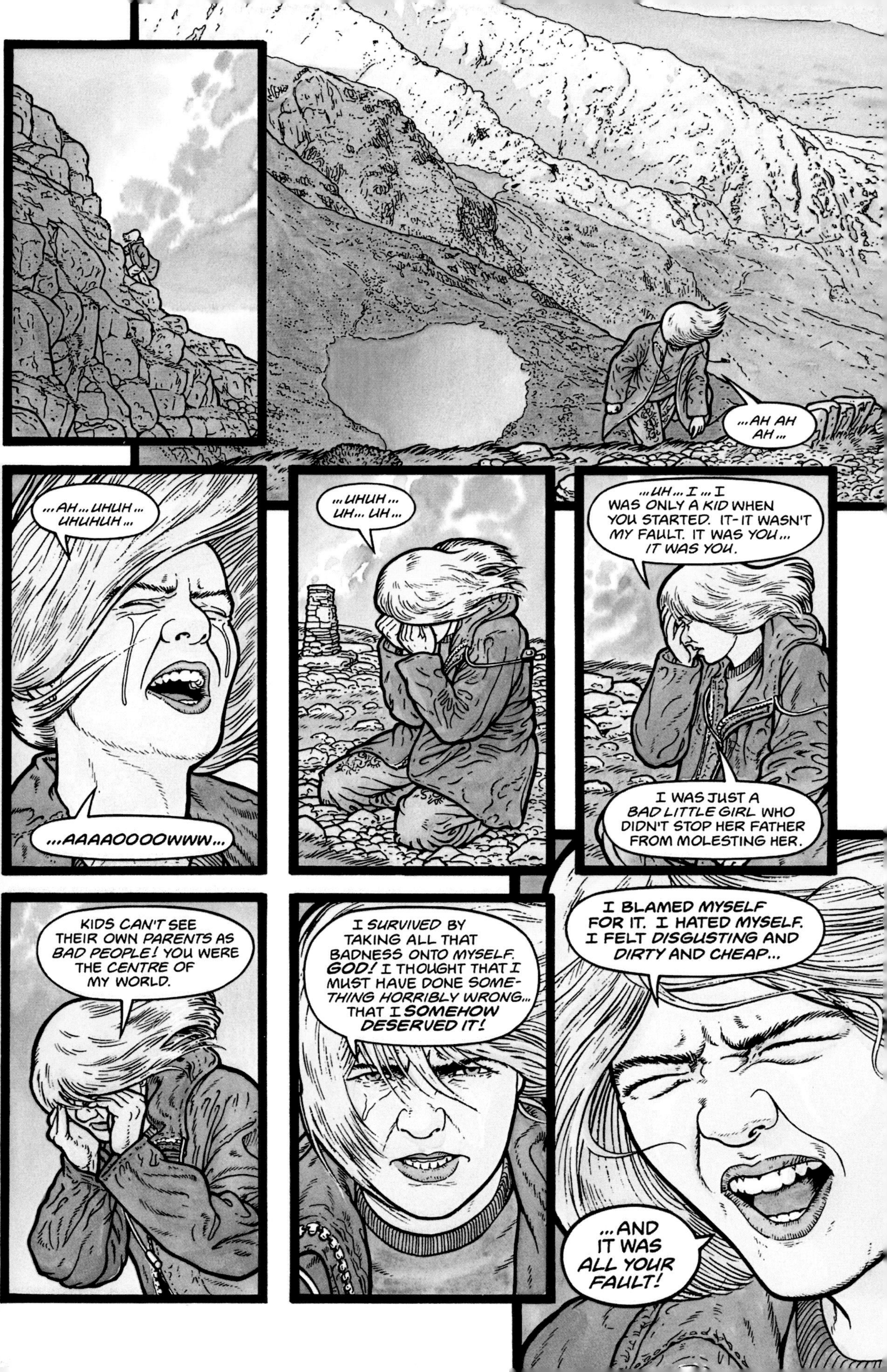
...AH AH AH...
...AH...UHUH... UHUHUH...
...AAAAOOOOWWW...
...UHUH... UH... UH...
...UH... I... I WAS ONLY A KID WHEN YOU STARTED. IT- IT WASN'T MY FAULT. IT WAS YOU... IT WAS YOU.
I WAS JUST A BAD LITTLE GIRL WHO DIDN'T STOP HER FATHER FROM MOLESTING HER.
KIDS CAN'T SEE THEIR OWN PARENTS AS BAD PEOPLE! YOU WERE THE CENTRE OF MY WORLD.
I SURVIVED BY TAKING ALL THAT BADNESS ONTO MYSELF. GOD! I THOUGHT THAT I MUST HAVE DONE SOMETHING HORRIBLY WRONG... THAT I SOMEHOW DESERVED IT!
I BLAMED MYSELF FOR IT. I HATED MYSELF. I FELT DISGUSTING AND DIRTY AND CHEAP...
...AND IT WAS ALL YOUR FAULT!

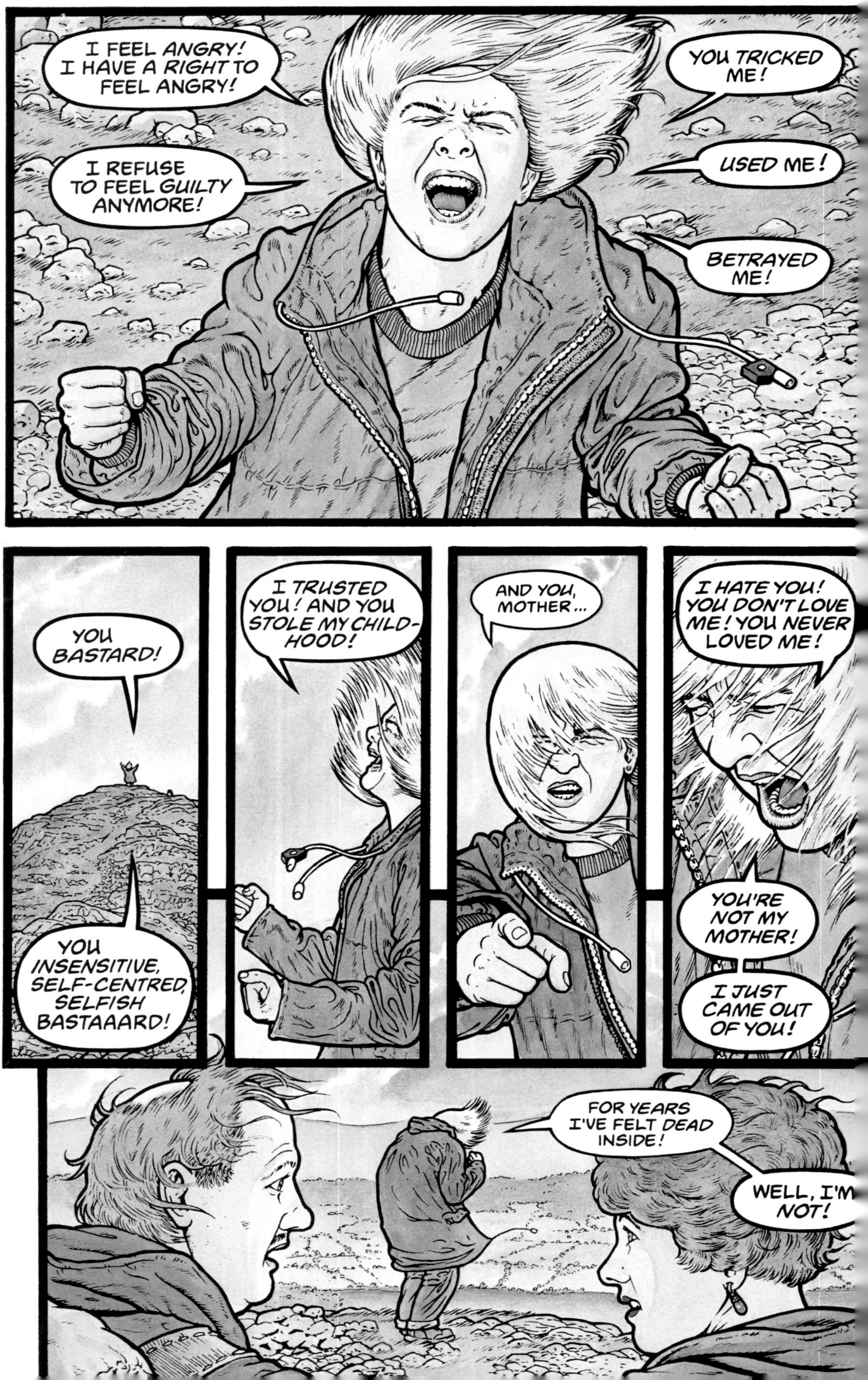
I FEEL ANGRY! I HAVE A RIGHT TO FEEL ANGRY!
YOU TRICKED ME!
I REFUSE TO FEEL GUILTY ANYMORE!
USED ME!
BETRAYED ME!
YOU BASTARD!
YOU INSENSITIVE, SELF-CENTRED, SELFISH BASTAAARD!
I TRUSTED YOU! AND YOU STOLE MY CHILD-HOOD!
AND YOU, MOTHER...
I HATE YOU! YOU DON'T LOVE ME! YOU NEVER LOVED ME!
YOU'RE NOT MY MOTHER!
I JUST CAME OUT OF YOU!
FOR YEARS I'VE FELT DEAD INSIDE!
WELL, I'M NOT!

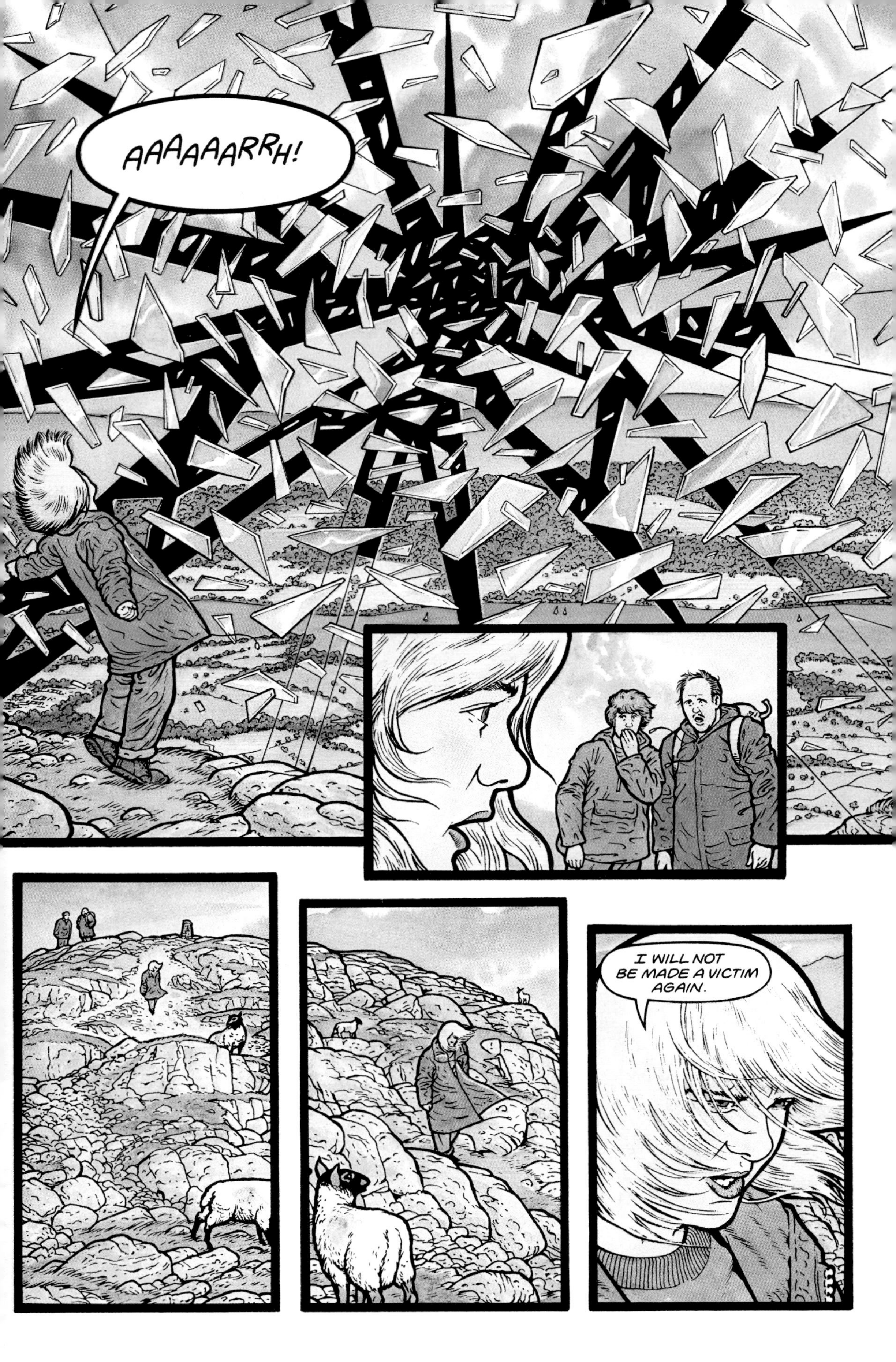
AAAAAARRRH!
I WILL NOT BE MADE A VICTIM AGAIN.

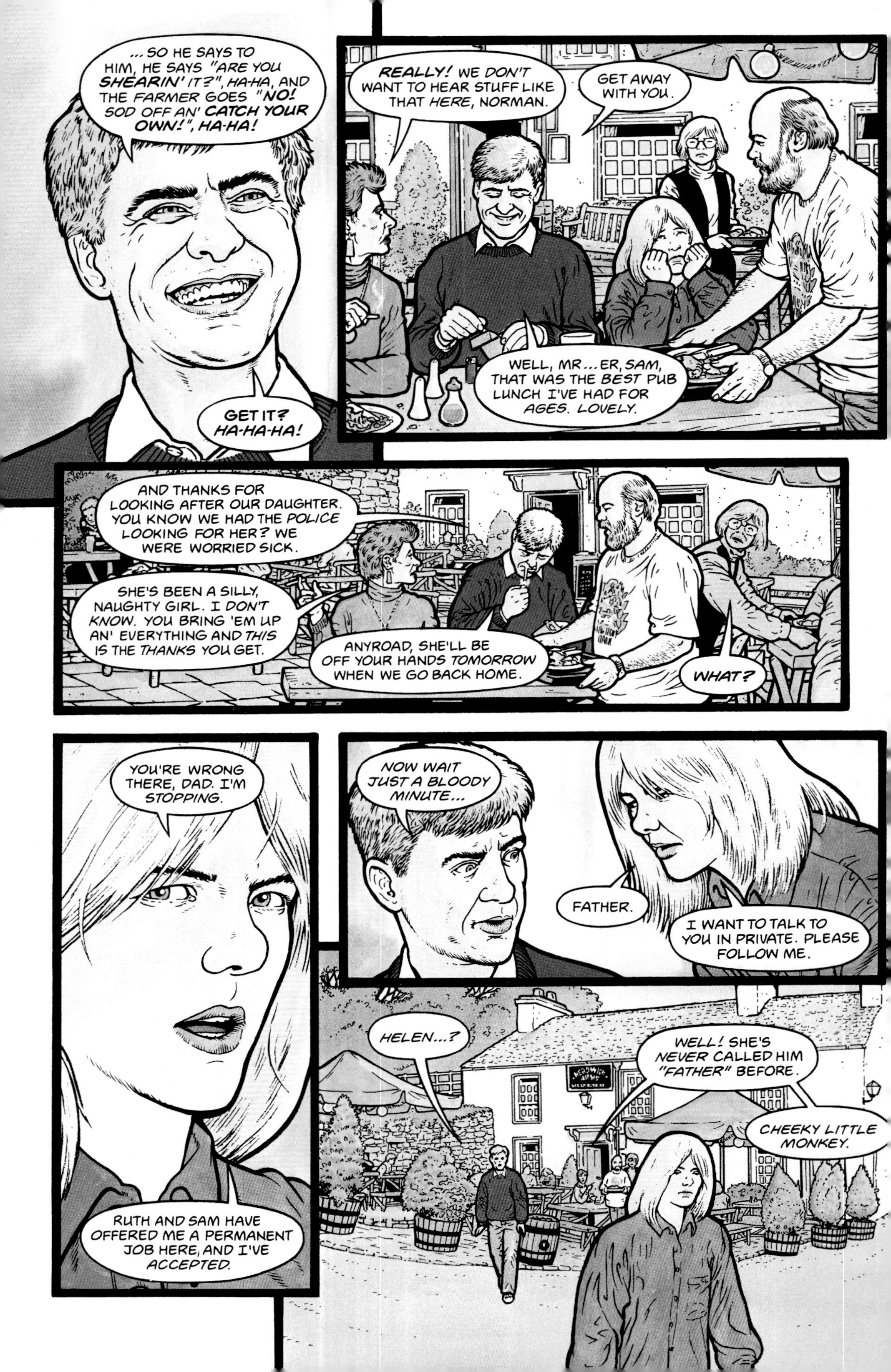
...SO HE SAYS TO HIM, HE SAYS "ARE YOU SHEARIN' IT?", HA-HA, AND THE FARMER GOES "NO! SOD OFF AN' CATCH YOUR OWN!", HA-HA!
GET IT? HA-HA-HA!
REALLY! WE DON'T WANT TO HEAR STUFF LIKE THAT HERE, NORMAN.
GET AWAY WITH YOU.
WELL, MR...ER, SAM, THAT WAS THE BEST PUB LUNCH I'VE HAD FOR AGES. LOVELY.
AND THANKS FOR LOOKING AFTER OUR DAUGHTER. YOU KNOW WE HAD THE POLICE LOOKING FOR HER? WE WERE WORRIED SICK.
SHE'S BEEN A SILLY, NAUGHTY GIRL. I DON'T KNOW. YOU BRING 'EM UP AN' EVERYTHING AND THIS IS THE THANKS YOU GET.
ANYROAD, SHE'LL BE OFF YOUR HANDS TOMORROW WHEN WE GO BACK HOME.
WHAT?
YOU'RE WRONG THERE, DAD. I'M STOPPING.
RUTH AND SAM HAVE OFFERED ME A PERMANENT JOB HERE, AND I'VE ACCEPTED.
NOW WAIT JUST A BLOODY MINUTE...
FATHER.
I WANT TO TALK TO YOU IN PRIVATE. PLEASE FOLLOW ME.
HELEN...?
WELL! SHE'S NEVER CALLED HIM "FATHER" BEFORE.
CHEEKY LITTLE MONKEY.

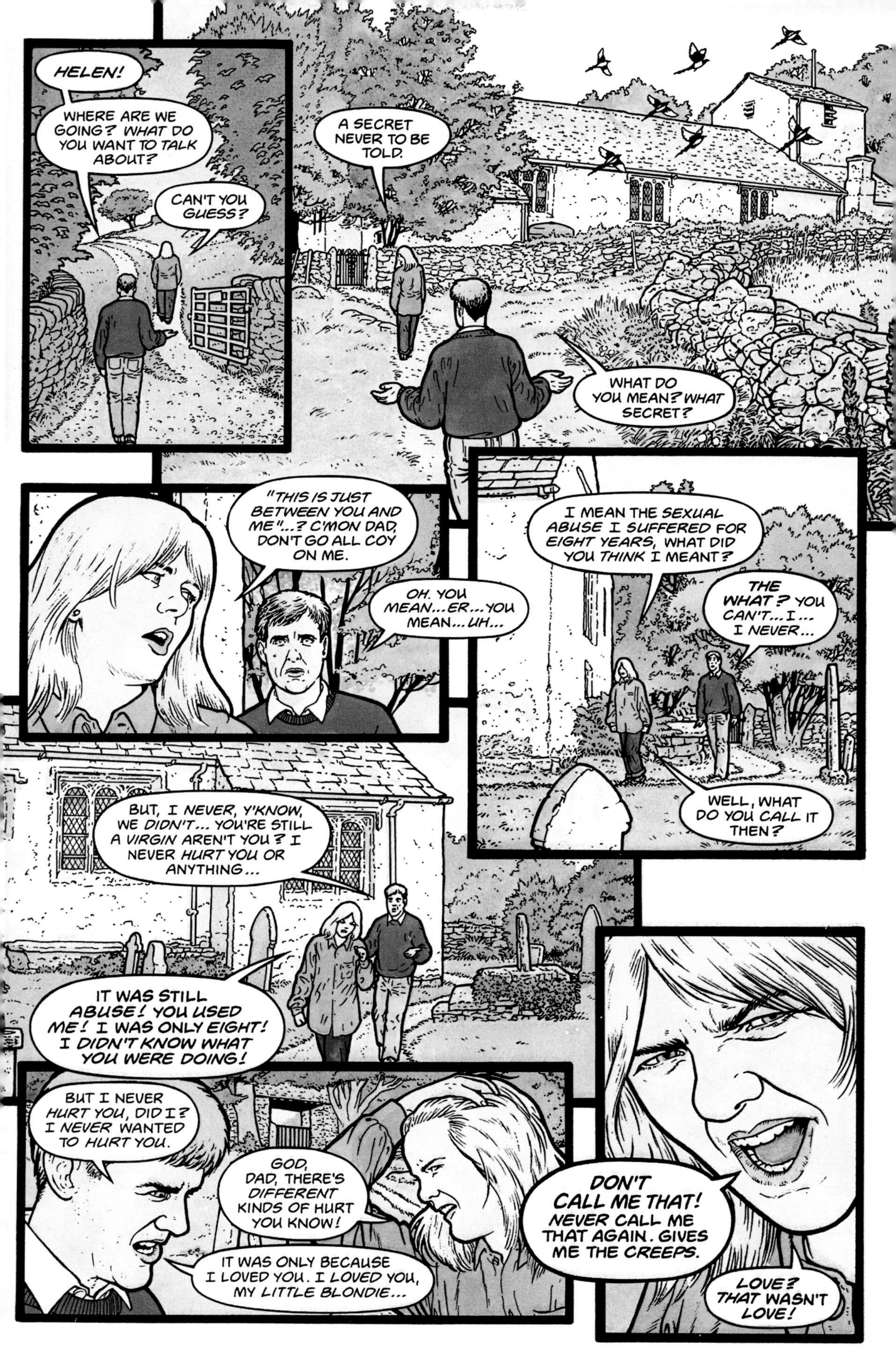
HELEN!
WHERE ARE WE GOING? WHAT DO YOU WANT TO TALK ABOUT?
CAN'T YOU GUESS?
A SECRET NEVER TO BE TOLD.
WHAT DO YOU MEAN? WHAT SECRET?
"THIS IS JUST BETWEEN YOU AND ME"...? C'MON DAD, DON'T GO ALL COY ON ME.
OH. YOU MEAN...ER...YOU MEAN...UH...
I MEAN THE SEXUAL ABUSE I SUFFERED FOR EIGHT YEARS, WHAT DID YOU THINK I MEANT?
THE WHAT? YOU CAN'T...I... I NEVER...
WELL, WHAT DO YOU CALL IT THEN?
BUT, I NEVER, Y'KNOW, WE DIDN'T... YOU'RE STILL A VIRGIN AREN'T YOU? I NEVER HURT YOU OR ANYTHING...
IT WAS STILL ABUSE! YOU USED ME! I WAS ONLY EIGHT! I DIDN'T KNOW WHAT YOU WERE DOING!
BUT I NEVER HURT YOU, DID I? I NEVER WANTED TO HURT YOU.
GOD, DAD, THERE'S DIFFERENT KINDS OF HURT YOU KNOW!
IT WAS ONLY BECAUSE I LOVED YOU. I LOVED YOU, MY LITTLE BLONDIE...
DON'T CALL ME THAT! NEVER CALL ME THAT AGAIN. GIVES ME THE CREEPS.
LOVE? THAT WASN'T LOVE!

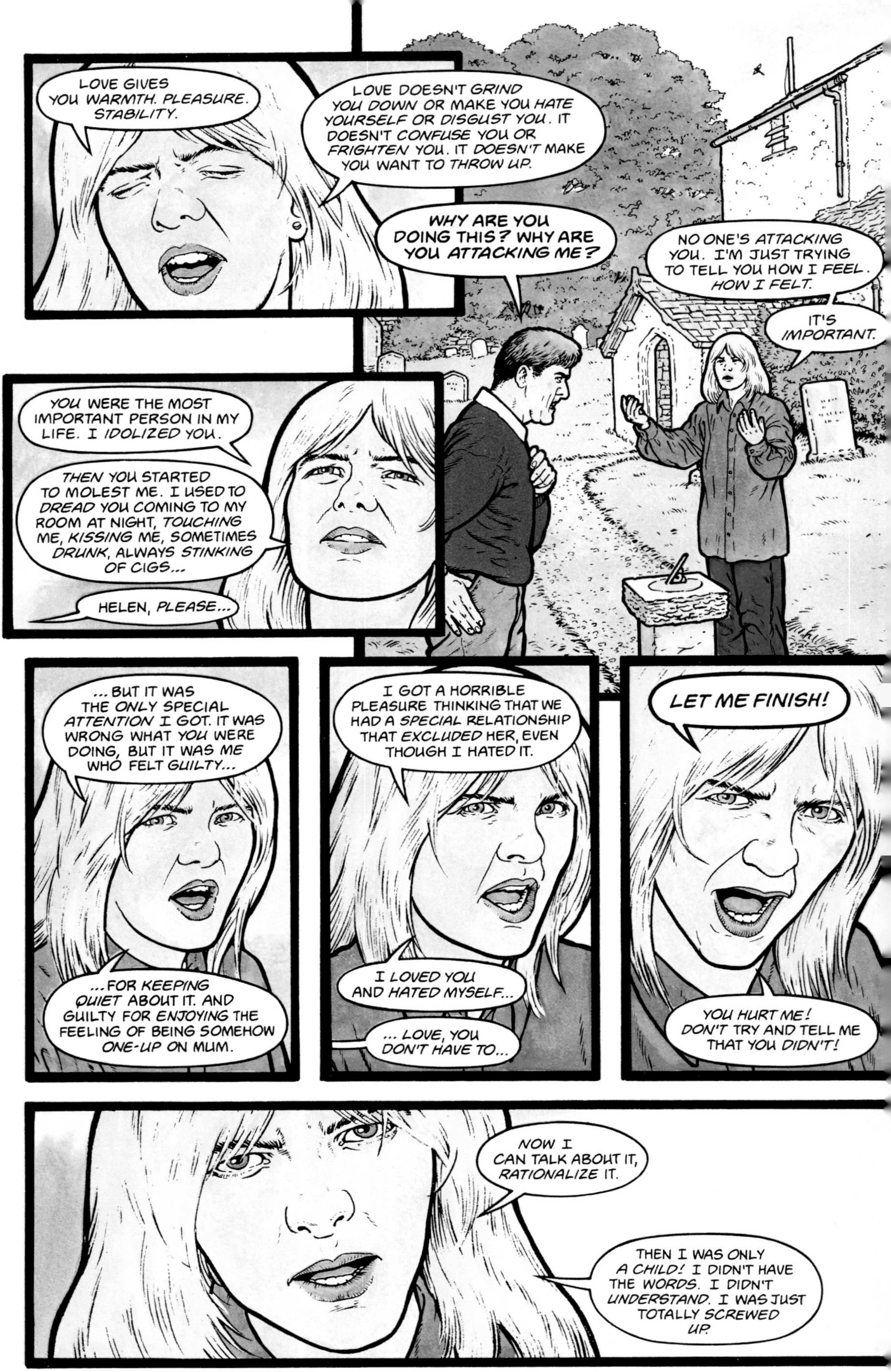
LOVE GIVES YOU WARMTH. PLEASURE. STABILITY.
LOVE DOESN'T GRIND YOU DOWN OR MAKE YOU HATE YOURSELF OR DISGUST YOU. IT DOESN'T CONFUSE YOU OR FRIGHTEN YOU. IT DOESN'T MAKE YOU WANT TO THROW UP.
WHY ARE YOU DOING THIS? WHY ARE YOU ATTACKING ME?
NO ONE'S ATTACKING YOU. I'M JUST TRYING TO TELL YOU HOW I FEEL. HOW I FELT.
IT'S IMPORTANT.
YOU WERE THE MOST IMPORTANT PERSON IN MY LIFE. I IDOLIZED YOU.
THEN YOU STARTED TO MOLEST ME. I USED TO DREAD YOU COMING TO MY ROOM AT NIGHT, TOUCHING ME, KISSING ME, SOMETIMES DRUNK, ALWAYS STINKING OF CIGS...
HELEN, PLEASE...
... BUT IT WAS THE ONLY SPECIAL ATTENTION I GOT. IT WAS WRONG WHAT YOU WERE DOING, BUT IT WAS ME WHO FELT GUILTY...
...FOR KEEPING QUIET ABOUT IT. AND GUILTY FOR ENJOYING THE FEELING OF BEING SOMEHOW ONE-UP ON MUM.
I GOT A HORRIBLE PLEASURE THINKING THAT WE HAD A SPECIAL RELATIONSHIP THAT EXCLUDED HER, EVEN THOUGH I HATED IT.
I LOVED YOU AND HATED MYSELF...
... LOVE, YOU DON'T HAVE TO...
LET ME FINISH!
YOU HURT ME! DON'T TRY AND TELL ME THAT YOU DIDN'T!
NOW I CAN TALK ABOUT IT, RATIONALIZE IT.
THEN I WAS ONLY A CHILD! I DIDN'T HAVE THE WORDS. I DIDN'T UNDERSTAND. I WAS JUST TOTALLY SCREWED UP.

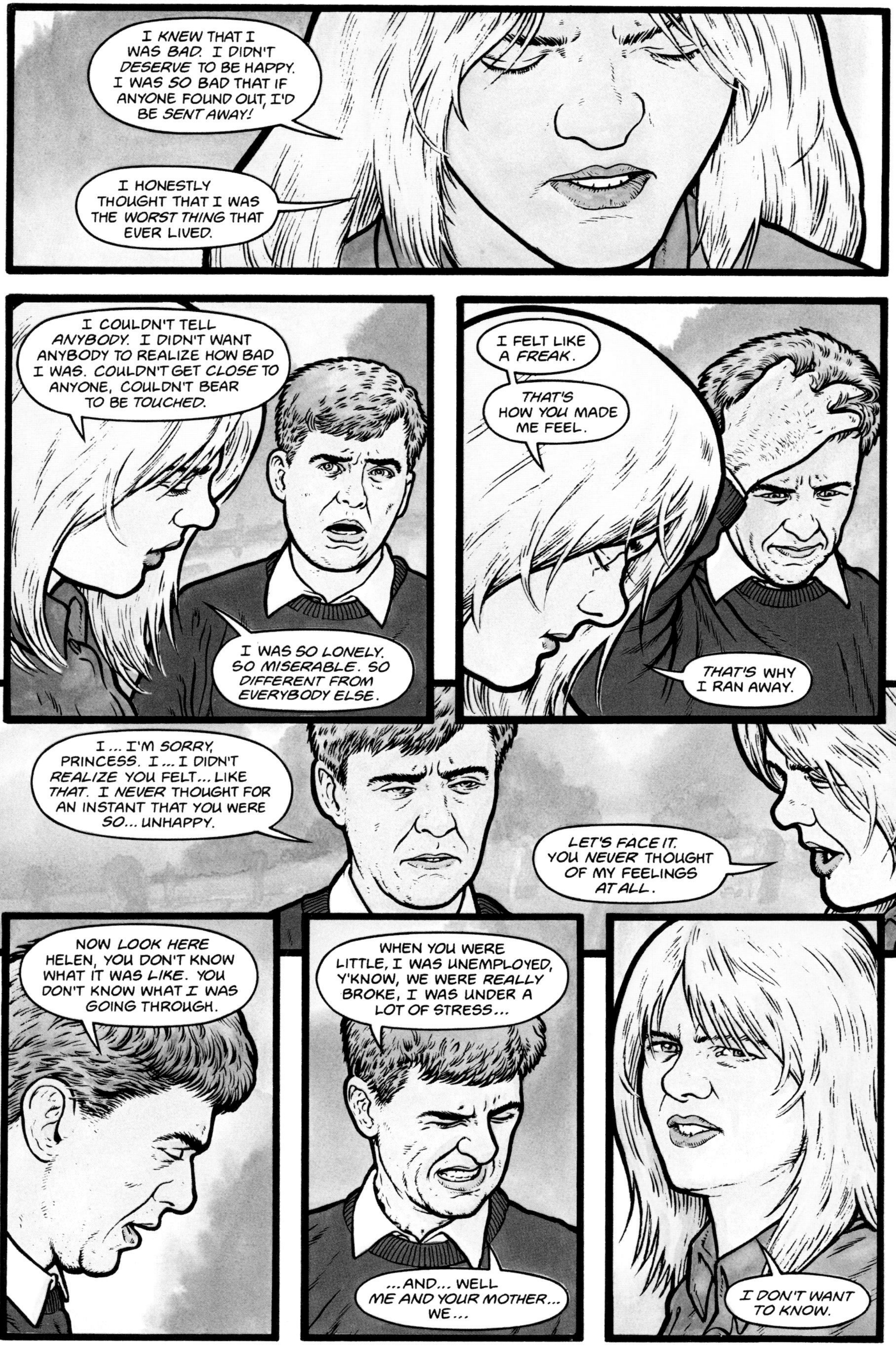
I KNEW THAT I WAS BAD. I DIDN'T DESERVE TO BE HAPPY. I WAS SO BAD THAT IF ANYONE FOUND OUT, I'D BE SENT AWAY!
I HONESTLY THOUGHT THAT I WAS THE WORST THING THAT EVER LIVED.
I COULDN'T TELL ANYBODY. I DIDN'T WANT ANYBODY TO REALIZE HOW BAD I WAS. COULDN'T GET CLOSE TO ANYONE, COULDN'T BEAR TO BE TOUCHED.
I WAS SO LONELY. SO MISERABLE. SO DIFFERENT FROM EVERYBODY ELSE.
I FELT LIKE A FREAK.
THAT'S HOW YOU MADE ME FEEL.
THAT'S WHY I RAN AWAY.
I... I'M SORRY, PRINCESS. I... I DIDN'T REALIZE YOU FELT... LIKE THAT. I NEVER THOUGHT FOR AN INSTANT THAT YOU WERE SO... UNHAPPY.
LET'S FACE IT. YOU NEVER THOUGHT OF MY FEELINGS AT ALL.
NOW LOOK HERE HELEN, YOU DON'T KNOW WHAT IT WAS LIKE. YOU DON'T KNOW WHAT I WAS GOING THROUGH.
WHEN YOU WERE LITTLE, I WAS UNEMPLOYED, Y'KNOW, WE WERE REALLY BROKE, I WAS UNDER A LOT OF STRESS...
...AND... WELL ME AND YOUR MOTHER... WE...
I DON'T WANT TO KNOW.

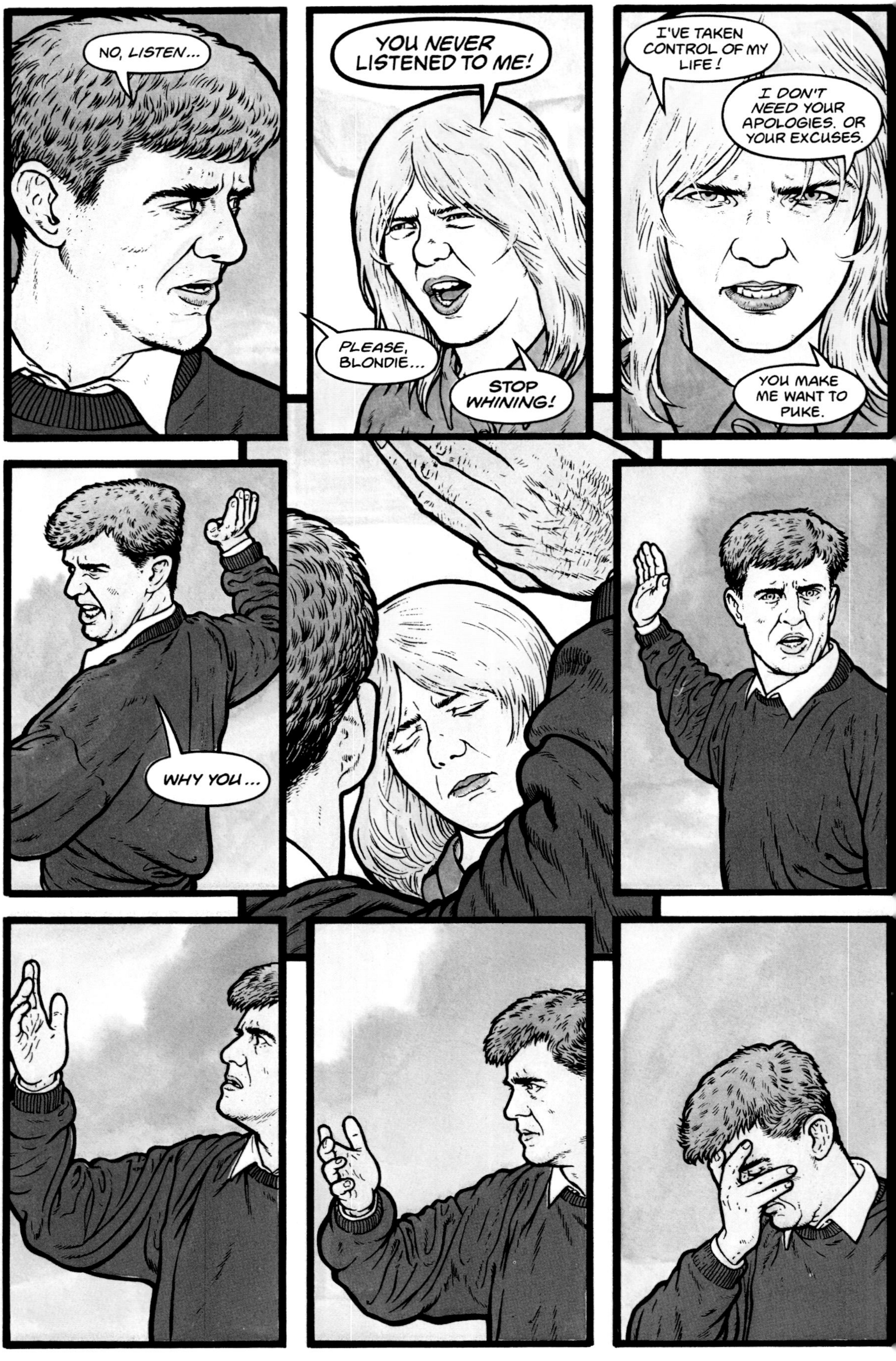
NO, LISTEN...
YOU NEVER LISTENED TO ME!
PLEASE, BLONDIE...
STOP WHINING!
I'VE TAKEN CONTROL OF MY LIFE!
I DON'T NEED YOUR APOLOGIES. OR YOUR EXCUSES.
YOU MAKE ME WANT TO PUKE.
WHY YOU...

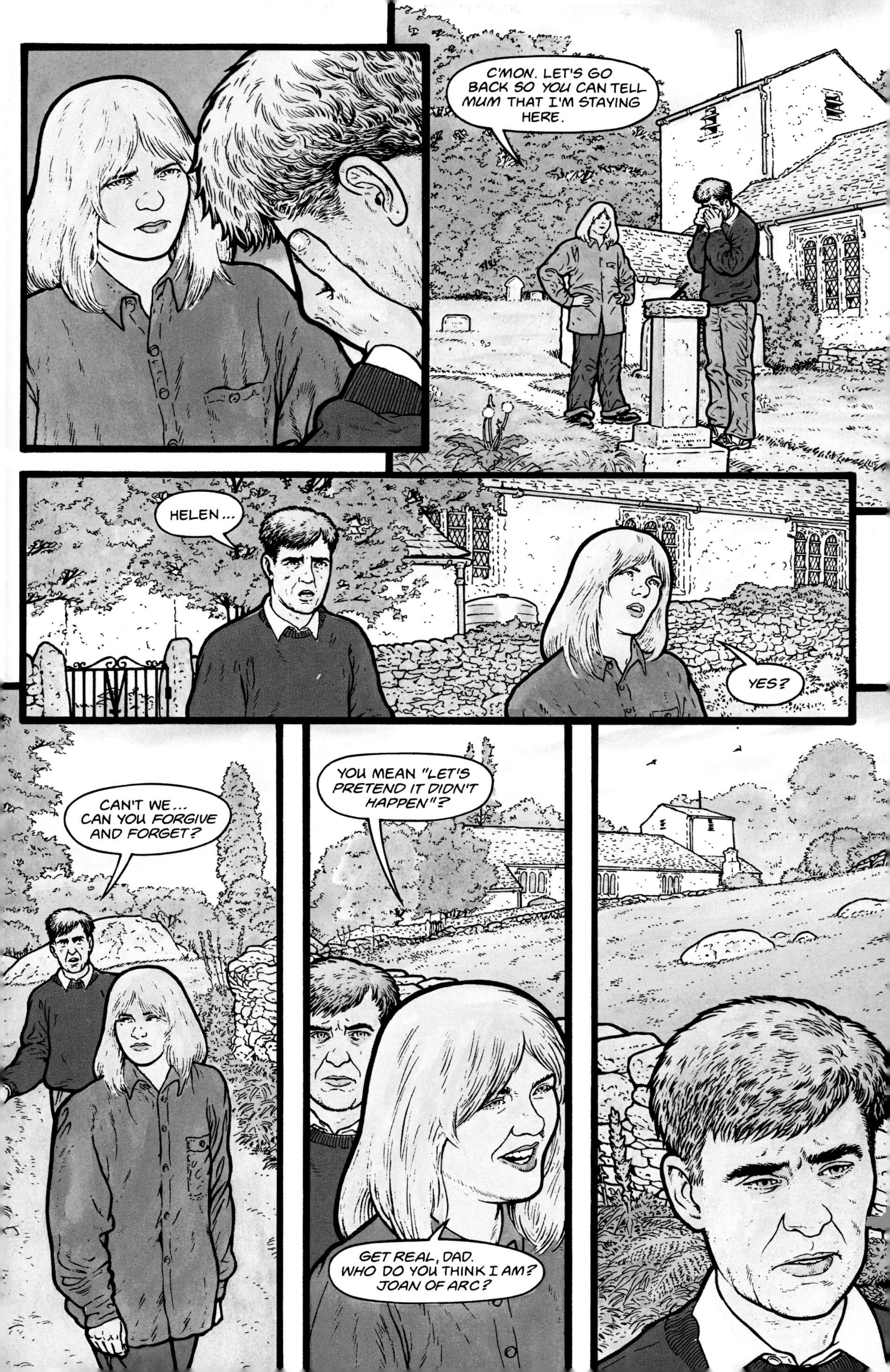
C'MON. LET'S GO BACK SO YOU CAN TELL MUM THAT I'M STAYING HERE.
HELEN...
YES?
CAN'T WE... CAN YOU FORGIVE AND FORGET?
YOU MEAN "LET'S PRETEND IT DIDN'T HAPPEN"?
GET REAL, DAD. WHO DO YOU THINK I AM? JOAN OF ARC?

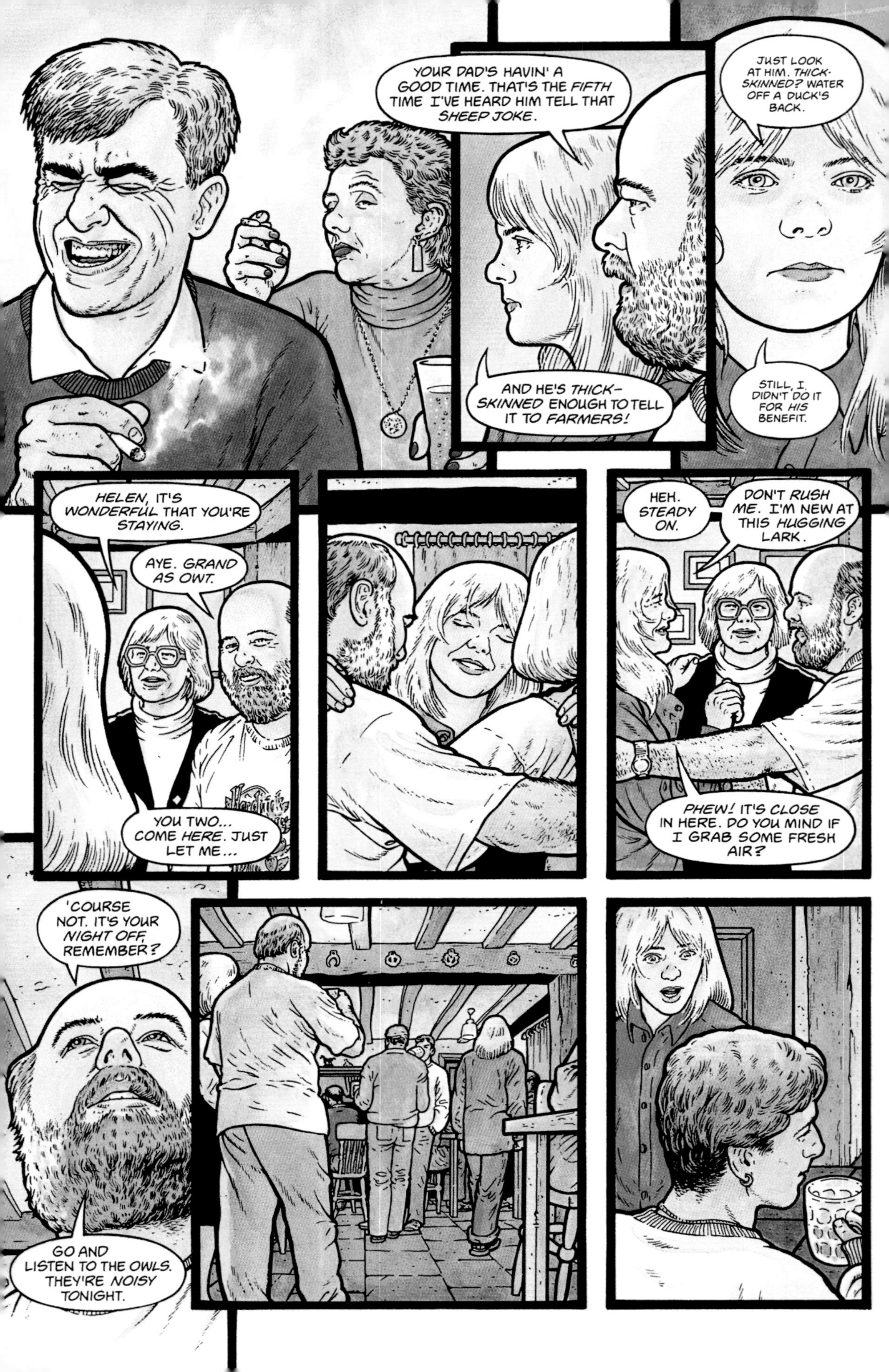
YOUR DAD'S HAVIN' A GOOD TIME. THAT'S THE FIFTH TIME I'VE HEARD HIM TELL THAT SHEEP JOKE.
AND HE'S THICK-SKINNED ENOUGH TO TELL IT TO FARMERS!
JUST LOOK AT HIM. THICK-SKINNED? WATER OFF A DUCK'S BACK.
STILL, I DIDN'T DO IT FOR HIS BENEFIT.
HELEN, IT'S WONDERFUL THAT YOU'RE STAYING.
AYE. GRAND AS OWT.
YOU TWO... COME HERE. JUST LET ME...
HEH. STEADY ON.
DON'T RUSH ME. I'M NEW AT THIS HUGGING LARK.
PHEW! IT'S CLOSE IN HERE. DO YOU MIND IF I GRAB SOME FRESH AIR?
'COURSE NOT. IT'S YOUR NIGHT OFF, REMEMBER?
GO AND LISTEN TO THE OWLS. THEY'RE NOISY TONIGHT.

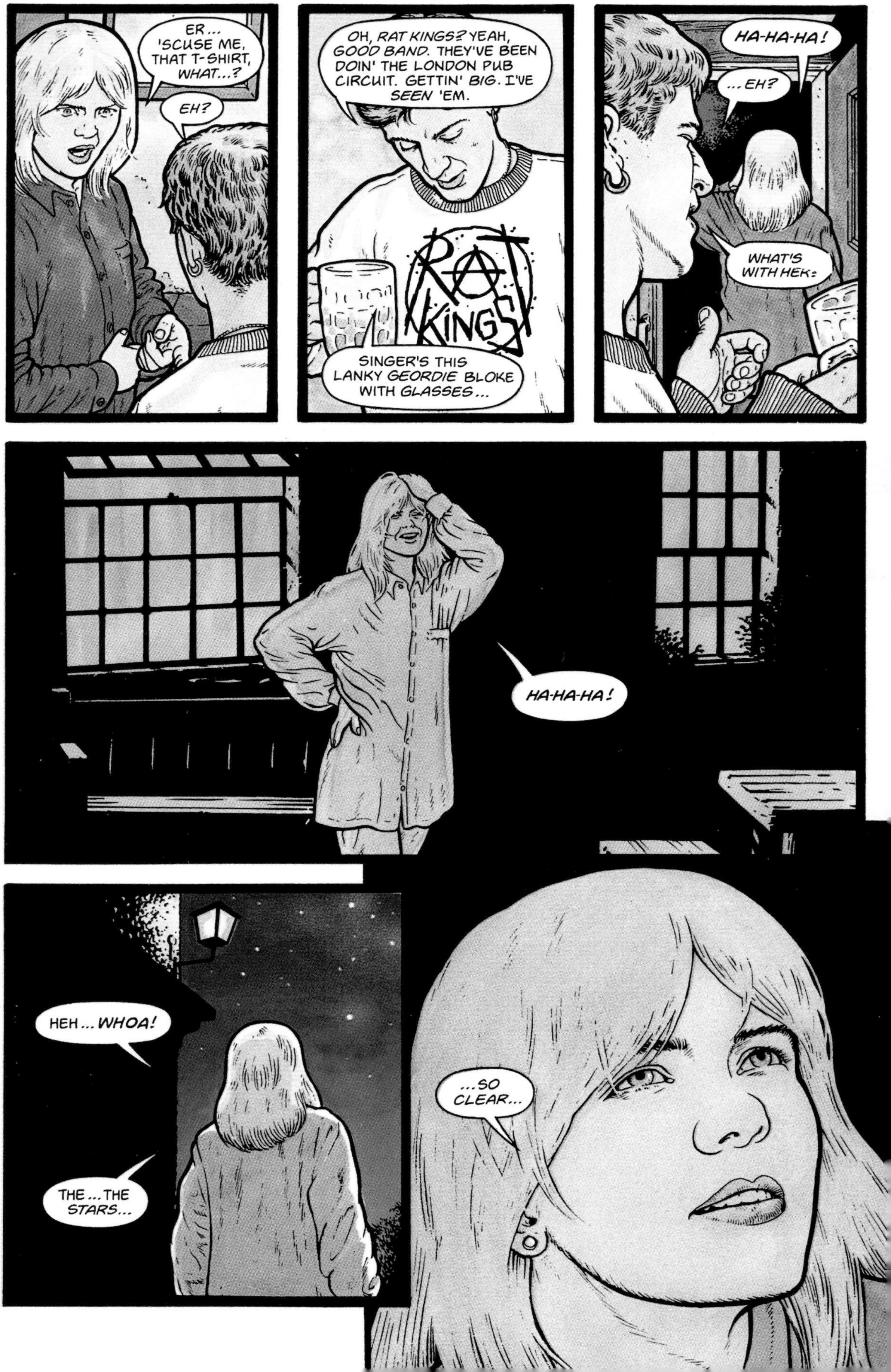

ER... 'SCUSE ME, THAT T-SHIRT, WHAT...?
EH?
OH, RAT KINGS? YEAH, GOOD BAND. THEY'VE BEEN DOIN' THE LONDON PUB CIRCUIT. GETTIN' BIG. I'VE SEEN 'EM.
RAT KINGS
SINGER'S THIS LANKY GEORDIE BLOKE WITH GLASSES...
HA-HA-HA!
...EH?
WHAT'S WITH HER?
HA-HA-HA!
HEH... WHOA!
THE... THE STARS...
...SO CLEAR...

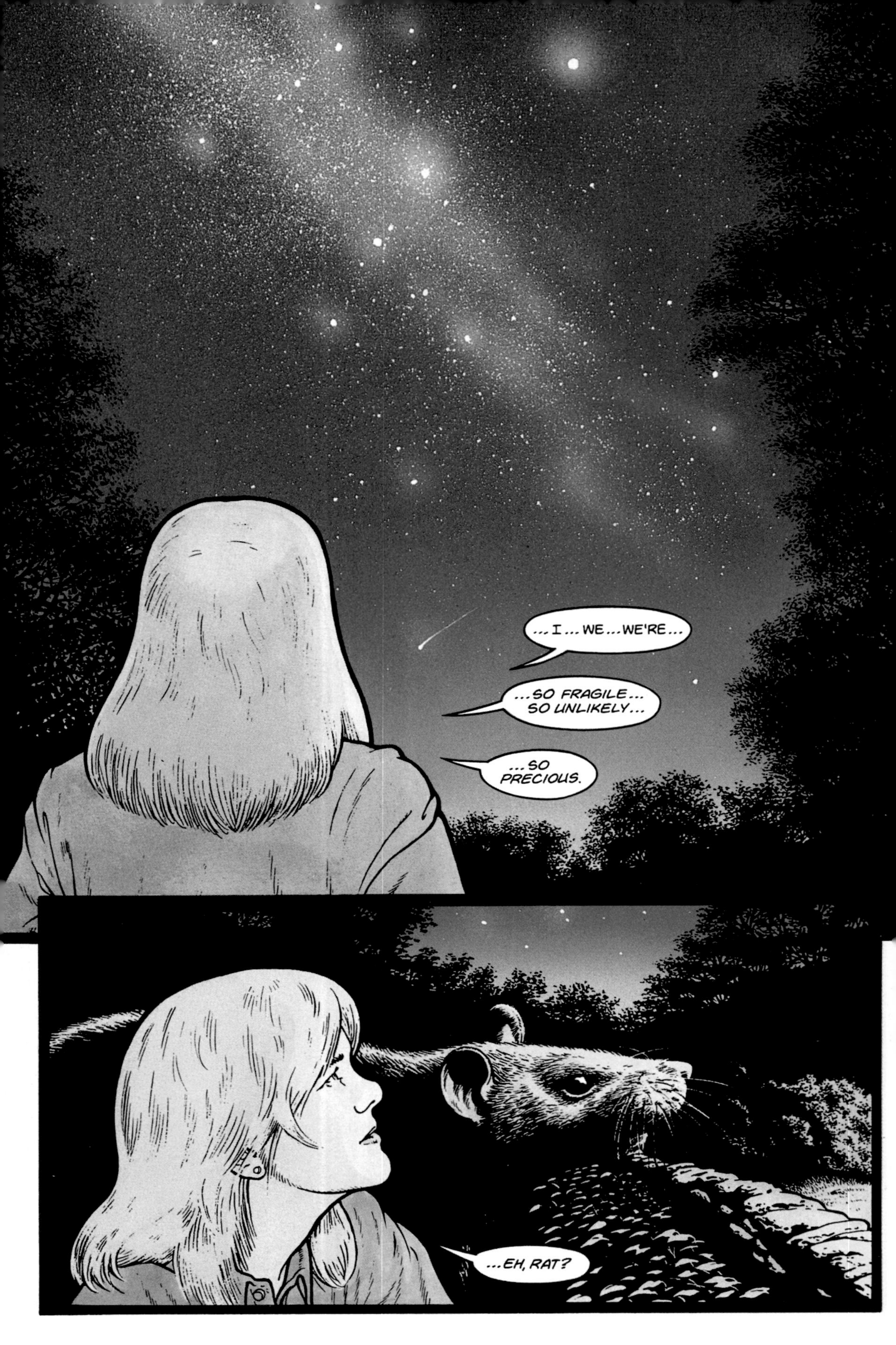
...I...WE...WE'RE...
...SO FRAGILE...
SO UNLIKELY...
...SO
PRECIOUS.
...EH, RAT?

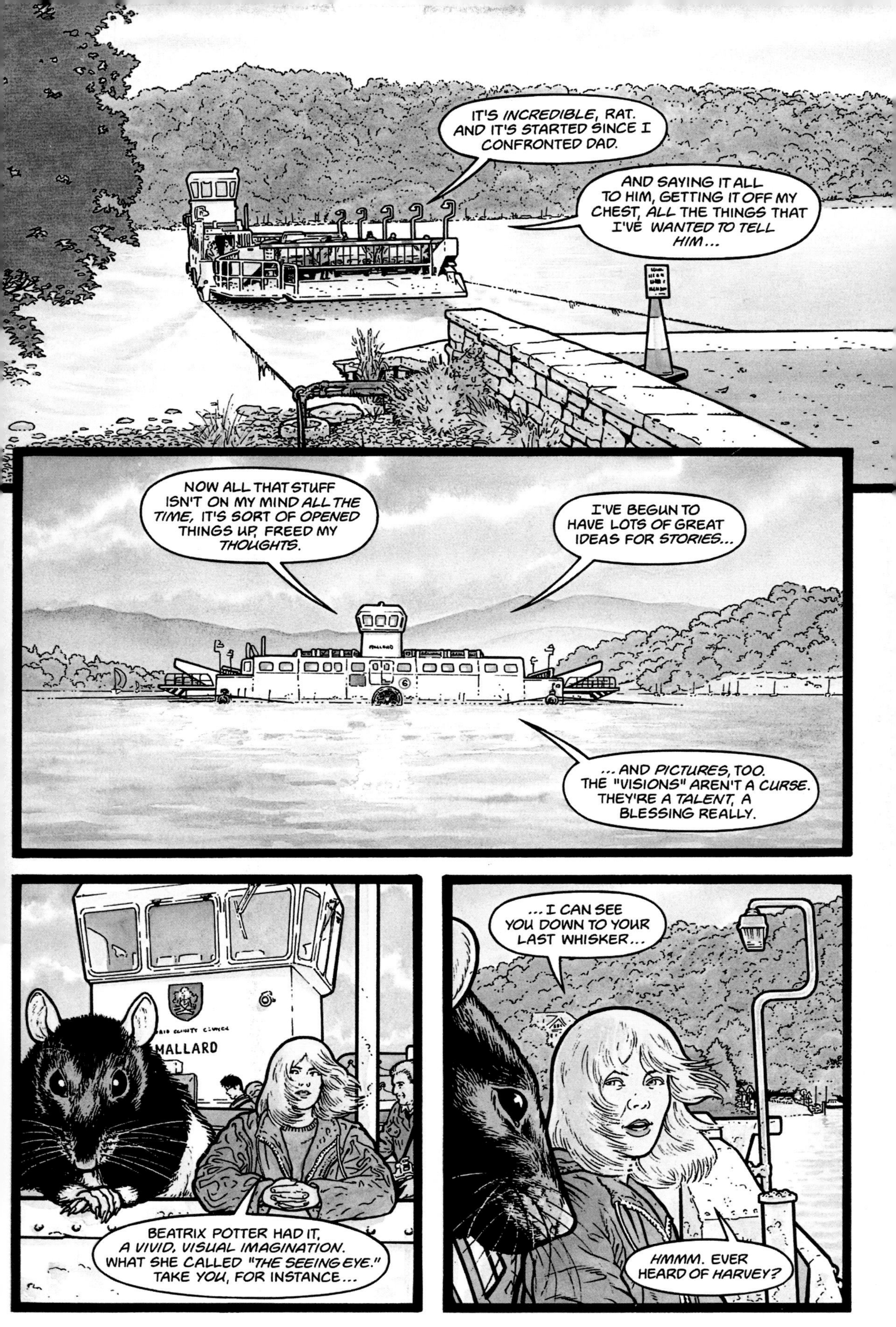
IT'S INCREDIBLE, RAT. AND IT'S STARTED SINCE I CONFRONTED DAD.
AND SAYING IT ALL TO HIM, GETTING IT OFF MY CHEST, ALL THE THINGS THAT I'VE WANTED TO TELL HIM...
NOW ALL THAT STUFF ISN'T ON MY MIND ALL THE TIME, IT'S SORT OF OPENED THINGS UP, FREED MY THOUGHTS.
I'VE BEGUN TO HAVE LOTS OF GREAT IDEAS FOR STORIES...
...AND PICTURES, TOO. THE "VISIONS" AREN'T A CURSE. THEY'RE A TALENT, A BLESSING REALLY.
MALLARD
BEATRIX POTTER HAD IT, A VIVID, VISUAL IMAGINATION. WHAT SHE CALLED "THE SEEING EYE." TAKE YOU, FOR INSTANCE...
...I CAN SEE YOU DOWN TO YOUR LAST WHISKER...
HMMM. EVER HEARD OF HARVEY?

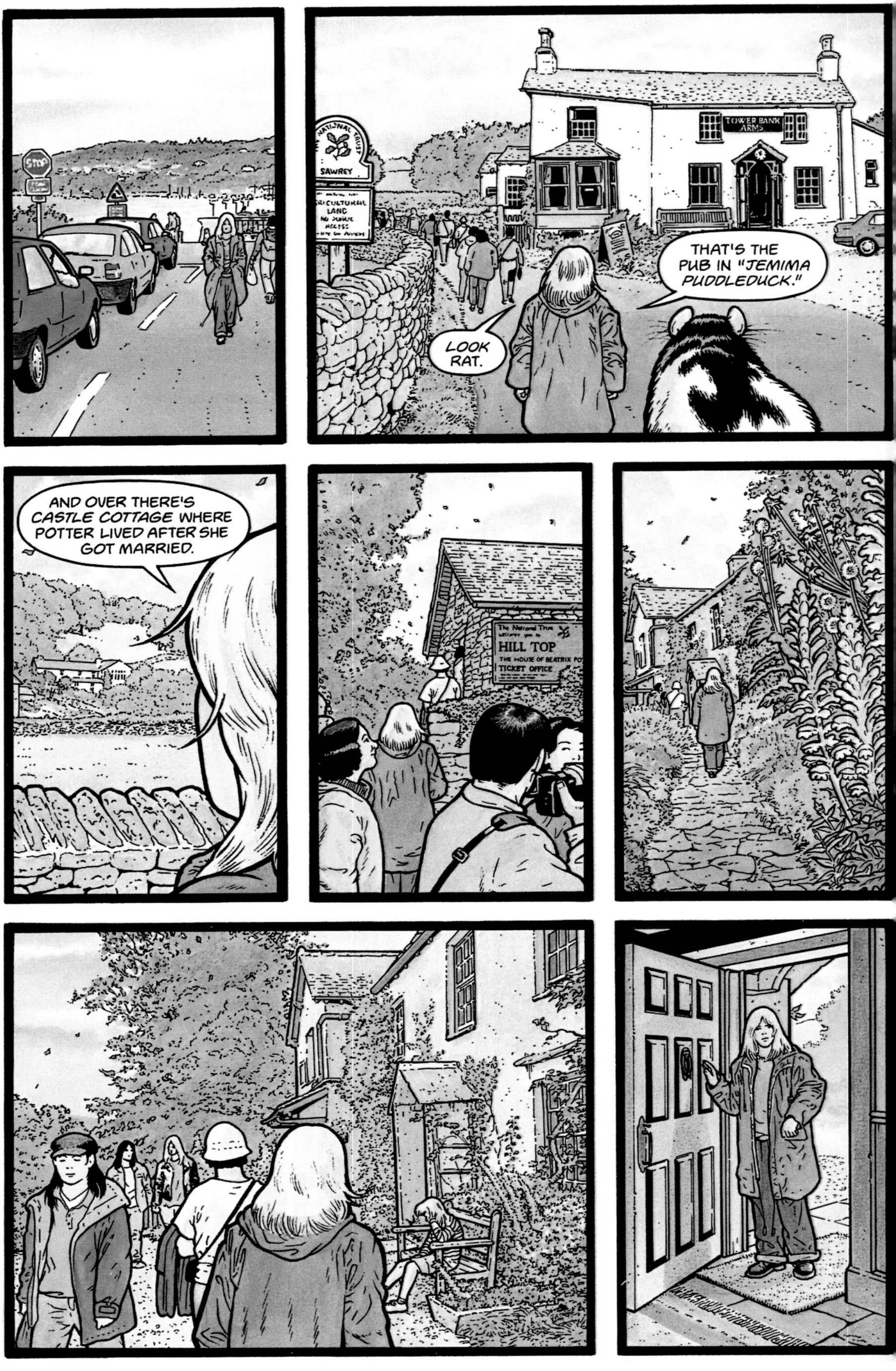
STOP
SAWREY
TOWER BANK ARMS
LOOK RAT.
THAT'S THE PUB IN "JEMIMA PUDDLEDUCK."
AND OVER THERE'S CASTLE COTTAGE WHERE POTTER LIVED AFTER SHE GOT MARRIED.
HILL TOP
TICKET OFFICE

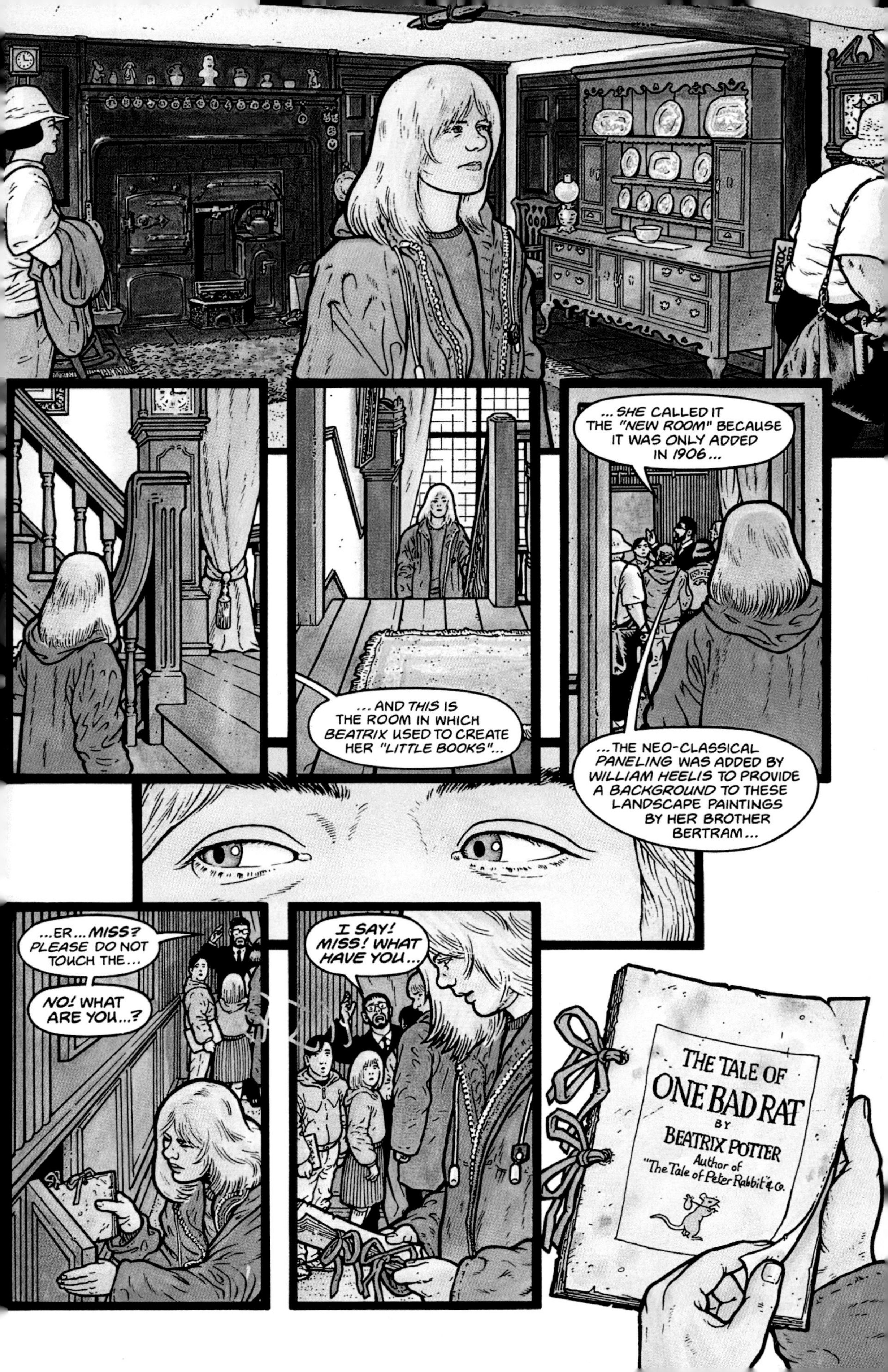
...AND THIS IS THE ROOM IN WHICH BEATRIX USED TO CREATE HER "LITTLE BOOKS"...
...SHE CALLED IT THE "NEW ROOM" BECAUSE IT WAS ONLY ADDED IN 1906...
...THE NEO-CLASSICAL PANELING WAS ADDED BY WILLIAM HEELIS TO PROVIDE A BACKGROUND TO THESE LANDSCAPE PAINTINGS BY HER BROTHER BERTRAM...
...ER...MISS? PLEASE DO NOT TOUCH THE...
NO! WHAT ARE YOU...?
I SAY! MISS! WHAT HAVE YOU...
THE TALE OF ONE BAD RAT
BY
BEATRIX POTTER
Author of "The Tale of Peter Rabbit" & Co.

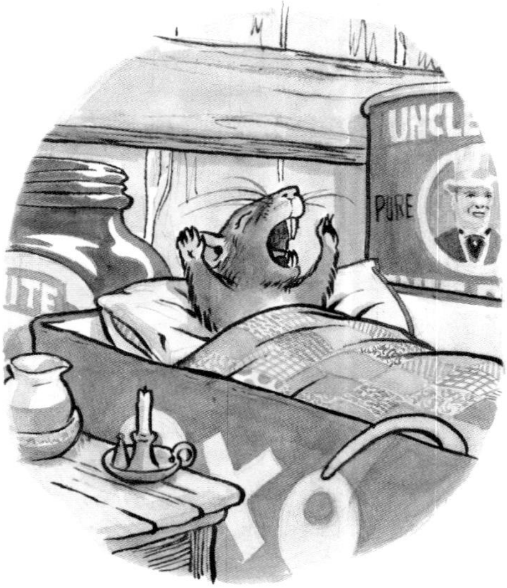
UNCLE
PURE

ONCE upon a time, there was a very bad rat.

Her name was Helen Barnrat. She knew that she must be a very bad rat because everybody told her so; Mr. and Mrs. Barnrat were constantly chastising her, and her teacher was cross because she always came bottom of the class.

One morning, she awoke to bright sunshine and the sound of throstles singing. Oh, what a yawny — stretchy rat that was!

All at once — she realized she had overslept!

SHE jumped out of bed and scurried to the living room. She was late for Rat School!

"Oh, why did I oversleep?" she cried. But she knew perfectly well.

Every night, Mr. Barnrat told Helen that if she did not behave herself, Owd Scratch would come and get her.

Owd Scratch was a notorious cat; a cat to be feared. He was a huge, one-eyed, mangy cat of many winters and a ferocious ratter.

She had heard the rhyme:

"Not last night, but the night before,
A big, fat tomcat came knocking at my door.
'I'm OWD SCRATCH,' he said to me,
'And I eat rats like thee for tea!'"

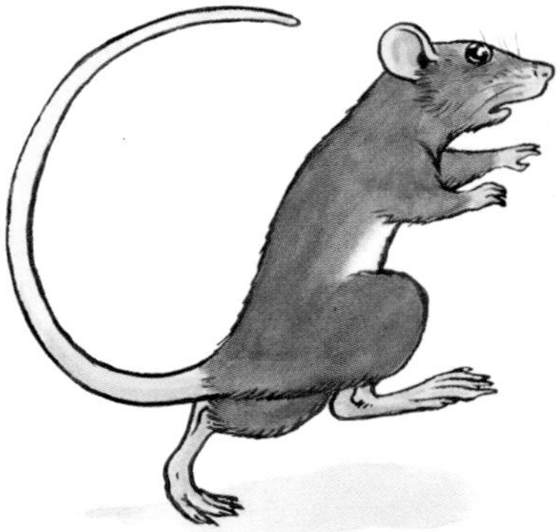

AND that was why Helen had overslept. She had been so frightened of the horrid Owd Scratch that she had been quite unable to get to sleep for most of the night.

Helen was in a fearful pickle. And she was so busy thinking about Owd Scratch that — BUMP! — she ran straight into Mrs. Barnrat.

"Oh, my whiskers!" her Mother exclaimed, dropping all the breakfast crockery. It fell with a SMASH! CRASH! TINKLE! CRASH!

Her Father, who had been quietly lighting a pipeful of rat-tobacco, was so surprised at the noise that he jumped up, burning his nose. "YOCK! YOCK! EEK!" he squeaked loudly.

MR. and Mrs. Barnrat were exceedingly annoyed.

"You bad little rat! You bad little rat!" her Mother scolded. "What a nasty little rat you are," said her Father, grinding his teeth.

This made Helen cry.

"Now go and get ready for school!" they squeaked. "No breakfast for you today!"

But when Helen went back to her room, do you know what she did? She did not get ready for school!

INSTEAD, she packed up her favourite books, some sunflower seeds, her acorn-cup, her toothbrush, her tortoiseshell hairbrush, some pine-needle pins, and her life's savings, which amounted to five peppercorns.

"I've had enough of this," she thought. "I'm going to run away from home, and BOTHER school!"

What a naughty, bad rat!

Then she sneaked out of her room, around a hay-bale, along a beanpole, down a stove-pipe, behind some rolls of old oilcloth, out of the barn (by way of her secret trapdoor), and pitter-pattered away down Toad Road.

IT was a beautiful, sunny day; Red Admiral and Peacock butterflies danced in the air, and somewhere a Yellowhammer was singing "A little bit of bread and NO CHEESE! A little bit of bread and NO CHEESE!"

Helen Barnrat followed Toad Road to the top of Cuckoo Brow, then turned to look back. She could see the rooftops of the farm where she had lived for all of her short life, and she felt sad.

"I wish I wasn't such a bad rat," she said to herself. "I don't want to leave home, but I cannot bear it anymore; I really can't stay. I must go over the hills and far away."

And with that, Helen descended the far side of Cuckoo Brow.

S HE was passing through a copse and starting to feel hungry when... Crack! The sudden snap of a breaking twig made her scramble for cover. And not a second too soon, for as she crouched beneath an old oak fern, a hunter appeared, sniffing the air.

All Helen could do was hold her breath, stay perfectly still, and hope that the sandy-whiskered squire would quickly pass by.

T HEN she nearly jumped out of her skin! For a voice behind her hissed — "Pssst! Little Rat!"

"Pssst!" It went again, "Over here!" And looking around, Helen could see a pair of black eyes twinkling at her from inside a hole in the bank.

The voice and the eyes seemed friendly and so, with a springy bound, Helen dived into the safety of the tunnel.

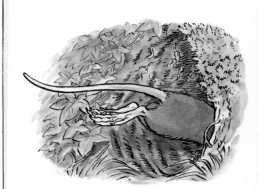

PRESENTLY, a soft light spread all around her as the occupant struck a lucifer and lit an oil lamp. Helen could now see that he was a spiny hedgehog and that she was in the hedgehog's home.

"Snuff! Pleased to meet you, Little Rat," he said, "Urchin Leafmould at your service. Absolutely! I was just about to commence lunch and it would give me great pleasure if you joined me in some raspberries. Snuff, snuff, snuff!"

HELEN politely accepted, although she was rather in awe of this prickly stranger. She was treated to some delicious raspberries in honeydew, but respectfully declined to partake of some horrid-looking ragworms, earwigs, and woodlice in slug sauce.

"So, Longtail, tell me — snuff — why did you run away from home?" asked Urchin Leafmould, crunching an earwig's leg.

Helen explained how she was so terrified at the thought of Owd Scratch that she could do nothing right.

"At home I can think of nothing else," — she squeaked. "My father threatens me with that cat nonstop. So I'm going where there are lots of other rats. My Aunt Janie lives at Hill Top Farm. I can stay with her."

Urchin Leafmould was very sympathetic in his snuffly way, and after lunch he showed Helen the path to Hill Top.

"OH, it's terribly, terribly close," he snuffled. "Absolutely! Just over there past the cow parsley, snuff, hemlock, snuff, jack-by-the-hedge, snuff, sweet cicely, snuff, hog-weed, snuff, and other assorted umbelliferie. But before you depart, Little Rat, please take the advice that I now — snuff — will freely offer."

The hedgehog wrinkled his nose and looked up at the racing clouds far overhead. "I ran away from home, when I was young you know. Oh, absolutely! For years I was a proper urchin! And there's something that I learned about — snuff — cats."

"There is one thing that cats will never do. And do you know — snuff — what that thing is?" he looked at her sharply, his black eyes glittering.

"I can't imagine!" said Helen.

"What they are told! Absolutely! No cat will ever do what it is told! Snuff, snuff, snuff!"

He seemed to think this tremendously funny.

And even when Helen had taken her leave and turned to wave back at him, Urchin Leafmould was still shaking with unbounded amusement.

BUT he was right about one thing; Hill Top was "terribly close," and after ten scampering minutes she arrived.

Now Hill Top Farm is where I live. And let me tell you, it was completely infested by rats. I had no end of trouble with them! But recently things had changed…

Helen Barnrat pitter-pattered across the farmyard feeling very self-conscious. Cows watched her, pigs watched her, the chickens watched her — but there was not another rat to be seen. Where on earth could they be?

Then she saw something that made her blood turn to ice. Nailed to the cowshed door were dozens and dozens of rats' tails! No rats, only the tails nailed there like trophies!

At that moment, a dark shadow fell across Helen and she smelt a smelly, fusky, musky, catty smell that made her eyes water.

"HOW now, a RAT?" a deep voice growled behind her. "Dead for a ducat, DEAD! Ha-ha-ha!"

It was none other than Owd Scratch himself.

Helen looked up, trembling. She was so dreadfully frightened that she durst not move.

"Such a leetle rat!" exclaimed Owd Scratch. "A gay young frisker! Yum yum!"

Helen was horrified — with popping eyes she saw the ugly gralloching knife in the cat's belt and the bird and rat skulls hanging around his neck.

Owd Scratch did not live at Hill Top. He had come to the farm as a hireling ratter after hearing of its enormous rat population.

CAT fleas squirmed under his stained mouseskin coat. He licked his lips with his rough cat tongue. "My favourite dish, with the possible exception of mouse sausages and tripe, is young rat-attouie!" he grinned. "An excellent starter!"

Now, it is contrary to rat nature to be able to think clearly in the presence of cats, but Helen tried to do her best in the circumstances.

"P-p-please, sir," she said, quaking with fear, "p-p-please don't eat me. I c-can pay you."

Helen opened the kerchief containing her few possessions. "H-h-here are f-f-five p-p-pepper-corns," she offered, laying them on the ground before the huge, old tom.

He snatched them up and tipped them into his purse. "What a foolish leetle rat," he laughed, "to think that you could bribe Owd Scratch! Money for nowt! Money for nowt! Ha-ha-ha!"

"DON'T you know," he sneered, baring his frightful teeth, "that I am the cat that killed the rat that ate the malt that lay in the house that Jack built? And now it is your turn!"

He flexed his cruel claws and drew them along the ground — scr-r-itch, scratch, scrit! Scr-r-itch, scratch, scrit!

Then he arched his back and bent down so close to the transfixed rat that she felt his hot cat breath on her face. She winced at his fat-cat halitosis.

ALL at once a queer thing happened. Helen thought to herself — "Why, he's nothing but a mangy, moggy BULLY!" And with one quick swipe she scratched his single eye with her sharp little nails.

"MEOOOW!" screamed Owd Scratch, "MEOOOW!"

He held up a paw to his eye and snarled and spat at her. "You vicious little rat!" he shrieked, stumbling toward her and clawing the air with his free paw. "Just you wait! I'll get you for that, even if you do escape me now. I'm the best ratter there is!"

"That's all flummery," said Helen calmly. "If you think I'm going to take to my heels now, then you're very much mistaken."

THIS infuriated Owd Scratch. "Little rubbish! Little rubbish!" he spat. "Where are you?"

"Right here!" Helen said. "TAKE THREE STEPS FORWARD!"

Of course, cats being contrary, Owd Scratch immediately took three steps backwards. His third step sent him tripping over a low stone wall, whereupon with a cat-aclysmic, cat-astrophic, cat-awauling, he plunged straight down the shaft of the Hill Top well!

BEFORE Helen knew what was happening, hundreds of rats appeared; from under the chicken coop, from lumber, from over bales and under, singing: "Ding-dong bell! Pussy's in the well!" (They must have been watching all the time.)

They bore Helen up on their shoulders and proclaimed her a brave rat, a good rat, a great rat, the best rat in the world!

IT was at this point that I heard their squeaking and marched into the farmyard with a broom. All the rats scuttled away but one; Helen Barnrat looked up at me, sniffing. I suppose that having seen off Owd Scratch, she was not going to be intimidated merely by one of the Big Folk who smelled of sheep!

I couldn't bring myself to hurt this brave little rat, so instead, I went to fish the humiliated tomcat, who was mewing piteously, out of the well.

Owd Scratch, now a bedraggled soggy moggy, slunk away in shame, never to be seen around Sawrey again.

AND as for Helen Barnrat?

Well, now that she was no longer terrified of Owd Scratch, she realized that she was a very good rat indeed!

The Congress of Rats awarded her the "Freedom of the Farmyard" and an annual income of one hundred peppercorns for ridding them of the N.C. (Nasty Cat).

She wrote and drew a story about her experience and called it *The Tale of One Bad Rat*. It was sold in the village store and become a rat best-seller. So from being a common, or garden, rat Helen became an uncommonly famous rat.

And now she is a perfectly contented rat. She writes rat stories, paints rat pictures, and…

…she is never bothered by cats!

THE END

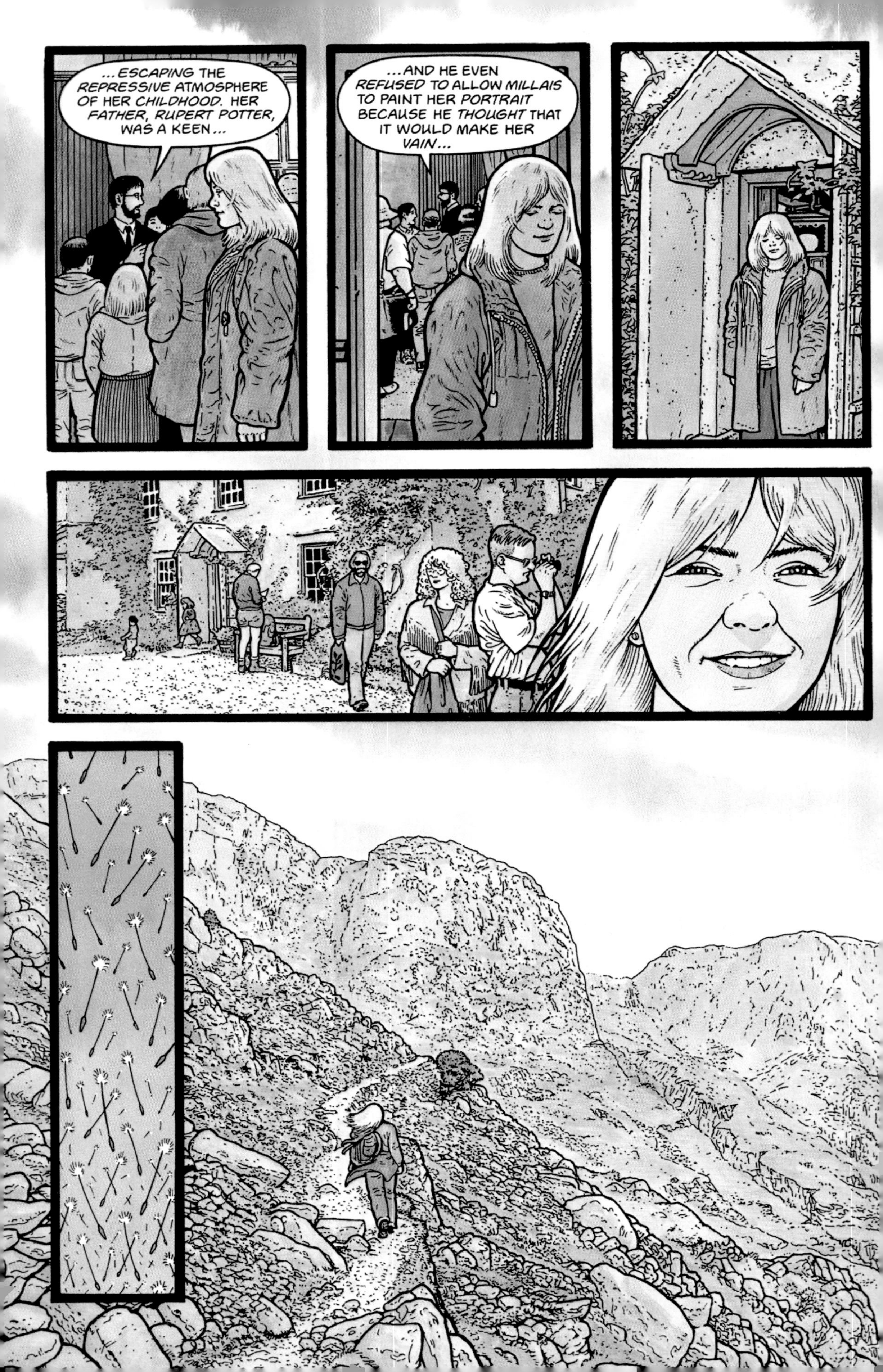
...ESCAPING THE REPRESSIVE ATMOSPHERE OF HER CHILDHOOD. HER FATHER, RUPERT POTTER, WAS A KEEN...
...AND HE EVEN REFUSED TO ALLOW MILLAIS TO PAINT HER PORTRAIT BECAUSE HE THOUGHT THAT IT WOULD MAKE HER VAIN...

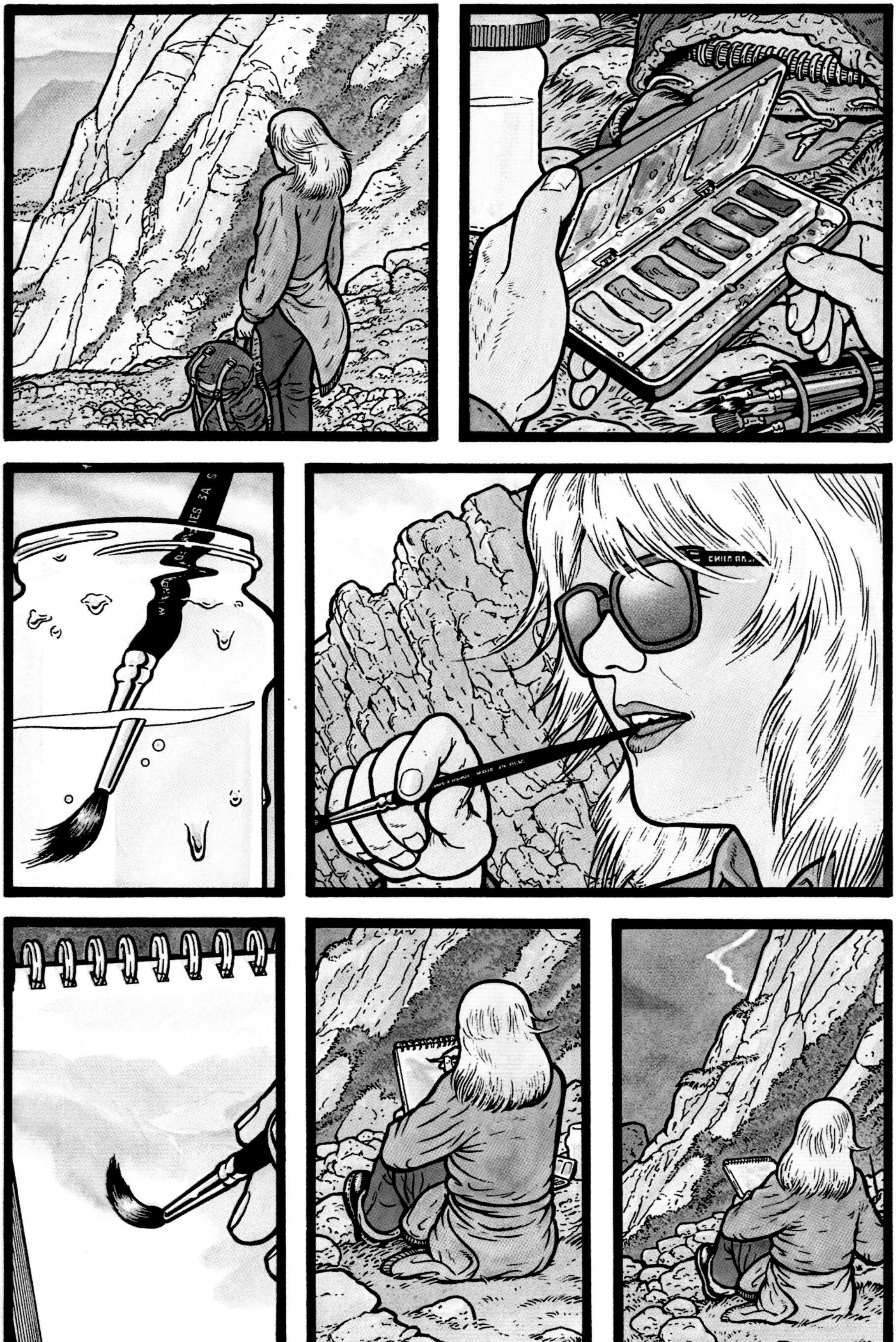

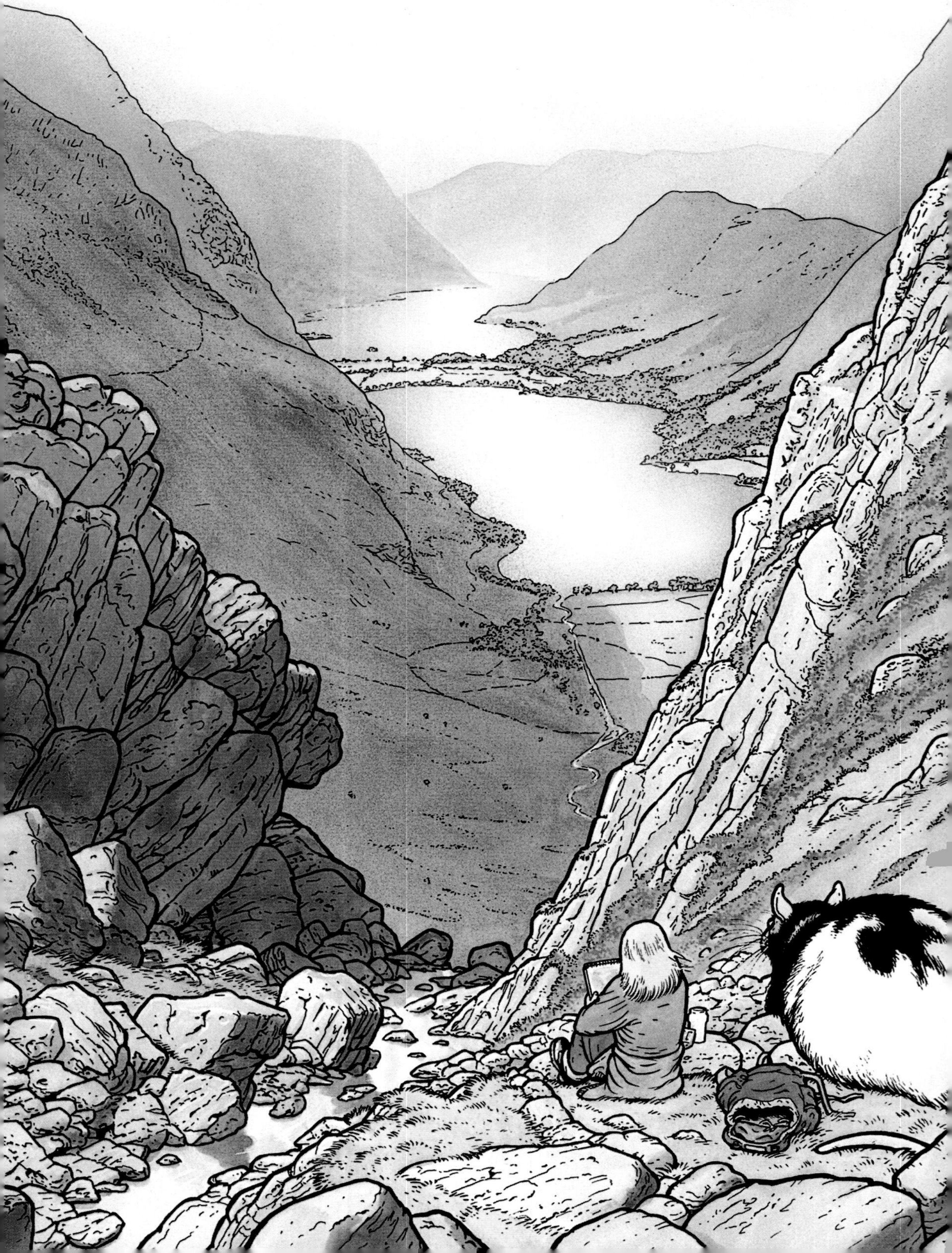

RAT'S TAIL

ONCE upon a time, I had the notion to write and draw a story about the English Lake District.

I'd been in love with the place since I was fourteen, when my parents bought a "static caravan" on a trailer park in the Winster Valley for holidays and weekends. On the days when we weren't motoring around the beauty spots and tourist magnets, I spent hours exploring the immediate area; Bowland Bridge, Strawberry Bank, Ravensbarrow, and Cartmel Fell are all there as depicted in *The Tale of One Bad Rat*.

I could have produced a documentary comic book. There's certainly no lack of material. The Lake District has the widest range of geological features and types of scenery in such a small area in the world. Wordsworth's "beauty lying in the lap of horror" — its lush valleys and spectacular crags — were an inspiration to the English Romantic Movement. Samuel Taylor Coleridge, writer of the *Ancient Mariner*, invented the sport of rock climbing there. Dr. Johnson, Shelley, Dickens, Ruskin, Turner, and many others all have connections with the area. Then there's the huntsman, John Peel; writer Arthur Ransome; film star Stan Laurel; Donald Campbell, who crashed whilst attempting to break his world water speed record on Coniston; and Canon Hardwicke Rawnsley, poet, co-founder of the National Trust and friend of the family of the young Beatrix Potter.

Now, Beatrix Potter — an expert at telling stories using a combination of words and pictures — *there* was a correlation with comic art. Being unfamiliar with her work, I began to research, starting with Margaret Lane's *The Tale of Beatrix Potter* and a visit to Hill Top. However, I didn't want to do a biography; I was just looking for a way in.

Potter was an oppressed child. Starved of affection, not sent to school, she was kept a virtual prisoner on the third story of the family house. As a young girl, she was "unnaturally lonely," "exceedingly shy and tongue-tied" in company, and her only true friends were the small animals she accumulated, studied, and drew.

I was reminded of a teen-age girl I'd seen begging on a platform of Tottenham Court Road tube station. She looked excruciatingly shy and was being hassled by a huge, bearded Jesus freak . . .

The rat theme seemed natural for it. We'd had a pet rat ever since my son Alwyn had pestered us into getting him one. Harpo was so intelligent that he immediately became the family pet. Beatrix Potter had a pet rat, famous through the dedication in her "rat book" *The Tale of Samuel Whiskers*; "In remembrance of 'Sammy,' the intelligent, pink-eyed representative of a persecuted (but irrepressible) race. An affectionate litle friend, and most accomplished thief." And *The Tale of One Bad Rat* sounded exactly like a Potter story.

Producing a proposal for the story with a color cover illustration based on my recollection of the girl at the tube station, I sent a copy to every publisher of illustrated books in Britain. It occurred to me that, since the story was non-genre, it had the potential to have a mainstream readership. These were all returned, mostly by return

Helen Beatrix Potter, 1866-1943, age 16

Kate Housden

of post, mostly unread. The submission editors had reached the words "graphic novel" or "comics" in the cover letter and cut off.

I did receive offers from comics companies. Michael Bennent, then editor for Dark Horse UK, liked the concept, and we had a meeting with publisher Mike Richardson at the Alexandra Palace Comic Convention. I'd worked with Dark Horse before and had a good working relationship with them. Mike gave me the go-ahead.

At that time, I was right in the middle of writing and drawing a Batman story for DC Comics and so *Bad Rat* had to wait. And I still had lots of research to do. By this point, I'd read a few books on the Lake District, four about rats, and approximately a dozen on Beatrix Potter. It was time to have a look at sexual abuse . . .

When putting together the proposal, I'd worked on the basic premise: a homeless girl with a synchronistic link with Beatrix Potter follows Potter's escape into her new life in the Lakes. The plot demanded a reason for her leaving home. Without much consideration, I keyed in "fleeing sexual abuse at the hands of her father." It was glib but, I thought, a pretty reasonable plot device. After all, it's one of the most common causes of teen-age homelessness. And it seemed to fit the character of the shy protagonist.

I read over a dozen books on the sexual abuse of children and its effect on psychological development. In fact, one book would have done. The same sort of coercion, an emotional blackmail, takes place; and the same results, the behavioral symptoms, recur with monotonous regularity. Reading transcripts of accounts by sexual abuse victims, even by those from different countries, you'll find the same situations described and the same feelings paraphrased. The utter selfishness of the abuser is the common denominator — not class, race, or creed. The psychological aftereffects — despair and withdrawal; low self-esteem; feeling worthless, dirty and bad — can last for life. The children take the badness onto themselves.

It's been estimated that one in three girls will be molested before they're eighteen. Approximately 90% of that abuse is committed, not by the stereotypical stranger in the raincoat, haunter of the schoolgates, but by a close, male relative. And less than one in twenty of reported offenders are prosecuted.

Ben Evans

Keith Marsland

This issue was far too important to marginalize; I needed to change the nature of the story in order to address it. It became *Bad Rat*'s raison d'être and the chief concern of the plot.

The story dictated the illustration technique. This is true for every comic I've worked on; I've always tried to adapt my drawing style to project the different atmospheres required by each individual story. With *Bad Rat*, this meant a drastic stylistic change. Because of the content and the mainstream nature of the story, I felt that it needed to be clear and accessible, easily readable by those without an acquired knowledge of comics grammar.

Usually I "create on the page." Working in the genres of science-fiction or super-hero adventure comics, it's perfectly acceptable to make up characters and landscapes. I felt very strongly that I had to ground *Bad Rat* firmly in reality, basing all the characters on real people and all the scenes on real locations. I carefully cast the story and used some of the methods of Frank Hampson: a mixture of invention, photo reference, and life drawing.

Within a week of having to start pencilling, I still hadn't found the model for Helen. Invited to give a lecture on comics art at a local college, I mentioned this to the organiser, Peter Hartley, head of drama. By the time of the lecture, Peter had three of his students lined up to audition for the role. I was astounded. There was Helen, as I had imagined her, in the person of Kate Housden. Kate was indispensable to this project. As I was telling Kate about *Bad Rat*, Ben — as described in detail in the script — walked past. I told him about the Ben character. "I'll pose," he said, "That's my name!"

The location shots I did over a couple of years, sometimes having to stop drawing to take the train to London or drive to Cumbria because I didn't have the correct reference. I followed Helen's walk from Chelsea to Kensington to the site of Beatrix Potter's natal home in Bolton Gardens, bombed during the London blitz. Like Potter, I occasionally resorted to artistic licence to "improve" the composition of some of the Lake District scenes, although the majority are faithful renditions.

Preparatory pencil study of dead rat

Bryan Talbot outside the Mason's Arms

In answer to several queries, the view at the beginning and end of the book is of Crummock Water and Buttermere, from just below Haystacks.

Sometimes stories really do take on a life of their own. Instead of creating a comic about the Lake District, I ended up writing and drawing a story about child sexual abuse. And I'm glad it turned out that way. This has been the most worthwhile book that I have been involved with and the best — not to mention the hardest — comics work that I've ever done.

Worthwhile?

"The first step towards prevention and to provision of supportive services for the girls who've been abused is bringing abuse into the open . . . Incest is not taboo. It seems to be that talking about incest is the real taboo." Miriam Saphira, *The Sexual Abuse of Children*.

It's only recently that abuse has been openly discussed in some small way in the media, and there's a backlash of opinion about even this. People don't want to hear it, don't want to have to think about it. I can only think of three, perhaps four, examples in the comic-book medium that have ever tried to deal with it, even in passing. This backlash is often expressed in dismissive terms, as if we all know about the subject now and there's no point bringing it up again. Sexual abuse occurs a great deal more frequently than murder, but watch television for a night, pick up a novel, go to the cinema, and what do you see? But then, talking about murder is not taboo.

The fact is, because the media largely ignores it, this abuse can still go on unhindered. It works in a conspiracy of silence. Most of the victims, the younger the more likely, believe that this frightening, confusing thing is happening to them alone. They dare not talk about it to anyone and become lonely and alienated. Read Helen's dialogue concerning her feelings. This was paraphrased from transcripts of interviews with abuse survivors. I tried to let the victims speak for themselves.

The more child abuse is discussed in society or fiction in whatever medium, the more likely it is that the victims will realise that it is something that happens all the time, that they can speak out, be believed, and get it stopped.

BRYAN TALBOT
Lancashire, England
May 1995

Bryan Talbot at the porch, Hill Top

ACKNOWLEDGMENTS

TO the following writers and artists for comment and encouragement on the work in progress: Leo Baxendale, Ramsey Campbell, John Coulthart, Al Davison, Glenn Fabry, Ben Hunt, Neil Gaiman, Stephen Gallagher, Colin Greenland, Gwyneth Jones, Steve Leialoha, Alan Moore, Eric Pringle, Roger Sabin, Dave Sim, Trina Robbins, Mary Talbot, and Tom Veitch.

To the abuse survivors who talked to me, for information, comment, and letting me know that I was getting it right.

To the London Metropolitan Police (Thames Division, Waterloo Pier), Stuart Mason (art teacher at Tulketh High School, Preston), Dick Hansom, and Dick Jude for help with location shots.

To Dave Frost, the late Frank McConville (Scouse advisors), Al Davison and Chris Moir (Geordie advisors).

To hairdresser Robin Simmons of Preston for calculating the monthly growth rate of Helen's hair.

To Pip and Julie Grundy and James and Pauline Brunton, cat wranglers.

To Nigel and Helen Stevenson, proprietors of The Mason's Arms, Crosthwaite, the real-life Herdwick Arms for allowing their pub to be used as a backdrop.

To Judy Taylor, author of *Beatrix Potter, Artist, Storyteller and Countrywoman* and Chair of the Beatrix Potter Society, for championing *The Tale of One Bad Rat*.

And to my models: Pete Applegarth; Krishnan Arya; James Barker; Benjamin Blackledge; Theresa Bond; Babu Chauhan; Jean Dixon; Ben Evans; Clair Flannery; Ellen, Marilyn, and Steve Gallagher; Sid Heathcote; Graham Holland; Kate Housden; Graeme Hurry; Les Isbister; Frank McConville; Keith and Sarita Marsland; Nick Robinson; Gary and Hilary Smith; Joan Smith; Jane Sorenson; Alwyn, Mary, and Robin Talbot; and Neil Wheeler.

The rats: Harpo, Vasquez, Daisy, Mad Mink Mortimer, and Beatrix.

BRYAN Talbot has worked in underground comics such as *Knockabout, Slow Death*, and *Brainstorm*. He produced SF humour strips *Frank Fazakerly, Space Ace of the Future* (for *Ad Astra*) and *Scumworld* (for *Sounds*).

First serialized in *Near Myths* and *Pssst!*, his seminal award-winning story *The Adventures of Luther Arkwright*, begun in 1978, was the hugely influential first British graphic novel. The sequel, the parallel-world historical fantasy epic *Heart of Empire*, was published in 2001.

In the eighties and nineties, Bryan worked for the British SF weekly comic *2000 AD* on *Nemesis the Warlock* and *Judge Dredd*. He also worked for DC Comics drawing *The Nazz, Hellblazer, Sandman, Dead Boy Detectives, Fables* and the *Paradox Big Books* as well as writing *The Dreaming* and *Batman: Legends of the Dark Knight*, which he also drew. He wrote and drew *Neil Gaiman's Teknophage* for *Tekno Comics*.

First appearing in 1994, *The Tale of One Bad Rat* is published in ten countries and has won numerous international awards. It featured in the *New York Times* annual list of recommended reading and is used as a resource in schools and child-abuse centres in several countries.

2007 saw his first prose book, *The Naked Artist*, and a collection of his book and magazine illustrations, *The Art of Bryan Talbot*.

His most recent graphic novel as writer/artist is the bestselling 'dream documentary' of Lewis Carroll, *Alice in Sunderland*, published in 2007. *Cherubs!*, a supernatural comedy-adventure appeared in 2008, written by Bryan and drawn by Mark Stafford.

Need help or counselling or
know someone who does?

Phone Childline's free helpline: 0800 1111

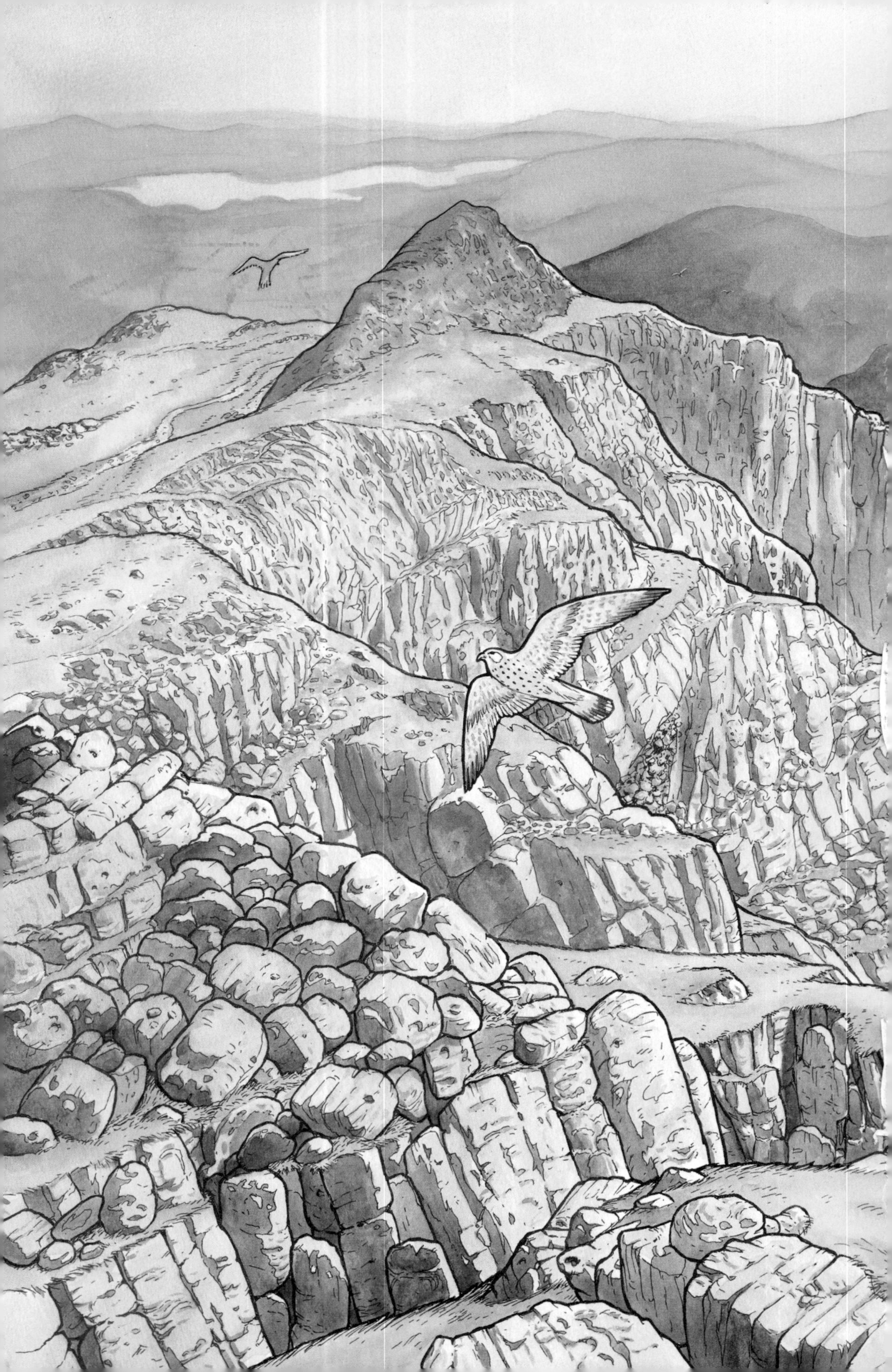